Pricing and Hedging Financial Derivatives

A Guide for Practitioners

Leonardo Marroni and Irene Perdomo

This edition first published 2014
© 2014 John Wiley & Sons, Ltd

Registered office
John Wiley & Sons Ltd, The Atrium, Southern Gate, Chichester, West Sussex, PO19 8SQ, United Kingdom

For details of our global editorial offices, for customer services and for information about how to apply for permission to reuse the copyright material in this book please see our website at www.wiley.com.

Library of Congress Cataloging-in-Publication Data

Marroni, Leonardo
  Pricing and hedging financial derivatives : a guide for practitioners / Leonardo Marroni, Irene Perdomo.
      pages cm. — (The Wiley finance series)
  Includes bibliographical references and index.
  ISBN 978-1-119-95371-5 (hardback)
  1. Derivative securities—Prices.   2. Hedging (Finance)   I. Perdomo, Irene   II. Title.
  HG6024.A3M367 2013
  332.64′57–dc23

                                                                                                    2013021914

A catalogue record for this book is available from the British Library.

ISBN 978-1-119-95371-5 (hardback) ISBN 978-1-119-95457-6 (ebk)
ISBN 978-1-119-95458-3 (ebk) ISBN 978-1-118-77321-5 (ebk)

Cover image: Shutterstock

Set in 10/12pt Times by Aptara Inc., New Delhi, India
Printed in Great Britain by CPI Group (UK) Ltd, Croydon, CR0 4YY

Contents

Preface

The study of derivatives is tough. The institutional and regulatory framework is evolving constantly, new products and structures are being developed daily, existing products are being refined and financial mathematicians regularly introduce new, more complicated techniques for pricing these products. Tough, but neither impossible nor inaccessible to those people who wish to learn. In fact, everybody involved in the derivatives market is caught up in a continual learning experience.

First, a word of warning. Our book is not meant to be a handbook for the derivatives market. It is light on the regulatory changes currently taking place in financial markets since this is not part of our aim. Indeed, any book written on this topic will very soon be out of date. Of course, for many, these changes are the most important developments taking place in the derivatives markets currently. We would not disagree. We just prefer someone else to write books on this.

On the other hand, our book aims to offer a practical introduction to the topic of pricing and hedging of derivatives. It is rigorous in its conclusions, although we may sometimes take a few liberties with academic rigour if it helps us to explain the intuition behind certain ideas. Where we do take poetic licence, however, we make it abundantly clear why we are doing so. Moreover, we would contend that, in recent years, had the majority of market participants had a more practical and intuitive understanding of derivative products, there would have been more respect for the risks inherent in the untrammelled expansion of the derivatives market and financial institutions may have been in less need of bail-outs.

Our book is light on complicated mathematics. We do not see the point of pages and pages of equations that we will never need again. One does not need, for example, to be able to derive the Black–Scholes pricing equation from scratch to understand the risks involved in trading and investing in derivatives and how to hedge these risks.

We hope that by the end of this book, the interested reader will have a clear understanding of the way that derivatives are priced and hedged and to be able to use this understanding in a practical manner.

Leonardo and Irene

Acknowledgements

We would like to thank the following individuals, without whose help we would not have been able to complete this project.

To Jesse McDougall and Patrick Boyle, principals of Palomar Capital Management LLP, we say a very big thank you for their patience in reviewing the entire book in such a timely fashion. Their comments were always helpful and almost all have been incorporated into the finished product. We wish them continued success with their fund, especially since one of us is an investor!

To Francesco Chiminello, we say a very big thank you for his sizeable contribution to Chapters 5 and 7. The three of us met when we worked together at Barclays Capital although we have all subsequently moved on to pastures new. We wish him well in his new role at Bloomberg. His new employer and its clients will benefit greatly from his knowledge of quantitative finance.

To Christopher Culp, Adjunct Professor of Finance at the University of Chicago's Booth School of Business, we say a big thank you for helping to review the book despite his many other commitments. As an expert in the field of derivatives and risk management, Christopher ensured that the liberties that we took with the theory in order to ease explanation were little ones. Irene also wishes to thank him again for making her time at Chicago University such a rewarding experience.

To Neil Schofield, principal of FMT Limited, a financial training company, we also say a big thank you for helping to review our book despite being halfway through writing his latest bestseller. Neil's Amazon page can be found at http://www.amazon.co.uk/Neil-C.-Schofield/e/B001IQZBC2.

To Jennie Kitchin, Vivienne Wickham, Werner Coetzee, Thomas Hyrkiel and the rest of the team at John Wiley & Sons, we say a very big thank you for their continued patience as we failed to meet all of the deadlines that we were set. They must have sighed heavily before reading every one of our e-mails in the past few months.

Finally, we would very much like to thank Troy Bowler for his significant contribution in editing the final draft. Troy is married to one of us and, as such, probably did not have much choice but to cooperate. Nevertheless, we are grateful that he was there since neither of us are native English speakers and we needed all the help we could get.

Although there were many people helping to put this book together, any mistakes are clearly our own.

Leonardo and Irene

1

An Introduction to the Major
Asset Classes

This introductory, and slightly eclectic, chapter focuses on the liquid investment asset classes in which derivatives and structured products are normally developed, priced and traded, namely equities, fixed income, commodities and foreign exchange. The aim is not to describe in detail the everyday products traded in these markets but more to give a sense of the general price characteristics of these markets, e.g., how they move through time. There are many excellent product books on the market and we would recommend readers interested in the range of products available to pick up a copy of one of them; we have listed some in the References.

In this chapter, we aim to make some observations on how to model underlying asset price behaviour for each asset class.[1] In order to have a real understanding of the value that can be extracted from financial derivatives, one must understand how prices behave in their composite parts. This is not a quantitative finance textbook, however, and we do not aim to be completely rigorous. Instead, in this chapter as in the others, we try to get across an intuitive (rather than an academic) understanding.[2]

On the way, we will also highlight some interesting features of the markets under review so that you, the reader, can feel more personal affinity with them; we think that, if your interest is tweaked, you will enjoy the book (and the chapter) much more. Many readers of this book will have experience in one or two of these asset classes but probably not all. If short on time, you could, of course, read the sections on the least familiar asset classes and skip the rest. That said, if you do have some experience but you are a little rusty, the following sections should be a good review.

1.1 EQUITIES

1.1.1 Introduction

Equities are perhaps the most familiar of the main asset classes. The shareholder capital or capital stock (or, merely, stock) of a company represents the capital paid into or invested in the business by its shareholders. Along with other assets in the firm, shareholder capital serves as security for the creditors of that company. The capital stock is divided into *shares* (also called *equity*). The company may have different types (*classes*) of equity, each class having distinctive ownership rules, privileges and/or prices.

Equity typically takes the form of *common* or *preferred*. Common shares typically carry voting rights, which shareholders can exercise at certain times to influence the company and its directors. Preferred shares typically do not carry voting rights but holders are legally entitled to receive their dividends before other shareholders. Since holders of preferred shares get preferential treatment, they are called *preference* shares in the UK.

---

[1] There will be a little mathematics but not much. Instead, we hope to explain the issues more intuitively.
[2] If you are looking for a quantitative finance textbook then probably anything by Wilmott is worthwhile.

Convertible preferred shares are preferred shares that include an option for the holder to convert them into a fixed number of common shares, usually any time after a predetermined date.

Preferred shares may sometimes have a hybrid structure, having the qualities of bonds (such as a fixed percentage dividend) and common stock voting rights.

1.1.2   Pricing equities

The price of a single stock/share/equity (the terms are interchangeable) is determined as always by the interaction of supply and demand. Factors that impact only on the single stock price are called *stock-specific*. These factors can include a change in CEO, new patents awarded to the company, new product development, etc. The prices of individual stocks are also influenced by factors that affect the entire equity market, however. These are *market-specific*. In fact, statistical analysis suggests that the majority of the variation in the prices of individual stocks usually comes about from events that impact the overall equity market, for example changes in monetary policy or the risk tolerance of investors, rather than stock-specific factors. Stocks that tend to move by more than the overall market moves are called *high-beta* stocks while those that move less than the market are called *low-beta* stocks. This is essentially a carry-over from the Capital Asset Pricing Model (CAPM),[3] which you do not really need to know much about for the purposes of this book. High-beta stocks tend to be in cyclical sectors, such as consumer durables, property and capital equipment. Low-beta stocks tend to be non-cyclical, such as food retailers and public utilities. Another way of describing low-beta stocks is *defensive*.

To be sure, there is a huge industry dedicated to predicting likely future movements in the price of a single stock or equity market. The three main approaches are *fundamental analysis*, *technical analysis* and *quantitative analysis*. We discuss these techniques below. There are some more esoteric theories of equity price determination, such as those predicated on sun spot activity or the Chinese horoscope, for example. What all these theories have in common, however, is that they have their fans as well as their detractors.

Of course, investors could just ignore forecasting entirely and invest passively, judging that the future direction of price movements is unpredictable in all but the long run. We will say more on this below.

1.1.3   Fundamental analysis

Fundamental analysis attempts to use economics and accountancy to value a single stock or the overall equity market (or sector), thereby obtaining the *fair value price*. Investors can then compare the actual price with the fair value price and then decide whether the stock price or index level is over- or undervalued. Put simply, analysts attempt to assess the likely flow of cash flows from the company or the market as a whole and discount these using a relevant discount rate. The net present value of the future cash flows is then the equilibrium (or fair value) price of the equity or the overall market.

---

[3] The beta is usually estimated by regressing the historic returns to the stock against the returns to the market over a given sample period (for example, or one business cycle). Alternatively, beta may be interpreted as a stock's contribution to the volatility of the total market portfolio. In this case, it is the covariance of returns between the stock and the "market portfolio", divided by the variance of returns to the market portfolio. Variance is a measure of dispersion and is the square of the standard deviation of returns. One of the problems with stock betas, however, is that they are notoriously unstable and significantly different estimates will be obtained depending on the sample period selected for the price return histories.

Although discredited by many, the Efficient Markets Hypothesis (EMH) suggests that equity markets are essentially rational. That is, the price of any stock (and, consequently, market index) at any given moment represents a complete evaluation of the known information that might have a bearing on the future value of that stock. In other words, stock prices are, at any point in time, equal to the sum of the discounted future cash flows. Furthermore, prices can only change if there is some "news" that has an effect on those future cash flows.[4] In a sense, the EMH supports the idea of fundamental analysis although there is a chicken-and-egg problem here. The EMH says that fundamental analysis to value a stock or equity market is unnecessary since current stock prices are already at their fair value. But, of course, how did the market arrive at the prices in the first place? Presumably some entity somewhere must be cranking out the numbers?

In recent years, even the most die-hard fans of the EMH have come to accept that the markets are not perfectly efficient, especially the least liquid ones. To quote Professor Robert Schiller, "the Efficient Markets Hypothesis is a half-truth".

1.1.4 Technical analysis

Technical analysis attempts to predict future price changes in a single stock or the overall equity market (or sector) by analysing past price movements. Technical analysis is extremely popular among certain market participants although there is considerable controversy attached to its use. Certainly, if you subscribe to the school of thought that says that equity markets are efficient, then there is no place for technical analysis. For a more in-depth discussion of this point, see Chapters 10 and 11 of *Financial Theory and Corporate Policy* (2003) by Copeland, Weston and Shastri.

Whichever approach you prefer, it is irrefutable that stock prices are determined by supply and demand. Although new stock can be issued, for example when a company is wishing to raise new capital for fixed investment, stock prices at the overall equity market level are likely to change from day to day because demand conditions are changing rather than because the net supply of equity is increasing. If equity investors are feeling particularly confident, then they may well allocate more capital to stocks and this will push up prices. On the other hand, if equity investors are feeling much less confident, then they may well take capital out of the stock market and this will push down prices. If changes in the confidence levels of investors are unpredictable, as seems the case empirically, then short-term price changes will tend to be random.[5] Of course, fundamental analysts will argue that the market or single stock has temporarily moved away from fair value and recommend buying (if cheap) or selling (if rich). The technical analysts, on the other hand, will try to explain these short-term movements with reference to past price patterns.

1.1.5 Quantitative analysis

But what about the passive investors, those who judge that the future direction of price movements is unpredictable in all but the long run? Empirically, single equity prices and stock market indices tend to follow a pattern that closely resembles what mathematicians call

---

[4] Although not recent, a 1988 NBER Working Paper, entitled *What Moves Stock Prices?*, found that "large market moves often occur on days without any identifiable major news releases (which) casts doubt on the view that stock prices movements are fully explicable by news about future cash flows and discount rates".

[5] "I can predict the motion of heavenly bodies but not the madness of crowds", Sir Issac Newton.

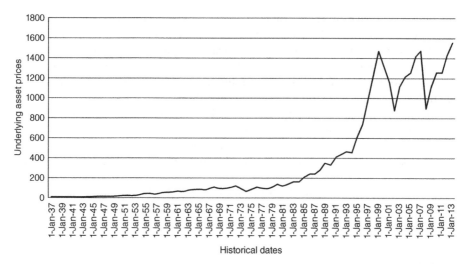

Figure 1.1   S&P 500 historical prices

a random walk (with drift). Predicting future price changes over anything but the medium to long term in such a world is likely to be unfulfilling. Investors can "predict" that they will earn a long-run average return above the risk-free rate (since equities are risky) but the intermediate path will be far from predictable. In this case, a single investor can only systematically "beat the market" by being incredibly lucky. This is the world of the quantitative analyst. Put very simply, quantitative analysts attempt to model the returns from assets, rather than their fair value prices since, empirically, price movements appear random but returns, over time, seem to follow something akin to a normal distribution (Figure 1.1).

More recently, academics have suggested that, in fact, equity prices may more closely resemble a first-order autoregressive process than a random walk. Without wishing to get too mired in mathematical-speak, such a process allows for mean reversion to the trend. If so, then there may be opportunities, after all, for savvy investors to beat the market. They just need to be able to determine the trend!

Neither the random-walk model nor the autoregressive model seems to be an entirely accurate description of the process of equity price determination, however. Stock markets are much more volatile than such models would seem to imply. In particular, they do not seem fully to be able to explain the prevalence of stock market crashes.[6] And, the models do not explain why technical analysis has so many fans. If equity prices change with a random walk, then technical analysis is useless. If equity prices follow a first-order autoregressive process, however, then it may be possible to predict price moves from statistical analysis but the "head-and-shoulder" and "double-bottom" formations popular with technical analysts the world over are likely to be little more than colourful nonsense. As Simon Beninga suggests in his book *Financial Modeling*, "if you are going to be a technician, you have to learn to say these things with a straight face".

---

[6] Many quantitative analysts argue that, in practice, it is not worth trying to model crashes, for example. While they can create significant damage, there is very little that we can actually do about them. They may appear more regularly than the normal distribution would imply but their prevalence still tends to be relatively limited. So, in practice, one can ignore them for modelling purposes as long as one is also aware of them and tries to account for their effects.

So, why does technical analysis appear to work at some level? Perhaps because it has lots of fans who follow the techniques and take investment decisions based on such. Is this rational, not entirely so but, then, humans are far from rational. How else can one explain the Dot-Com Bubble?

We have described the processes driving actual equity prices in some detail since those same processes are at work in the other asset classes, most especially commodities, foreign exchange and indices. Fixed income products are much less easy to model, however.

1.1.6   The equity risk premium and the pre-FOMC announcement drift

The equity premium is the difference between the "average" return on the stock market and the yield on short-term government bonds. Most academic research into the size of the premium finds that it is too high to compensate for the average riskiness of equities. The *equity premium puzzle* is the name given to this phenomenon. Mehra (2008) provides a review of the literature on this topic.[7]

A recent New York Fed staff report suggested that since 1994 more than 80% of the equity premium on US equities was earned during the 24 hours preceding scheduled Federal Open Market Committee (FOMC) announcements (which generally occur just eight times a year).[8] The researchers called this phenomenon the *pre-FOMC announcement drift*.

The interesting aspect to note is that the pre-FOMC announcement drift is generally earned *ahead* of the Fed's announcement and so it is not directly related to the actual post-meeting monetary policy actions. The historical record suggests that equity prices rise in the afternoon of the day before FOMC announcements and then rise even more sharply the next morning. Following the announcement, equity prices can vary widely but, on average, they tend to finish the day around the same levels prevailing at the time of the announcement. In other words, unchanged. The gain over the 2 days as a whole, however, averages about 0.5%.

On the other hand, since 1994, historic returns from equities are in line with the returns on government bonds if the windows around scheduled FOMC announcement days are excluded.[9] Note that similar patterns are found in other equity markets,[10] although, in these cases, they are reacting to the FOMC announcements rather than announcements from their own central banks.

Finally, while one might expect similar patterns to be evident in other major asset classes, the researchers concluded they were not. In other words, the pre-FOMC drift seems to be restricted to equities.

1.2   COMMODITIES

1.2.1   Introduction

What is a *commodity*? The standard definition of a commodity is "any marketable item produced to satisfy wants or needs" and can include goods and services. For most of us, however, a commodity is essentially a basic resource that we use that comes out of the ground

---

[7] See http://www.academicwebpages.com/preview/mehra/pdf/FIN%200201.pdf.

[8] See http://papers.ssrn.com/sol3/papers.cfm?abstract_id=1923197.

[9] The return on the 24-hour period ahead of the FOMC announcement was about 3.9% per year, compared with only about 0.9% per year for all other days combined. In other words, more than 80% of the annual equity premium is earned over the 24 hours preceding scheduled FOMC announcements.

[10] The FTSE 100, DAX, CAC 40, SMI, IBEX and the TSE.

(e.g., wheat, corn, sugar, coffee, copper, aluminium, gold, silver, crude oil, natural gas, coal, diamonds, uranium, etc.). Obviously, this description is far from rigorous but it is intuitive. We can go one step further and say that soft commodities are grown, while hard commodities are extracted through mining or drilling.

Commodities generally have actively traded derivative markets while the spot markets tend to be less liquid. The most active derivative markets are the commodity futures exchanges in the USA and the UK, although the first real futures market was probably the rice futures market that began in seventeenth-century Osaka, Japan. Spot markets provide for the immediate delivery of the relevant commodity while the derivative markets provide for or accommodate delivery at some point in the future; in some cases, as much as 10 years out. These markets help to determine "world" prices although most transactions in commodities do not actually take place "on market". Instead, they are bilateral arrangements undertaken directly between a buyer and a seller. The prices at which these trades take place are generally not made public, since they are private transactions, but they will tend to be determined to some extent in reference to the prices traded on the public markets.

Most commodity products will have undergone some form of basic refining before they are traded publically. For example, the copper that is traded on the London Metal Exchange (LME) is 99% pure, is in the form of cathode (a flat sheet of metal) and is quoted in lots of 25 tonnes (if one buys one lot, one is buying 25 tonnes of copper). Other commodities that will have gone through some form of refining include gasoline and fuel oil (both derived from crude oil), orange juice, lean hogs, sugar (refined from raw sugar), etc. Another important commodity is electricity. Electricity is derived from other fuel sources (oil, coal, nuclear, renewables, etc.) and has the particular characteristic that it is uneconomical/difficult to store. Hence, electricity is produced as and when it is demanded/consumed.

The main participants in the commodity markets are producers (mining companies, farmers, refiners, oil companies, etc.), manufacturers (who use the raw materials to make consumer durables and non-durables), households (who use electricity or gasoline), traders (who help the producers and consumers to hedge) and investors. Governments are also involved since they tend to intervene, perhaps to build strategic reserves in the case of the US government or to manipulate the price in the case of OPEC. We discuss the main participants in later sections describing their typical activity.[11]

Another aspect of commodities is that, although they tend to be lumped together under one single heading, there is no such thing as an average commodity. Their prices behave differently and they are influenced by commodity-specific factors. Gold prices will be impacted by the festival season in India, oil prices by the driving season in the USA, Australian natural gas prices by tsunamis in northern Asia, global grain prices by droughts in the USA, Russia and Australia, copper prices by earthquakes in Chile and coffee prices by the frosts in Brazil and Colombia. As the global economy expands, we can assume that commodity prices will rise but the actual path of prices will be heavily dependent on the forces of nature.[12]

1.2.2 Hedging

Producers and consumers of commodities will use the derivative markets to hedge their future production or consumption. Producers will want to lock in the prices of their future output

---

[11] An excellent book on the real life world of commodities is *The King of Oil, The Secret Lives of Marc Rich* by Daniel Ammann.

[12] In the short run, prices will be volatile and this volatility will tend to outweigh the underlying growth rate. In the medium to long run, however, prices will still be volatile but this volatility will tend to be outweighed by the underlying growth rate.

so that they have certainty of revenue. This certainty is required since their capital spending requirements are enormous and spread out over many years. Likewise, consumers will look to lock in the supply of raw materials over time since they will not want to risk not being able to find the materials they need to manufacture their finished goods. This is hedging. The producers will generally sell their future output using prices determined today. They will deliver their output at predetermined dates in the future and receive the price at the level set today. The consumers will generally buy their future needs at prices determined today. They will receive the raw materials at predetermined dates in the future and pay the price at the level set today.

The hedging actions of the producers and consumers very rarely match. The producers tend to hedge their output 3 to 5 years out while the consumers tend to hedge their demand out to 2 years. Moreover, the producers will tend to want to hedge when average prices are high (locking in high prices), while consumers will want to hedge when average prices are low (locking in low prices). Someone will need to sit in the middle, the *speculators*.

The traders generally get a bad press from governments, regulators, consumer bodies and charities since they are perceived as profiting from some kind of unfair activity in commodity prices. Such complaints are ill-targeted, however. Producers and consumers need to hedge. Without this hedging, producers and consumers would not be able to plan effectively. By stepping in to offset the mismatch between the hedging activities of the producers and the consumers, the traders are providing a publically undervalued service.

1.2.3 Backwardation and contango

Backwardation describes a situation where, for a given commodity, short-dated prices are higher than longer-dated prices. For example, if the price for delivery of copper today is $8,000 per tonne and the price for delivery 5 years into the future is $6,000 per tonne, then the copper curve would be backwardated. In this situation, one can argue that prices are assumed (or discounted) to fall over time (Figure 1.2).

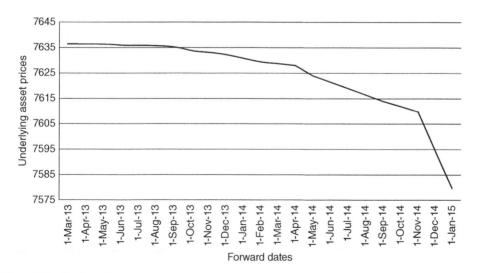

Figure 1.2   Backwardation curve

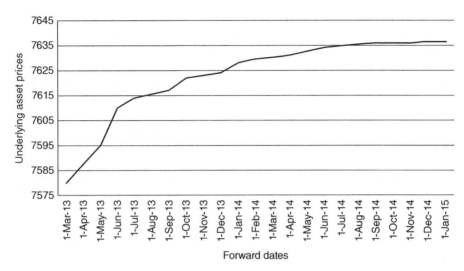

Figure 1.3   Contango curve

In a curve that is in *contango*, short-dated prices are lower than longer-dated prices. For example, if the price for delivery of copper today is $8,000 per tonne but the price for delivery 5 years into the future is $10,000 per tonne, then the copper curve would be in contango (Figure 1.3).

Which curve shape is the natural state of affairs? When there is excess supply of a particular raw material available, perhaps because the world economy is in recession and demand is weak, then the curve for that commodity may be in contango. Prices for immediate or near-immediate delivery will be low since producers will be happy to sell their excess inventories. Over time, however, producers will tend to cut back on their production, especially the high-cost producers. This will reduce the available supply, bringing supply and demand into balance at higher prices. The commodity markets will anticipate this and so longer-dated prices, prices for delivery further into the future, will be higher than short-dated prices.

When there is excess demand for a particular raw material, perhaps because the world economy is booming and demand is strong, then the curve for that commodity may be in backwardation. Prices for immediate or near-immediate delivery will be high since producers will demand high prices for their production. Over time, however, consumers may switch to substitutes or completely alternative products. This will reduce demand over time, bringing supply and demand into balance at lower prices. The commodity markets will anticipate this and so longer-dated prices, prices for delivery further into the future, will be much lower than short-dated prices.[13]

The ability to store or warehouse commodities (with the notable exception of electricity) might suggest to the average market participant that the "normal" state of commodity curves should be gently upward-sloping, i.e., in gentle contango. If a particular commodity curve

---

[13] Some commodity analysts interpret the long end of the commodity curve as a guide to the long-term marginal cost of production for that commodity. Empirically, when we look at forward curves at different points in time, long-term prices tend to cluster within a smaller range of prices.

were too steeply upward-sloping and prices for the immediate or near-immediate delivery of the commodity were much lower than longer-dated prices, then speculators could buy the commodity, store it in a warehouse and simultaneously sell for future delivery at the higher longer-dated price. Short-dated prices would tend to rise relative to longer-dated prices as the excess supply was taken out of the market and stored. The profit from such a transaction would depend upon the difference between short-dated and long-dated prices, the cost of warehousing the commodity (such as the rental cost of the warehouse and the insurance premium to insure it) and the interest cost of all the capital tied up in the commodity. Theoretically, then, there is a limit to the extent to which a commodity curve can be in contango.

But what if the curve is in backwardation? In this case, traders who are holding inventories may release their inventories in the spot market (i.e., for immediate delivery), selling at the high short-dated prices and buying back the inventory that has sold for future delivery at lower prices. By not having to warehouse the inventories, they would save on warehouse rental, the insurance premium and the interest cost of the capital deployed. Such flows would tend to cause a backwardated curve to move less into backwardation (or more into contango). The problem is that this trade cannot continue indefinitely. Once the available inventories have been sold off, there will be pressure on the curve to return to the original extent of the backwardation. It is easier to amass inventories than it is to keep selling them; once they have gone, they have gone. Hence, there is a limit to the extent of the contango but perhaps not to the extent of the backwardation.

Indeed, it is probably not an unreasonable statement to make to say that near-arbitrage situations are more likely to exist (and persist) in commodity markets than in other asset classes. This can occur for many reasons – for example, the activities of commodity consumers, the actions of index players in the futures markets, the inability to take advantage of the arbitrage opportunity (e.g., is there enough storage or transportation capacity?) and/or the inability to access sufficient finance.

1.2.4   Investment in commodities

The past 5 to 10 years have seen increased interest in commodities as a form of investment. Commodities are now demanded not just for the production of goods, say, but as a potential source of asset returns. Pension funds, insurance companies, sovereign wealth funds and wealthy individuals have been investing increasing amounts of money into commodities partly because they believe that commodity prices are likely to trend higher over time (as the world demands more and more of these scarce resources) and because they are believed to offer portfolio diversification benefits relative to financial assets. Equity-like returns from uncorrelated assets is the lure.

At first, this investment took very simple forms, perhaps investment in a financial product offered by one of the many investment banks involved in commodities. These financial products were, and still are, often based on the average price of a basket of commodities. Later, investors might have moved onto slightly more esoteric products offered by these same banks or they may have invested in one of the many commodity hedge funds that started in the mid to late part of the last decade. Next, they might have invested in the underlying commodities themselves, possibly trading them on a public exchange. Finally, as their experience in commodity products grows, they might have invested in non-listed assets such as commodity-related infrastructure; for example, buying timberland, mines, agricultural land, refiners, etc.

Note that the investment world has long been involved in commodities. Many investors have long held equity in commodity producers and traders, such as the major oil producers (BP, Shell, etc.), the mining companies (Rio Tinto, Xstrata, etc.), commodity traders, electricity producers and the like. For equity investment, however, the main risk tends to be the general level of the world's major stock markets. The prices of commodity-related equities tend to be highly correlated with the prices of equities issued by financials, utilities, producers of consumer goods and services, etc. So, investment in commodity-related equities tends to have returns that are only indirectly related to commodity prices. This may explain why governments often complain about direct investment in commodities while not complaining about investment in commodity companies, although this may be giving governments a little more credit than they perhaps deserve.

The experience of many investors in the commodity sector has not been a rewarding one. The early part of the last decade saw commodity prices rise rapidly, in large part due to the industrial emergence of China and the other BRIC nations. Those investors who were in from the start were able to ride the tremendous growth in prices in the 2000–2007 period. Those investors who became involved from 2007 onwards, encouraged by the gains of the previous years, have lived through a very volatile period for commodity prices. The sought-after diversification benefits of direct commodity investment have not been as evident as predicted since the financial crisis has, for example, hit commodity prices as much as it has hit equity and property prices. A number of high profile commodity hedge funds opened and closed in this latter period as investors first flocked to them and then departed from them, discouraged by the extreme volatility of returns.

Nevertheless, the amounts invested in commodities have continued to rise as more and more asset managers look for ways to increase investment returns in the current low interest-rate environment.

1.2.5 Commodity fundamentals

Producers and consumers of commodities tend to think of commodity prices being determined by demand and supply fundamentals and, on top of this, by investor flows. They tend not to think of investor flows as being "real" supply and demand. One will hear statements such as "copper prices are too high relative to supply/demand fundamentals". Clearly, however, the current copper price is determined solely by supply and demand. That is how prices are determined. Commodity researchers will spend much of their professional lives analysing Chinese commodity imports, Chile's copper output, cheating on production quotas by individual countries within OPEC, maintenance schedules for oil rigs, weather patterns, etc. Then using these supply and demand *fundamentals*, they will forecast prices. In the past, commodity prices were much more stable and researchers tended to have more success in forecasting prices. With the recent increased volatility in prices, however, comes greater propensity for forecasting errors.

The investment community is an easy target to explain those errors. "If it were not for those pesky investors, prices would be lower", might be one refrain from a researcher who has under-predicted prices. Is this fair? Possibly, but perhaps one should ask why these same researchers are not trying to model the impact of investor flows, if investors do indeed have an impact (see below).

One issue with commodity prices is that the demand and supply schedules are inelastic (in an economics sense). Shifts in these schedules will have significant impacts on commodity prices

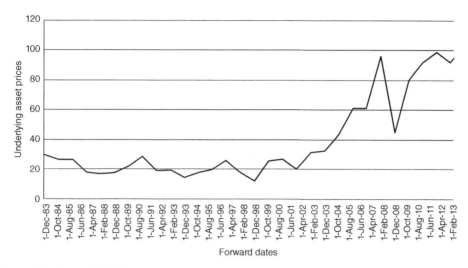

Figure 1.4   Crude Oil WTI

and, unfortunately, these shifts are unpredictable and unobservable except through the prism of price changes. Could it be that unobservable movements in the fundamentals are really to blame for recent volatility of prices? After all, as demand increases with the industrialization of the BRIC economies and the rest of the newly industrialized economies (NIEs), there will be a whole set of demand schedules that researchers know little about. This is especially the case for China where the actual level of inventories is a multiple of the amount recorded in official warehouse statistics.

The truth of the matter is that commodity prices are becoming more and more random in the short term and this is not the fault of the investor. As commodity markets become tighter and tighter, with the growth of the NIEs and the depletion of the more easily accessible commodity supply, one has to accept greater volatility in prices. This does not mean that the fundamentals no longer apply. It just means that forecasting prices will become more and more difficult; as difficult as forecasting FX or equity prices (Figure 1.4).

1.2.6   Super-cycles in commodity prices

A paper published in February 2012 by the *United Nations' Department of Economic and Social Affairs*[14] reviewed the literature around *super-cycles* in commodity prices.

What are super-cycles? They are decades-long periods of significantly above- or below-trend movements in prices. Super-cycles differ from short-term fluctuations that come about from microeconomic factors in that they tend to span "20–70 year complete cycles". These long cycles can see commodity prices varying between 20 and 40% above or below their long-run trend. The authors of the UN report argued that approaching the analysis of commodity prices from a super-cycle framework is "an important innovation over the more traditional analysis

---

[14] http://www.un.org/esa/desa/papers/2012/wp110_2012.pdf.

of trends and structural breaks (since) it allows us to analyze the gradual change in long-term trends instead of a priori assuming a constant deterministic or stochastic trend".[15]

1.2.7 Future regulation

Although evidence to support the view that direct investment in commodities leads to higher prices is patchy, there is a belief among many that those people who do not directly use commodities in the production process should not be allowed to buy them since these people obviously (sic) push commodity prices higher than they otherwise would be to the detriment of all. As noted earlier, however, many traders, especially those who help producers and consumers to hedge, provide a very valuable service. Hence, there is a begrudging acceptance of such activity although it is still viewed with suspicion by some politicians, regulators, charities and consumer bodies.

Investment in commodities to turn a profit, however, wins few fans outside of the investment business despite there being conflicting evidence as to whether or not investors themselves push up prices. A review by the last Labour government in the UK found that investment flows did not impact commodity prices on average but did increase the overall liquidity of the marketplace while a recent study by the Commodity Futures Trading Commission (CFTC) found that investor flows were the main determinant of the moves in agricultural futures prices in the USA.

Consider the case of commodity futures markets, however. If investors are buying, someone must be selling since futures contracts are a zero-sum game. The buyers always equal the sellers. Are the investors merely hedging producer supply? To be fair, much of the work done in this area tends to be politically motivated and, as such, the results will have a political bias. Interestingly, when prices are rising, the investor tends to get the blame, when prices are falling, however, it is the state of the world economy. Nevertheless, the upshot is that investors in commodity futures will find themselves more and more limited in what they can and cannot do. Some regulators would clearly like to be in a position where only "real" commodity people trade commodities even if liquidity is harmed in the process.

1.3 FIXED INCOME

1.3.1 Introduction

Fixed income products can be split into three broad categories, *rates*, *credit* and *inflation*. For all these, a significant driver of the equilibrium price of the product will be the general level of interest rates, as determined in a large way by the relevant central bank. For rates products (government bonds and interest rate swaps), changes in the general level of interest rates are essentially the only significant driver of equilibrium prices. Credit products, however, are those where there is a second, significant driver of prices, i.e., credit risk – for example, in the case of a bond issued by a highly-geared corporate or by a lowly-rated emerging market sovereign (in the last few years, credit risk has become a major factor also in the sovereign bond market of some Euro Zone countries). By extension, inflation products are those where

---

[15] As an aside, the authors also note that there is a short-run relationship running from crude oil prices to changes in world output. This finding supports the widely held view that oil price hikes constrain economic growth in the short run. This is in sharp contrast with non-oil prices, which tend to follow world GDP and are thus more demand determined.

the second significant driver of prices is the future development of some inflation index, such as Consumer Price Index (CPI) or Retail Price Index (RPI) – for example, in the case of an inflation-linked bond issued by a sovereign or the case of an inflation swap offered by an investment bank.

Fixed income products may also be thought of as *flow* or *structured*. Flow products are essentially those products that are traded by many market participants and they have simpler cash flow structures. A flow product, for example, would be a government bond, a bond issued by a corporate or an interest rate swap (we discuss swaps in some detail later in the book). Structured products, on the other hand, are essentially those with relatively complex, non-linear cash flows, although, with the passage of time, the distinction between what is flow and what is structured has become a little blurred. Products that were once considered to be structured are now thought of as flow, such as Credit Default Swaps (CDS), Mortgage Backed Securities (MBS) or basic options.

1.3.2   Credit risk

Credit risk is the risk that a borrower will not be able *or willing* to meet its interest or principal repayment obligations. Historically, the risk for many borrowers has been assessed by ratings agencies, such as Standard and Poor's or Moody's. Each of the ratings agencies has a slightly different approach to valuing credit risk, although their qualitative assessments tend to be very similar.

How does one measure credit risk? There are many ways to measure credit risk depending, to some extent, on how the enquiry is framed. In simple terms, however, credit risk can be thought of as the probability of a *credit event* occurring (e.g., a default) multiplied by the loss incurred as a result of that credit event.[16] Credit events include bankruptcy, failure to pay, default or repudiation (a polite term for sovereign default).

As noted above, for all fixed income products, one would expect their prices to be influenced *directly* by the general level of interest rates. However, credit risk (and inflation) will also be impacted *indirectly* by the level of interest rates. As interest rates are reduced, for example, one would expect that the ability of a borrower to meet his or her obligations will improve, i.e., credit risk would decline. On the other hand, if interest rates are increased, one would expect the ability of the same borrower to meet his or her obligations to deteriorate, i.e., credit risk would increase. In a sense, the prices of credit products are influenced both directly and indirectly by the overall level of rates and by factors related to the specific borrower.

1.3.3   The empirical pattern of yield curve moves

Until 2010, the historical record showed that yield curves bull steepened or bear flattened.[17] When yields fell, they tended to fall across the entire yield curve and to be led by moves in short-tenor instruments. Not only that but the absolute moves in short rates were greater than the absolute moves in long rates, hence, the yield curve steepened. Conversely, when

---

[16] Credit risk (or spread) = probability of default × (1 – recovery rate). What you expect to lose multiplied by the probability that you will lose it.

[17] Since the start of 2010, central banks around the world have held short-term interest rates at very low levels as they have tried to combat the *balance sheet recession*. With short rates held in place, interest-rate volatility that would usually manifest itself along an entire yield curve has been transmitted into the medium to long end of the curve. Consequently, higher yields have tended to be associated with steeper (rather than flatter) curves and vice versa for lower yields. This pattern is likely to remain the case until the central banks refrain from holding short rates at abnormally low levels.

yields rose, they tended to rise across the entire yield curve and to be led, again, by moves in short-tenor instruments. Again, the absolute moves in short rates were greater than the absolute moves in long rates and, hence, the yield curve flattened. At the same time, however, yield curves would see significant changes in their shape. As rates fell, they tended to become more convex (imagine an upside-down bowl). As rates rose, yield curves tended to become less convex and more concave (imagine a normal bowl).

The key driver in most cases was central bank activity. If central banks are in control of anything, it is short-term interest rates. Short rates are raised and lowered in order to control macroeconomic variables. As short rates are changed, the entire yield curve follows but long rates typically move by less; they tend to be more stable.

1.3.4   Modelling interest rate movements

Modelling stock or commodity price movements is relatively easy; assume a random walk, with an element of mean reversion and some capacity for occasional (random) jumps to "explain" market crashes. Modelling interest rates is a lot more complicated, however. In fact, we include this section (and the next) for completeness but most readers will probably prefer to skip it (them) and move straight to the section on foreign exchange.

In *Quantitative Finance*, Paul Wilmott notes, "... there's no reason why interest rates should behave like stock prices, there's no reason why we should use the same model for interest rates as for equities. In fact, such a model would be a very poor one; interest rates do not exhibit the long-term exponential growth seen in the equity markets." A thorough description of the leading interest rate models is beyond the scope of this book but interested readers may want to take a look at Rebonato's classic *Interest-rate Options Models*.

In the jargon, interest rate models either attempt to model the future movements in a liquid, "short rate", such as the Ho & Lee approach, or they attempt to model movements in the entire forward curve,[18] such as the Heath, Jarrow & Morton (HJM) approach. When modelling the path of the short rate, this will be something like a 1-month or 3-month rate rather than the overnight rate since changes in the latter tend not to be a very good guide for other short-term rates. Just as with modelling equity or commodities, the interest rate modeller will need a "drift" parameter, i.e., by how much will interest rates tend to change from period to period, and a "volatility" parameter that measures the random changes in interest rates around the drift. Unlike models for equities and commodities, however, there will also need to be mean reversion to some kind of constant value (rather than to a trend). Finally, if one can model the future path of the spot rate, then one can, of course, create an entire yield curve.

1.3.5   Modelling the risks of default

When modelling default, it is generally assumed that the probability of default is exogenous to the asset under consideration. Such an approach is popular since it is simple to use even if it does not sound very clever. Think about simultaneously tossing three coins every month. If you get three heads, then assume default.

Now think of a corporate bond and a risk-free bond of equal maturity. In the world just described, where the risk of default is exogenous, the incremental yield that the corporate bond

---

[18] Forward rates are those future short-term interest rates implied by the current yield curve.

needs to earn to compensate for the default risk can be thought of as a fixed spread added to the yield on the risk-free bond.[19]

For example, a 5-year risk-free bond has a yield to maturity of 6% while the yield to maturity of a 5-year risky bond is 7.5%. The extra 1.5% is the compensation for the risk of default. In this example, if we have 100% loss at default, then the implied probability of the company default is approximately 1.5% per year.

A slight refinement to this model is to assume that the probability of default changes with time. For example, one could assume a Poisson distribution so that there is a very small chance of a default initially, rising over time to some maximum value before tailing off indefinitely. This seems to mirror the empirical record. Over the long term, companies either do well or have already gone bust; it is unusual for well-established companies to go into default, they are generally taken over beforehand.

In practice, loss on default is not 100% and there is usually some recovery value and one can assume a recovery value given the historical record. Such data is easily obtained from the ratings agencies. Of course, alternatively, the recovery rate could be modelled but this is probably a digression too far.

Finally, as an aside, we note that there is the possibility of a re-rating, either positive or negative. The ratings agencies publish data on the likelihood of transition from one rating to another and this data could also be incorporated into models to price credit risk.

1.4 FOREIGN EXCHANGE

1.4.1 Introduction

An exchange rate is the ratio of the price of one currency versus another. In most cases, exchange rates between the currencies of the developed economies are freely floating although there are occasional bouts of central bank intervention.

Empirically, the best forecast of tomorrow's exchange rate is today's spot rate. In other words, short-term changes in exchange rates tend to be random. This does not cause too much worry for the FX forecasting profession, however, which makes a great living from making short- and long-term forecasts. As with equities, there is fundamental analysis, technical analysis and quantitative analysis.

There are many fundamental models of exchange rates. Unfortunately, despite the efforts of many academic researchers in particular, such models fail to explain the following real world experiences:

1. Exchange rate movements very often tend to be unrelated to changes in macroeconomic variables over periods exceeding a year.
2. Exchange rates are excessively volatile relative to the underlying economic fundamentals (assuming that we can agree on what these are).[20]

---

[19] The spread to the risk-free rate is not all credit risk. There are other issues to take into account such as the relative liquidity of the credit bond versus the risk-free bond but, as a means of understanding, it is probably a fairly reasonable approximation.

[20] A 2011 IMF Working Paper argued that inflation and growth rates are the two principal fundamental factors used by foreign exchange forecasters in the formation of exchange rate expectations. The prominence of inflation points to broad acceptance of purchasing power parity. Other oft-mentioned factors, including the current account balance, do not appear to play a common role in the formation of exchange rate expectations. See http://www.imf.org/external/pubs/ft/wp/2011/wp11116.pdf.

Note also that excess returns (i.e., returns over and above the risk-free interest rates) from speculating in currencies tend to be predictable but inexplicable; what academics call the *forward bias puzzle*.

Given the weaknesses inherent in fundamental analysis of exchange rates, it is surprising that it is still popular, although, of course, we all like to have some kind of prop to support our decision-making. When the forecasts support the investment view, they are popular. When they do not support the investment view, they can be ignored.

Technical analysis is also very popular for foreign exchange markets, perhaps because the fundamental models have such a poor forecasting record. Nature abhors a vacuum and it is human nature to try to explain the world through repeated patterns. There are many adherents and some techniques within technical analysis do seem to work for foreign exchange forecasts because of this. If enough market participants expect a certain exchange rate level to hold, then it will very likely hold. The problem is, we tend to remember the successes more than the failures and most testing of the value of technical analysis tends to be undertaken in hindsight.

Surveys of foreign exchange market participants suggest that they generally base their short-term forecasts on recent trends, i.e., they extrapolate recent behaviour. This is why moving averages are so popular as technical analysis tools. Moving averages are essentially extrapolative, i.e., they extrapolate the recent trend. Longer term, however, i.e., 1 to 2 years, market participants tend to focus more on fundamental models in their assessment of value. Nevertheless, foreign exchange trading tends to be short-term trading, given the sensitivity of most players to large mark-to-market swings. As a consequence, while fundamental models may matter, they have little relevance for near-term price developments.

1.4.2   How foreign exchange rates are quoted

Foreign exchange rates are always defined in currency pairs, e.g., EUR/USD. The first currency in the pair is called the *base currency* and the second is called the *term currency*. The foreign exchange rate represents the number of units of the term currency that must be surrendered in order to acquire one unit of the base currency. So, a foreign exchange rate defined as CCYA/CCYB and equal to X means that X units of the CCYB (term currency) can be exchanged for 1 unit of CCYA (base currency). In other words, if the EUR/USD rate is 1.27, it means that 1.27 units of USD can be exchanged for 1 unit of EUR.

When expressing foreign exchange rates against USD, the standard market conventions are as follows:

- When quoting EUR, GBP (Great Britain pound), AUD (Australian dollar) or NZD (New Zealand dollar) against USD, the USD is the term currency. Consequently, the standard market convention is to quote EUR/USD, GBP/USD, AUD/USD or NZD/USD respectively, i.e., number of US dollars per unit of the other currency.
- When quoting the remaining currencies against USD, the USD is the base currency. Consequently, the standard market convention is to quote the number of units of the foreign currency per 1 US dollar, e.g., 1 USD = 0.89 CHF in the case of Swiss franc.
- When quoting EUR crosses, EUR conventionally tends to be the base currency, i.e., one will generally see market prices such as EUR/AUD, EUR/CHF, EUR/JPY (JPY is the Japanese yen).

SUMMARY

In this chapter, we focused on the liquid investment asset classes in which financial derivatives are normally traded, namely equities, fixed income, commodities and foreign exchange. The aim was to give a sense of the general price characteristics of these markets, e.g., how they are quoted and how they move through time. We also aimed to make some observations on how to model underlying asset price behaviour for each asset class since investors must understand how prices behave in their composite parts in order to have a real understanding of the value that can be extracted from multi-asset derivative products.

2

Derivatives: Forwards, Futures and Swaps

In this chapter, we introduce the standard derivative products of forwards, futures and swaps. We will go through key definitions and the most common jargon and we will subsequently start discussing the pricing and hedging framework for derivatives, with examples taken from a variety of asset classes. In particular, the notion of a forward contract and its pricing is crucial to fully understand the concepts presented in the following chapters of this book. Given its importance, we will discuss it with reference to different asset classes (such as equity, foreign exchange, commodity and fixed income), trying to develop a framework based on intuition rather than a formal proof. The drawback of an approach focused on intuition is that, from time to time, our discussion may not be theoretically rigorous, although we will reach exactly the same conclusions. In particular some of the instruments presented in this chapter (such as futures and swaps) will be discussed only in relatively basic terms and to the extent that they are linked to other sections of the book.

2.1 DERIVATIVES

A derivative is a financial instrument whose value is dependent upon, or derived from, one or more other financial instruments or observable variables; these instruments or observable variables are generally known as underlying assets. Derivatives are financial instruments in their own right with their own price dynamics. Consequently, we can say that the price of a derivative is determined (among other things) by fluctuations in the prices of the underlying asset or assets.

A derivative can be seen either as a private contract between two or more parties or it can take the form of an exchange-traded instrument. Futures contracts, forward contracts, options and swaps are the most common types of derivatives. Although derivatives are instruments derived from other underlying assets, they can be traded in their own right and can be used for hedging and speculative purposes. They range from fully standardized to very bespoke, tailor-made products. The most standardized derivatives (i.e., futures) are traded on exchanges (as we will see in more detail in section 2.3), whereas customized contracts are traded over-the-counter (OTC). An over-the-counter contract is a private, bilateral contract between two parties in which they agree on the economic terms of the particular trade, as we will see in the case of forwards and swaps.

A key feature of most derivatives instruments is that they allow market participants to take leveraged exposures to the underlying asset. This means that the amounts that can be earned or lost in a derivative transaction could exceed the amounts that are exchanged when the transaction begins. In fact, in an ideal world, where it is assumed that all market participants are not subject to the risk of defaulting on their obligations, many derivatives transactions would not even require an initial financial outlay. This is very uncommon for non-derivatives transactions. For instance, buying stocks or bonds requires an initial cash disbursement while exchanging a certain amount of one currency for another currency requires an initial exchange of cash. This may not necessarily be the case for many derivative instruments, at least in an ideal world. In practice, things are a bit more complicated because the risk that market participants default on their future obligations cannot be ignored. Therefore, even when trading instruments that, in principle, should not require a financial outlay (such as futures contracts, as we will see), market participants are often required to post margins as guarantees of their potential future obligations.

2.2 FORWARD CONTRACTS

2.2.1 Definition

A forward contract, or simply a forward, is an over-the-counter contract between two parties to buy or sell an asset at a specified future date at a fixed price determined at the time when the contract is agreed. This is different from a spot contract, which is an agreement to buy or sell an asset immediately.[1]

The party agreeing to buy the underlying asset in the future is said to *go long* or to assume a *long position*. The party agreeing to sell the asset in the future is said to *go short* or assume a *short position*. The price agreed upon is called the *delivery price* or the *forward purchase price*. Usually, the delivery price is equal to the *implied forward price* prevailing at the time when the contract is agreed. We will define and explain how to calculate the implied forward price later in the chapter, although, at this stage, it is worth noting that if the delivery price is the same as the implied forward price at the inception of the trade, then the current value of the forward contract will be zero when it is negotiated. Such a forward contract is said to be "at market". This does not mean, of course, that the forward contract is not valuable to one of the parties involved in the transaction. It must provide some service otherwise there would be no trade. When we say that the current value of the forward contract is zero, what we really mean is that the cost of entering into the contract is zero at the time of the trade; neither party has to pay any money to the other at that time to initiate the trade. As market prices move, however, the value of the forward contract will change and one party will see a profit on the trade and the other one will see a loss.

Like other OTC derivatives, forward contracts can entail significant counterparty credit risk. There are clearly ways to mitigate exposure to counterparty risk, however, such as collateralization. Under collateralization, there is regular marking to market (i.e., calculations of valuation/profitability for each side) of OTC positions just as exchanges use margining to mark-to-market futures positions (as we will see in section 2.3). With collateralization, the two parties to a trade will make regular payments between themselves so that neither party has a significant outstanding financial debt to the other prior to the expiry of the contract.

Let us show a simple example of a forward contract. Table 2.1 lists the quotes for spot and for selected forward contracts for the EUR/USD rate prevailing in the interbank market on 12 Jan 2012.

The spot bid indicates the level at which the bank showing the highest bid is willing to buy EUR in the spot market, i.e., for immediate delivery. The quoting bank is prepared to spend

---

[1] When we say "immediately", we do not mean on the same day but, rather, within a few days. This is because a certain amount of time has to be allowed for the trade to be settled, i.e., for paperwork to be completed and for any cash flows or exchange of assets. In most FX trades, a spot transaction is settled within 2 days.

Table 2.1   Example of EUR/USD forward prices

	Bid	Offer
Spot	1.2778	1.2782
1-month forward	1.2755	1.2759
3-month forward	1.2725	1.2728
6-month forward	1.2695	1.2699
1-year forward	1.2635	1.2640

$1.2778 to buy 1 EUR. The spot offer indicates that the bank showing the lowest offer is willing to sell 1 EUR for $1.2782 in the spot market. The 1-month forward bid indicates that the bank is willing to buy EUR for delivery in 1 month at $1.2755 per EUR and the 1-month forward offer indicates that it is willing to sell 1 EUR for delivery in 1 month for $1.2759. And so on.

The difference between the spot and the forward price is called the *forward premium* or *forward discount* (in the foreign exchange market, such a difference is generally described as the "forward points"). Forward contracts, like other derivatives, can be used for hedging purposes or speculation purposes.

To illustrate how a forward contract can be used, let us assume the following scenario. A US corporation knows today that it will have to pay EUR 500,000 in 3 months. It can go long a 3-month EUR/USD forward (i.e., long EUR, short USD) where it commits to buy EUR 500,000 at the rate of $1.2728 per EUR (this is taken from the 3-month forward price in Table 2.1). The bank counterparty on the other side of the forward contract will go short the contract. Both parties have made a binding commitment but, as we said earlier, there is no exchange of cash at the time of the trade since the initial cost of entering the forward contract is zero. In this example, the US corporation is hedging itself. It needs to buy EUR at some point in the future but it is arranging today to buy it in the future at a delivery price known/fixed today.

2.2.2 Payoffs of forward contracts

The forward contract obliges the corporation to buy EUR 500,000 in 3 months at $1.2728 per EUR, a total spend of $636,400. Whether or not the decision to hedge will end up being the correct one will depend somewhat on the actual level of EUR/USD when the forward contract comes due.

Table 2.2 should help to illustrate this point. If the EUR/USD rate rises to 1.2810 then the corporation will have benefited. By hedging, it will have saved itself $4,100 since it has ended up buying EUR at a better level than the level currently prevailing in the market. If, however,

Table 2.2   Payoff of forward contract

EUR/USD rate when forward contract comes due	1.2600	1.2728	1.2810
Payoff in USD	500,000 × (1.2600 − 1.2728) = − 6,400	0	500,000 × (1.2810 − 1.2728) = 4,100

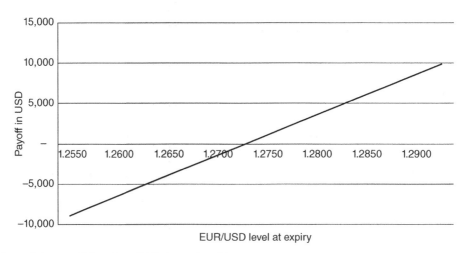

Figure 2.1   Payoff from long EUR forward position

the EUR/USD rate falls, the corporation will be $6,400 worse off than it would have been if it had not hedged itself and merely traded the spot rate when it needed to do so.

Of course, the decision to hedge does give the corporation peace of mind.[2] Ex-post, if the corporation loses money from the hedge then it may wish that it had not put it on but, ex-ante, the hedge may well have been worthwhile. The real worth of the hedge is in protecting the corporation against significant adverse movements in the EUR/USD exchange rate. For example, if the EUR/USD rate had risen to 1.4000 and the corporation had not hedged, then it would have had to pay $700,000 to buy EUR 500,000 rather than the $636,400 that it had to pay under the terms of the forward contract.[3]

Of course, the forward can also be used as a speculative instrument rather than a hedging instrument. In this case, the value of the decision to buy or sell the forward should be seen in terms of how much money was made or lost given the amount of risk that was taken. If the corporation were speculating, then a decision to buy the forward at $1.2728 might be seen as a good trade if EUR/USD subsequently moves to $1.2810. At this point, the US corporation would be able to buy EUR 500,000 at $1.2728 (it is obliged to do so in the forward contract) and simultaneously sell EUR 500,000 at $1.2810 (in the spot market) for a $4,100 profit. On the other hand, if EUR/USD falls to, say, $1.2600 then the corporation would end up losing $6,400 since it would have to buy EUR 500,000 at $1.2728 (in its previously agreed forward contract) and simultaneously sell EUR 500,000 at $1.2600 in the spot market to get its dollars back.

Figures 2.1 and 2.2 show the terminal payoff from the perspective of the corporation (long EUR forward position) and its counterparty (short EUR forward position).

---

[2] Technically, a corporation is merely a paper entity. It does not have any personality. Nevertheless, although we may incur the wrath of the academics by treating the corporation as if it were an individual or a group of individuals, it will do no harm right now for us to treat the corporation and its officers in the same way.

[3] One could argue also that an advantage of the hedge is to create "known future cash flows", which helps the corporation to budget more effectively. So, even if it is wrong about the future, at least it had "known" cash flows for that timeframe.

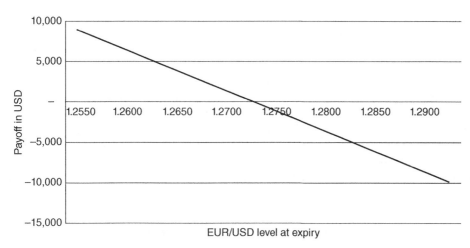

Figure 2.2   Payoff from short EUR forward position

We can generalize as follows. The final payoff from a long position in a forward contract on *one unit* of the underlying asset is given by:

$$\text{Payoff} = S - K$$

where S is the spot price of the asset at the maturity of the contract and K is the delivery price agreed at the inception of the trade. Likewise, the payoff from a short position in a forward contract on *one unit* of an asset is:

$$\text{Payoff} = K - S$$

2.2.3   Forward price versus delivery price

Let us return to the difference between the *delivery price* and *the implied forward price*. The delivery price is simply the price agreed between two parties at the point of trade to buy or sell the asset at some point in the future. It does not change when the contract has been agreed. Market conditions can clearly change afterwards, but the delivery price specified in the contract is fixed once the contract details have been agreed.

On the other hand, the implied forward price is the quantity that, if used as the delivery price when the forward contract is traded, makes the monetary value of the forward contract equal to zero.

In other words, we could say that the delivery price is part of the contractual agreement between the two counterparties, whereas the implied forward price is a function of the market conditions prevailing at any time (as we will see).

At the time of the trade, it is very likely that the delivery price will be set to be the same as the implied forward price, but this is by design only and it will imply a zero monetary value for the forward contract traded.

That said, it is not necessary that the delivery price be set to equal to the prevailing forward price since the two parties to the transaction can choose a delivery price to be anything that they wish. If the delivery price is not the same as the forward price, however, then there will need to be a cash flow at the time of the trade between the two parties to reflect the fact that the forward contract will now have an explicit non-zero monetary value. In summary, if the delivery price and the implied forward price are the same, then the forward contract will have no monetary value at the inception of the trade. As market conditions change subsequently, however, then it is very likely that the monetary value of the forward contract (for a given delivery price) will change, moving either into positive or negative territory.

In the example of the US corporation, the delivery price of the forward is $1.2728. It is clearly likely that, after the trade has taken place, the 3-month implied forward price will move. This is just a fact of life. There is no reason to believe that the forward price will stay constant, since it is a derivative and it moves with the general FX market level. In fact, it is also true that there is little reason to believe that the spot price will actually converge over time to the original delivery price.[4]

2.3 FUTURES CONTRACTS

A *future* is a contract traded on a derivatives exchange[5] which fixes the price for the delivery of a specific asset at a specific date in the future. As with a forward contract, the parties to a futures contract must fulfil the terms of the contract on the delivery date. Also, as with a forward contract, the price is set at the point of trading. Unlike a forward contract, however, the asset that is delivered for each contract will be of standardized quantity and quality, both of which are determined by the exchange on which the future is traded. Consequently, a future is a standardized contract and can be used for hedging, investment or speculative purposes, just like many other financial assets.

The price agreed at the point of trade is called the *futures price* and the delivery of the asset will occur on the *delivery date*. The delivery date is also determined by the exchange; each future will have a cycle of possible delivery dates, perhaps on a set day every month or on a set day specified for every quarter.

The exchange also determines the way the delivery will take place. Some futures contracts require *physical delivery* of the underlying asset (in which case the exchange will define the key features of the underlying that can be delivered and, in case of physical commodity delivery, also the location of the delivery); alternatively other futures contracts are *cash settled*, implying monetary transfers that reflect the profit and loss of the trade for each counterparty involved. Usually cash settlement is adopted when it would be impractical to deliver the underlying physical asset, for example stock index futures. A buyer of the future on an equity index, say, will not want to receive all the stocks in the index. Instead, he or she would prefer to receive a cash payment based on any profit made from the trade. In practice, a cash payment will be made from the party who sustained a loss to the one who made the profit.

Irrespective of the way in which it is settled, the party that is agreeing to buy the underlying asset on the predetermined date in the future (or to settle a monetary amount representing the profit and loss of the purchase of the underlying asset in case of cash-settled contracts), the *buyer* of the contract, is said to be *long the future* and the party agreeing to deliver the asset

---

[4] In other words, forward prices are not the same as expected future spot prices. The forward prices are determined under the condition of no-arbitrage. The best prediction of where FX prices will move over short periods of time, for example, is the current spot price. This is why FX speculators will often sell forward points when they are very high or buy them when they are very low since they do not expect the spot price to move to or past the forward value.

[5] Think of an exchange as a highly supervised market where buyers and sellers trade highly standardized contracts that have been specified by the exchange.

in the future (or to settle a monetary amount representing the profit and loss of the sale of the underlying asset in case of cash-settled contracts), the *seller* of the contract, is said to be *short the future*.

The parties involved in trading futures do not necessarily know each other and the exchange's clearing house sits between them and guarantees to each party involved in the transaction that the contract will be honoured, i.e., settled. Sometimes, the exchange will own its own clearing house. In this case, the exchange not only provides a centralized place where all trades are conducted, it acts as the central counterparty to all trades. This does not mean that exchanges actively buy and sell their products themselves, however. Rather, exchanges sit in the middle of all trades that take place on them. For example, assume a trader is offering to sell 1,000 contracts of a particular future on, say, the EUREX exchange, and another trader comes in to buy them. Although the buyer has bought the 1,000 contracts offered by the seller, EUREX effectively sits in the middle of the transaction so that both the buyer and the seller will face it as their ultimate counterparty when it comes to the delivery date/settlement of final profits or losses.

In particular, a mechanism for "margining" will be in place such that neither the buyer nor the seller of the contract has counterparty credit risk.[6] Broadly speaking the margining is structured as follows:

- When a futures contract is traded, both the buyer and the seller have to post an *initial margin*; this amount will be different for each future. It is determined by the rules of the exchange and, in general, it will be a function of the estimated expected future volatility of the underlying asset.
- During the life of the trade *variation margin* payments (also known as pay/collects) are made daily and are, in effect, the mechanism by which profits or losses from futures positions are crystallized. If the futures price subsequently falls, for example, the buyer of the future will have made an implied loss on the trade while the seller will have made an implied profit. In this case, the buyer of the future will have to pay variation margin to the exchange while the seller of the future will receive variation margin from the exchange. The converse is true in the case of a gain in the futures price. These margin payments mitigate the counterparty credit risk. Clearly, the exchange is unable to protect itself and its customers from every possible eventuality but the initial and variation margin together should ensure that all financial obligations can be honoured.

Since futures are standardized products, the holder of a futures position can always take out an equal and opposite position in the same underlying contract. The two positions would then offset each other and the difference between the futures prices would determine whether a profit or loss is made. So, for example, assume that, in a particular January, a trader sold 1,000 lots of the September EUREX Bund future, held the position until May and then bought them back. The trader no longer had a net position in the Bund future. There will be no obligation to deliver any bonds to the exchange in September and the profit or loss from the trade will depend upon the price at which the trader sold the future in January and the price paid to buy them back in May. These prices are unlikely to be the same. Since there is no exchange of bonds at delivery date, there will be no exchange of cash to settle the bond trades. So, how

---

[6] Counterparty risk is the risk that a counterparty in a derivatives transaction will not be able to honour its obligations. Clearly, any party owed money in such an event will be at a disadvantage. Counterparty risk mitigation has seen increased emphasis since the onset of the financial crisis in 2007.

will the trader realize his or her profit or loss? It is realized through the process of margining which we have just described. At this stage, it is also worth noting that in practice only a small percentage of traded futures contracts are kept until the delivery date (when either cash settlement or physical delivery will take place); most positions are closed out before or "rolled" to a subsequent expiry when the delivery date approaches.[7]

If cash-settled futures contracts are kept until the delivery date, the last transfer of funds between the buyer and the seller taking place through the margining mechanism will be based on a final settlement price determined by the exchange soon after the trading activity for that specific contract has been halted. On the other hand, if futures contracts based on physical delivery are kept until the last trading day of that contract, the seller will have to deliver the underlying asset to the exchange (which will then deliver it to the buyer) and, in return, he or she will receive a cash payment based on a final settlement price determined by the exchange. Economically, this is equivalent to the buyer paying the original traded price to the seller because all subsequent price changes have been reflected in the daily margining activity.

2.4   CALCULATING IMPLIED FORWARD PRICES AND VALUING EXISTING FORWARD CONTRACTS

We are able to determine implied forward prices (and futures prices, see section 2.5) for most financial assets from prices prevailing in the market place.[8] These "prevailing" prices will include the spot prices of the assets themselves as well as interest rates determined in the money markets. If implied forward prices were not related to prevailing market prices, then arbitrage opportunities could arise.[9] In the following analysis, we will look at the calculation of forward prices for various asset classes but we will work under a couple of simplifying assumptions. First, while there are bid–offer spreads, there are no other explicit transaction costs. Second, we will assume that tax rates are zero. These assumptions do not impact the core analysis, however, and ignoring them will make it easier to understand the key concepts.

2.4.1   Calculating implied forward prices on equities

In general, stocks pay dividends. For simplicity, however, we will approach the analysis by assuming non-dividend paying stocks; in any case, over some time periods, it may be the case that single stocks do not make dividend payments.

Non-dividend paying stocks

Let us assume the following. Today's spot price of a stock issued by company XYZ is $106.0–$106.2. Investors can buy the stock at $106.2 and sell it at $106.0; the spread is the revenue

---

[7] When "rolling" a futures position, one closes out the existing position and opens up a new position in a future with a different (later) delivery month. For example, if an investor is long a September crude oil future, then he or she can "roll" this future into the October contract by selling the existing September contract and buying the October contract. In this case, the investor has replaced a long position in the September contract by a long position in the October contract.

[8] This is not necessarily the case for some specific types of transactions, such as non-deliverable forwards in foreign exchange (see section 2.4.2) and some variables that, even if observable, do not have a deliverable nature (for instance, weather-related variables).

[9] In practice, arbitrage opportunities rarely exist. Consequently, one can generally assume, for example, that quoted forward prices are in line with the fair value forward prices. In other words, it may not be necessary for most market participants to know how to calculate forward prices; they just need to know how to use them. Nevertheless, understanding how to calculate forward prices for the various asset types, rather than just taking them as a given from screen quotes, will be crucial in providing a backdrop for the appreciation of option pricing and option Greeks (we will discuss this in great detail later in the book).

made by the equity trader who makes a market on this particular stock. Let us also assume that we can borrow money at 5% (annually compounded) and lend money at 4% (annually compounded). Finally, the current 2-year forward bid–offer quote observed in the market for stock issued by XYZ is $118.5–$119.0. Do these implied forward prices represent fair value? In other words, are they fair in the sense that there are no arbitrage opportunities available?

In order to answer this question, we need to know the total cost of buying and selling a share today and holding that position for 2 years.

First, let us look at the case of buying the share. We will have to pay $106.2 today and borrow the money to pay for it at 5% p.a. for 2 years. Under annually compounded interest rates, the repayment on the loan after 2 years (capital repayment and interest) will be $106.2 \times 1.05^2 = $117.09. What about the case of a short sale? We borrow one share, sell it in the market at $106.0 today and invest the proceeds at 4% for 2 years. We know that, under annually compounded interest rates, we will receive $106.0 \times 1.04^2 = $114.65 in 2 years (capital repayment and interest).[10]

Since the quoted forward bid price in the market, $118.5, is higher than the amount needed to buy the share in the spot market and carry the position for 2 years ($117.09), then we can do the following trade today. Borrow $106.2, buy one share in XYZ and simultaneously enter a forward contract to sell the share 2 years forward at $118.5. Then, after 2 years, we will sell share X for $118.5 (i.e., as agreed in the forward contract) and repay the loan at $117.09. In this trade, we make a riskless profit of $118.5 − $117.09 = $1.41. In other words, if the forward price is higher than the price required to purchase the share and to finance the position, an arbitrage opportunity will arise. The arbitrage opportunity can be exploited by buying the equity in the spot market and selling it in the forward market.

Conversely, what if the current 2-year forward price were quoted at $112.0–$112.5 given the same $106.0–$106.2 spot price? Since the forward offer price is lower than the amount received from selling the share spot and investing the proceeds for 2 years ($114.65), we can do the following trade today. Borrow share XYZ, sell it at $106.0 in the spot market, lend/deposit the proceeds at 4% and simultaneously enter into a contract to buy share XYZ 2 years forward at $112.5. Then, after 2 years, we simply buy the share for $112.5 as agreed in the forward contract, return the share to the counterparty who lent it to us initially and get our loan back, whose value is now $106.0 \times 1.04^2 = $114.65, including interest. In this case, we will make a profit of $114.65 − $112.5 = $2.15.

From these two simple examples, we can conclude that, in order to avoid arbitrage opportunities, the 2-year forward bid cannot be higher than $117.09 and the forward offer cannot be lower than $114.65. In all other cases, it would be possible to build a riskless portfolio with a guaranteed profit.

---

[10] In practice, the actual transaction might be for the short-seller to agree to lend money at 4% to an equity counterparty against taking the stock in XYZ as collateral. The stock would then be sold in the spot equity market for cash proceeds and this cash subsequently used to finance the loan. It sounds very circular but all the parties involved expect to benefit from the individual trades. The equity counterparty has raised some money at 4% that, presumably, it can now invest profitably elsewhere. In addition, it still has recourse to its share in XYZ, which it gets back after 2 years once the loan is repaid. The short-seller, meanwhile, has been able to short sell the stock in XYZ and, presumably, he or she expects to make a profit on this trade. He or she will have to buy it back at some point in the future, however, so that it can be delivered back to the equity counterparty once the loan is repaid. Finally, the buyer of the stock in the spot equity market presumably expects to profit from the purchase. This is about as close as we will get to financial alchemy. There are three happy participants to transactions that appear to cancel out. The value of the entire transaction comes from the fact that each market participant will have different assessments about the prospects for XYZ and they will have different investment opportunities and, hence, different needs for cash.

Generalizing, we can conclude that the upper and lower bound of the forward price on a non-dividend paying stock are:

$$\text{Upper bound: } F_{up} = S_{ask} \times (1 + r_{ask})^T$$

$$\text{Lower bound: } F_{low} = S_{bid} \times (1 + r_{bid})^T$$

where S_{ask} and S_{bid} are respectively the offer and bid spot price of the stock, r_{ask} and r_{bid} are respectively the offer and bid interest rates and T is the maturity of the forward contract measured in years.

Assuming no bid–offer in the spot price (S) or in the interest rate (r), we get the sample formula for the implied forward price (F) as follows:[11]

$$F = S \times (1 + r)^T$$

To be clear, when assessing the fairness of the implied forward price based on the idea of no-arbitrage pricing, we are not incorporating any sort of market expectation about the future price of the underlying asset. The implied forward price is not an expected price. It is merely a breakeven price. The forward price is the delivery price for the forward contract such that, if we simultaneously enter into a spot and a forward transaction (borrowing and lending money as appropriate), then we will break even; i.e., we will neither make nor lose any money. The straightforward no-arbitrage condition says nothing about market participants' opinions regarding the future value of the share (which are usually considered to be embedded in the spot price, at least in an efficient market). Moreover, the arbitrage opportunities described above are completely independent of the attitude towards risk shown by market participants.[12]

Dividend-paying stocks

In practice, companies pay dividends to their shareholders. So, let us revisit the previous example. Today's bid–offer for share XYZ is still assumed to be \$106.0–\$106.2 with a 5% borrowing rate and a 4% lending rate. There is, however, a dividend payment of \$3 paid annually. The current 2-year forward quote for XYZ observed in the market stands at \$112.5–\$113.0. Are there any potential arbitrage opportunities?

First, what is the total cost of buying one share today and carrying the position for 2 years? In this case, we will have to pay \$106.2 today and we can borrow that amount at the 5% interest for 2 years. However, we will receive \$3 in 1 year's time (which we can invest at 4% for the second year) and \$3 in 2 years, when our forward contract expires. The proceeds from the dividends (including the interest on the dividend reinvestment) will be \$3 × 1.04 + \$3 = \$6.12. The net amount that we need from the share sale to be able repay the loan will now be \$117.09 (which we calculated in the previous example) less the \$6.12 from the dividend payments, i.e., \$110.97.

---

[11] If we define r as the continuously compounded interest rate, the formula for the forward would become $F = S \times e^{rt}$.

[12] The price that an investor pays for an asset is such that he or she expects to earn the risk-free rate *plus* a risk premium that reflects the degree of risk involved. This does not mean, of course, that, ex-post, the investor will earn the risk premium. Future returns on risky assets are, by their very nature, uncertain. It means only that the investor expects, at trade inception, to earn the risk premium. In the long run, investors will need to earn risk premiums otherwise they will stop investing in risky assets. When pricing derivatives, however, the usual approach is to invoke the idea of no-arbitrage. There is a risky asset and a derivative. Generally, there will also be a cash investment and the investor is assumed to earn the risk-free rate on this investment. The investor earns the risk-free rate because the entire portfolio is hedged against movements in the underlying market. In calculating the price of the derivative, it is irrelevant whether the investor is risk averse, risk neutral or risk loving since there is no market risk in the portfolio. In a sense, the derived price fits with all three types of investor risk preference. Knowledge of investor risk preferences is, thus, irrelevant for the mechanics of derivative pricing. Assuming risk neutrality for pricing derivatives is, therefore, not the same as assuming that investors are risk neutral.

What about a share sale? We will have to borrow one share that we can sell in the market at $106 today that we can invest at the prevailing lending rate of 4% for 2 years' time. We will also have to finance the dividend, however, (i.e., we will have to pay the dividend amounts to the stock lender) and the total amount needed at the end of the second year to cover the dividends will be $3 × 1.05 + $3 = $6.15. Therefore, the net amount that will be received in 2 years will be $114.65 (calculated previously) less $6.15 (the value of the dividend flows), i.e., $108.5.

Since the forward bid price in our example is higher than the amount needed to buy the share in the spot market and carry the position for 2 years, we could make a risk-free profit of $1.53 ($112.5 − $117.09 + $6.12).

From this simple example, we can conclude that, in order to avoid arbitrage opportunities, the 2-year forward bid cannot be higher than $110.97 and the 2-year forward offer cannot be lower than $108.5. If so, it is impossible to build a riskless portfolio with a guaranteed profit.

Generalizing, we can conclude that the upper and lower bounds of the implied forward price on a dividend paying stock are:

$$\text{Upper bound: } F_{up} = (S_{ask} - PV\_Div_{bid}) \times (1 + r_{ask})^T$$
$$\text{Lower bound: } F_{low} = (S_{bid} - PV\_Div_{ask}) \times (1 + r_{bid})^T$$

where S_{ask}, S_{bid}, r_{ask}, r_{bid} and T are as before and PV_Div_{bid} and PV_Div_{ask} are the present values of the dividend cash flows discounted respectively with r_{bid} and r_{ask}.

Assuming no bid–offer spreads in the spot price or in the interest rate, we get the formula for the implied forward price of a discrete dividend paying stock:

$$F = (S - PV\_Div) \times (1 + r)^T$$

In this example, we worked under the assumption of discrete dividends paid at specified dates. This is consistent with common practice, although, in academic texts, it is also very common to observe the notion of a continuous dividend yield, i.e., under the assumption that a company distributes dividend in continuous time. Such a dividend distribution is far from being practical (dividends are usually paid annually, semi-annually or quarterly but not continuously) but this approach does enjoy a certain analytical tractability.

In case of continuous dividend yield q and continuous compounding interest rate r, the formula for the implied forward price becomes:

$$F = S \times exp\left[(r - q) \times T\right]$$

2.4.2 Calculating implied forward prices on foreign exchange rates

We will now consider a simple[13] example of how to calculate the implied forward price of a foreign currency rate in order to avoid an arbitrage opportunity or risk-free gain. We will assume that any currency will be associated with an interest rate and any amount denominated in a currency allows the holder to earn an interest rate (which we assume to be risk free) on that currency. For simplicity, we will work with the EUR/USD cross and assume the following: the effective 1-year EUR and USD interest rates are respectively 5% (base currency interest rate) and 3% (term currency interest rate).

Let us assume that the current EUR/USD spot rate is trading at $1.3825–$1.3830. As in the case of single stocks, we can assess if quoted forward prices are "fair" or if arbitrage opportunities exist. In order to do this, we need to calculate the total cost of buying one unit

---

[13] We are ignoring day-count conventions.

of base currency (EUR in this case) today and carrying the position into the future as well as the cost of selling it and keeping the short position into the future.

So, let us take a look at the 1-year forward. In the case of a purchase of EUR, we will have to pay \$1.3830 today. Since we are starting with a zero cash balance, we will have to borrow that USD amount at 3% for 1 year. Therefore, we know that we will have to pay back \$1.3830 × 1.03 = \$1.4245 in 1 year. At the same time, the unit of EUR purchased can be invested at the EUR interest rate of 5%, resulting in a holding of 1.05 units of EUR at the end of the year. To sum up, at the end of the first year we will have EUR 1.05 asset and a USD 1.4245 liability. This suggests that any EUR/USD forward rate higher than 1.4245/1.05 = 1.3567 will lead to an arbitrage opportunity.

In the case of the sale of EUR, we will have to borrow it first (financing the position at the prevailing EUR rate of 5%) and exchange it for 1.3825 units of USD that we can invest at the prevailing USD rate of 3% for 1 year. As a result, at the end of the first year, we will have a EUR 1.05 liability versus a USD 1.4240 asset. This suggests that any EUR/USD forward rate lower than 1.4240/1.05 = 1.3562 will lead to an arbitrage opportunity.

To check if this is correct, assume the 1-year forward EUR/USD quote observed in the market is \$1.4000–\$1.4010. Since the forward bid price (1.4000) is higher than the amount needed to buy one EUR/USD spot and carry the position for 1 year (the 1.3567 calculated above), we could do the following trade. Borrow USD 1.3830 at the prevailing USD rate of 3% (we will therefore have to pay back USD 1.4245 after 1 year), convert the 1.3830 units of USD into EUR at the spot rate and invest at the EUR interest rate of 5%. Simultaneously, we can enter a forward contract to sell 1.05 units of EUR against USD in 1 year at the forward rate (bid side) of 1.4000, resulting in a purchase of 1.05 × 1.40 = USD 1.47 on a forward basis.

After 1 year, we have a EUR 1.05 asset and a USD 1.4245 liability. However, we will now sell our 1.05 units of EUR for USD 1.47 (i.e., as agreed in the forward contract), resulting in a zero EUR cash balance but 1.47 − 1.4245 = USD 0.0455 left over after repaying the loan of 1.4245 units of USD. So, we make a profit of USD 0.0455 for each EUR nominal at trade inception.

Remember, if the forward price is higher than the price required to purchase the currency and to finance the position, an arbitrage opportunity arises. It can be exploited by selling the forward and buying spot.

What about the opposite case? If the implied forward price is lower than the price required to sell the currency and to finance the position, an arbitrage opportunity will arise. It can be exploited by buying a forward and selling spot.

Generalizing, we can conclude that the upper and lower bounds of the implied forward price are:

$$\text{Upper bound: } F_{up} = S_{ask} \times (1 + r_{left\,CCY} - r_{right\,CCY})^T$$

$$\text{Lower bound: } F_{low} = S_{bid} \times (1 + r_{left\,CCY} - r_{right\,CCY})^T$$

where S_{ask} and S_{bid} are respectively the offer and bid spot price of the base currency expressed as the number of units of term currency, r_{right} and r_{left} are respectively the interest rate of the *term currency* and the *base currency* and T is the maturity of the forward contract measured by number of years.

Assuming no bid–offer spread in the spot price, we get the simple formula for the implied forward price of foreign exchange:

$$F = S \times (1 + r_{left\,CCY} - r_{right\,CCY})^T$$

As we noted in the case of single stocks, when assessing the fairness of the implied forward price based on the no-arbitrage pricing condition, we are not incorporating any sort of market expectation about the future price of the underlying nor are we expressing any sort of judgement regarding its future performance. The straightforward no-arbitrage relationships that we have been discussing are completely independent of market participants' opinion regarding the future value of the exchange rate.[14]

That said, there is a notable exception in foreign exchange that is worth mentioning at this stage: the non-deliverable forward (NDF). In some countries, the circulation of the domestic currency is restricted, meaning that the domestic currency may not be delivered offshore (examples include the Indian rupee, the South Korean won and the Brazilian real). For example, it is possible to open a USD-denominated bank account in the UK but it is not possible to open an Indian Rupee denominated bank account in the UK. The inability to get delivery (or to deliver) the currency is such that the approach we have used so far (which is based on entering a spot transaction against a forward transaction whenever arbitrage opportunities arise) may not necessarily be applicable. For some of these currencies, an offshore forward market has developed and the related transactions are called *non-deliverable forwards* or *NDFs*. When a non-deliverable forward is negotiated, there will be no delivery of the underlying currency at expiry but a cash amount representing the profit or loss of the transaction will be exchanged. The absence of a specific no-arbitrage relation between the spot price of a currency and the level of its non-deliverable forward is such that it is impossible to derive an explicit relation between spot and non-deliverable forward prices. In this case, the level of the non-deliverable forward price will be a function of supply and demand factors, as well as the risk aversion of the market participants active in the NDF transactions.

2.4.3   Calculating implied forward prices on commodities

Within the broad asset class of commodities, we can distinguish two types; those used for mainly investment/speculation and those that are used mainly for consumption or production. The most obvious examples of commodities used for investment are gold and silver, although they can also be used to make consumer durables such as jewellery. Typical examples of commodities used for consumption are sugar, coffee and soybeans, although, of course, they can also be used for investment purposes. There are two factors that impact forward prices of commodities in addition to interest rates, storage costs and convenience yields.

Let us look at storage costs first. The analysis of storage costs for consumption and non-consumption commodities will be fundamentally different as the following examples will show.

---

[14] We said earlier that, when pricing derivatives, the usual approach is to invoke the concept of no-arbitrage and that knowledge of investor risk preferences is irrelevant for the mechanics of derivative pricing. Unfortunately, this statement makes it sound as if the absolute price of the derivative will be the same in each state. This is definitely not the case. The absolute price of the derivative will be different in each risk state because the spot price of the underlying security will be different in each state. Calculating the price of the derivative is a relative price calculation; i.e., the price of the derivative is calculated using the underlying spot price of the asset. Investor risk preferences are relevant to the absolute price of the derivative but they are irrelevant to the price of the derivative in relationship to the price of the underlying asset, i.e., the formula for pricing the derivative, given the underlying asset price, is invariant to the assumed risk preference of investors who hold the underlying asset. When pricing the derivative, the spot price of the underlying asset is taken as a given. The spot price of the underlying asset will depend very much on the risk preferences of investors. In a world of risk-averse investors, the spot prices of assets will generally be lower than those that would prevail in a risk-neutral or a risk-loving world. Moreover, using risk neutrality to derive a pricing model does not mean that absolute derivative prices are invariant to risk preferences. In fact, absolute derivative prices are quite sensitive to risk preferences.

Consider a 6-month futures contract on silver. We will assume the following:

- The 6-month storage cost for silver is $0.5/oz, paid on the last day.
- The current bid–offer spot quote is $33/oz–$33.5/oz.
- The 6-month risk-free rate is 5% annualized and, hence, the present value of the storage cost is $0.49/oz; $0.5/oz $\times$ $1.05^{-0.5}$.
- The current 6-month forward is quoted at $34.9/oz–$35.1/oz.

So, today, we borrow $33.5 and buy one ounce of silver. The storage costs $0.49 since, presumably, we need to put the silver in storage and we have to borrow this amount too. If we can enter a 6-month forward contract to sell one ounce of silver in 6 months at $34.9/oz then what is the potential gain? First, we need to pay back the loan. The repayment is ($33.50 + $0.49) $\times$ $1.05^{0.5}$, i.e., $34.83. So, at $34.9/oz, we would make a profit of $34.9 less $34.83, i.e., $0.07 for each ounce of silver traded.

As before, so that there are no arbitrage opportunities, the fair bid of the 6-month forward has to be ($33/oz + $0.49/oz) $\times$ $1.05^{0.5}$ = $34.31 and the fair offer has to be ($33.5/oz + $0.49/oz) $\times$ $1.05^{0.5}$ = $34.83.

Generalizing, the formula to calculate the implied forward value for a non-consumption commodity is:

$$F = (S + U) \times (1 + r)^T$$

where F is the fair forward value of the non-consumption commodity, S is the spot price, r is the risk-free interest rate, U is the present value of all the storage costs incurred during the tenor of the forward contract and T is the tenor of the transaction. The storage cost can actually be seen as a negative dividend payment associated with holding the commodity for a certain period of time.[15]

Given that assets such as silver and gold are used mainly for investment rather than consumption, any arbitrage opportunities would not exist for long. If $F > (S + U) \times (1 + r)^T$ then arbitrageurs will keep buying the asset at today's spot price and entering into forward contracts to sell the asset. The spot price will increase and the forward contract price will decrease. If $F < (S + U) \times (1 + r)^T$ then arbitrageurs will keep on short selling the asset at today's spot price and entering into forward contracts to buy the asset. The spot price will decrease and the forward contract price will increase.[16]

When commodities are used mainly for consumption and production purposes, however, arbitrage opportunities may linger. In this case, the "equilibrium" forward prices determined by the actions of consumers and producers may not be as the formulas above would imply. This is where the concept of a convenience yield arises.

For those commodities held mainly for consumption – e.g., soybeans used for food, oil used for energy – holding the physical asset brings benefits in case of production shortages, low inventories, etc. These benefits are commonly referred to as convenience yield provided by holding the physical commodity rather than a financial contract on the asset. This convenience yield explains why apparent arbitrage opportunities may linger. If the storage costs are known and have a present value U, and assuming that we face an apparent arbitrage opportunity arising from the fact that the market price is such that:

$$F < (S + U) \times (1 + r)^T$$

---

[15] In the same way that we can treat the dividend, we can also think of the storage cost as being applied in continuous time (which may actually be fairly realistic since storage costs are often applied on a daily basis). If we define u as the storage cost expressed in continuous time and r as the continuously compounded interest rate, the formula for the forward will become $F = S \times e^{rT} \times e^{uT} = S \times e^{(r+u)T}$.

[16] Clearly, the same logic can be applied to the continuously compounded versions, $F < S \times e^{(r+u)T}$ and $F > S \times e^{(r+u)T}$.

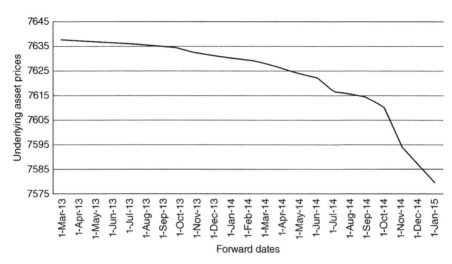

Figure 2.3   Curve in backwardation

However, this potential arbitrage opportunity may be impossible to exploit, as it would require to sell spot a commodity that may actually be necessary for consumption (i.e., not available for sale). If now we "add in" a convenience yield, c, the forward pricing equation becomes:[17]

$$F \times (1 + c)^T = (S + U) \times (1 + r)^T$$

Note that the convenience yield is observable only implicitly from the prices prevailing in the market. In a sense, the convenience yield is somewhat of an implied concept that creates a no-arbitrage condition when arbitrage seems to exist. Of course, arbitrage can only take place if delivery risks are eliminated. This is also why apparent arbitrage opportunities can linger.[18]

For investment assets the convenience yield should be zero, as otherwise there are clearer arbitrage opportunities.

The convenience yield is indicative of the market's expectations regarding the future availability of that commodity. If the forward curve of a commodity is in backwardation, i.e., the closest to expiry contract is higher than a contract further out on the curve, then the convenience yield, c, is greater than $r + u$ for that commodity. If a consumer thinks that there will be a shortage of a commodity in the future, e.g., low inventories, then he or she will prefer to hold that commodity now instead of waiting to buy it in the future. This explains why the prices of the commodity at the front of the curve will be much higher than those along the curve, as illustrated by the Figure 2.3.

On the other hand, if the forward curve of a commodity is in contango, i.e., the closest to expiry contract is cheaper than a contract further out along the curve, then the convenience yield, c, is smaller than $r + u$ for that commodity. If a consumer thinks that there will be

---

[17] Or, with continuous compounding, $F = (S + U) \times e^{(r-c)T}$. Likewise, when the storage costs u are proportional to the price of the commodity, the inequality is $F < S \times e^{(r+u)T}$. If we "add in" the convenience yield, c, the forward pricing equation becomes $F \times e^{cT} = S \times e^{(r+u)T}$ or $F = S \times e^{(r+u-c)T}$.

[18] Even with no delivery risk "apparent arbitrage" opportunities linger because it takes time for prices to reach equilibrium and the infra-marginal participants to perceive arbitrage violations. For example, if the convenience yield is zero, the current oil price is $100 and the cost of storage for a major oil company is $5 (and interest rates are zero), then the fair forward price is $105. If, for all other market participants, however, storage is $5.1, then they will see an arbitrage opportunity.

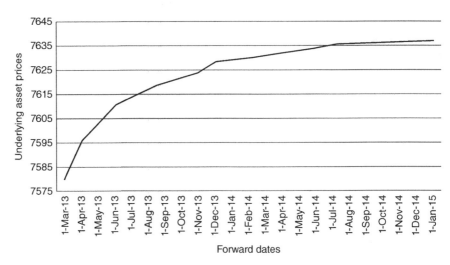

Figure 2.4   Curve in contango

enough supply of a commodity in the future, e.g., high inventories, then he or she may prefer to buy in the future and pay the corresponding $r + u$ involved in the future price (Figure 2.4).

2.4.4   Valuing existing forward contracts

Now that we are able to derive the implied forward price for a variety of assets, it should be straightforward to identify the monetary value of an existing forward transaction. In general, for an existing forward transaction, the delivery date and the delivery price have been already agreed (typically such that the value of the forward contract was zero when it was traded). As market conditions change, however, the implied forward related to the agreed delivery date may change. When this happens, the value of the existing forward contract will be non-zero. In general, on any given date before the delivery date, if we are able to calculate the new implied forward price related to the delivery date using the formulae presented in the previous sections, we can calculate the value of the existing forward contract by simply taking the difference between the new implied forward price and the agreed delivery price and then discounting this quantity with the appropriate discount factor.

If we define T as the agreed delivery date, K as the agreed delivery price, t as the valuation date and F as the new implied forward price for the delivery date T, the value at t of the existing forward contract for a long position in one unit of the underlying asset is given by:

$$DF(t, T) \times (F - K)$$

where $DF(t, T)$ is the discount factor applicable at t to cash flows payable at T. Likewise, the value of a short position in the same existing forward contract is:

$$DF(t, T) \times (K - F)$$

2.5   PRICING FUTURES CONTRACTS

Futures are little more than exchange-traded forward contracts and, in a practical sense, the mathematics behind the pricing of a futures contract are essentially the same as the mathematics behind the pricing of a forward.[19] Even if, from a purely theoretical point of view, there is a fundamental difference between forward and futures contracts (arising from the fact that futures transactions embed a margining mechanism that creates intermediate cash flows during the life of the trade), if one thinks of the futures price as the no-arbitrage price of a similar forward contract on the underlying asset for the specific delivery date determined by the exchange, then one will not go too far wrong. The price of a futures contract referencing a particular asset is just the discounted forward price for that asset adjusted for any intermittent cash flows.

With respect to bond futures that are physically settled, however, there is the added complexity of the value of *the delivery option*. When settling a German Bund future, for example, those market participants who are short the future (i.e., the shorts) have the right to deliver any particular Bund that they wish from a predetermined list,[20] set by EUREX.[21] The shorts will deliver Bunds to EUREX, which, in turn, will deliver these on a pro-rata basis to the longs (i.e., those people who are long the future). The longs do not know which specific bonds they will receive although they will probably have a very good idea since they will expect the shorts to act rationally and deliver the bonds that are "cheapest" within the basket.[22] These bonds are known as the *cheapest-to-deliver*.

Since the shorts have the right to deliver any bond they wish from the basket, they are *long an option*. This will be clearer when we discuss options in subsequent chapters but, for now, think about it this way; those people who sell the future implicitly receive something with tangible benefits while those people who buy the future implicitly give something away. The people who give something away will want to be compensated for this. In practice, this happens automatically and it happens via the prevailing futures price, which tends to trade below the price suggested by the no-arbitrage forward price for the underlying Bunds. In other words, the sellers of the future get less money for the bonds they deliver (than would be suggested by the no-arbitrage forward price) and the buyers of the future pay less money for the bonds they receive (than would be suggested by the forward price). The size of the price discount (i.e., how much the futures price trades below the fair value forward price) should be equal to the value of the delivery option.[23]

2.6 SWAPS

2.6.1 Introduction

A swap is a contract that involves an exchange of cash flows or an exchange of cash for an asset (e.g., a commodity) over a specific period of time between two parties. At specified dates, the two parties (party A and party B) will exchange specific cash flows determined according to the pre-agreed contract. Typically, the two parties exchange a fixed amount against a floating

---

[19] Again, we may incur the wrath of the academics here but we want the reader to understand the intuition rather than get overly worried about the concepts of futures as Martingales, etc.

[20] Colloquially called the *basket*.

[21] http://www.eurexchange.com/exchange-en/.

[22] Since the buyers will not know, when they buy the futures, with any certainty which bonds they will receive on the delivery date, they cannot determine exactly the price of the bonds under the no-arbitrage condition. They will know that there is a basket of bonds that can be delivered and they can calculate a forward price for each individual bond in the basket. The futures price will be a weighted average of these forward prices, with the weights determined by the likelihood of a particular bond being the cheapest-to-deliver. Given this uncertainty, the buyers will pay less to buy the future than is suggested by the forward price on the cheapest-to-deliver bond.

[23] Readers interested in more detail on bond futures may wish to look at pages 98–117 of the book by Schofield and Bowler (2011). For those interested in calculating the value of the delivery option, take a look at *The Treasury Bond Basis* by Burghardt and Belton.

amount. The latter depends on a reference price that is specified in the swap contract and can be linked to an easily observable financial variable, such as the level of interest rates, the performance of an equity index or a commodity index, etc. Swaps where both parties exchange floating amounts (i.e., there are no fixed payments) are also used. When the cash flows from the two parties occur on the same date, the net amount is usually exchanged.

In the following, we will give several examples to cement the idea of what a swap is. For the time being, it is worth stressing that, because of the link to an uncertain variable, observable in the future, a swap can be seen either as a hedging or as a speculative instrument and the flow of uncertain payments represents its payoff. At this stage, it is also worthwhile observing that, in general, there is a relationship between swaps and forward contracts. A forward contract can be considered as a single-period swap and, in general, a swap (and its value) can be decomposed into a portfolio of forwards.

2.6.2   Interest rate swaps

The most common type of swap used across the various asset classes is the interest rate swap. In the following, we will give a brief description of how this instrument works and how to calculate the value of a swap contract. We will present the most common examples of interest rate swaps. At this stage, it is worth mentioning that the approach that we are following here is not theoretically rigorous. The conclusion that we will reach is identical, however, and we believe that this approach tends to be closer to the intuition.

The simplest example of an interest rate swap (known as a "plain vanilla" rate swap) takes place when two parties agree to exchange a stream of fixed payments against a stream of floating payments linked to a specific interbank lending rate calculated on a certain notional. Typically the interbank lending rates used to calculate the floating payments are the 3-month and 6-month US Libor, Euribor, JPY Libor and Sterling Libor rates on notionals denominated in USD, EUR, JPY and GBP respectively. Obviously, for amounts denominated in other currencies, the appropriate floating rate will be used. In general, the frequency of the floating payments is the same as the frequency of the lending rate used. So, we will have two floating payments each year when the 6-month lending rate is used and four when the 3-month lending rate is the underlying. On the floating side, the floating rate of each payment tends to be observed at the beginning of each period and the payment related to this observation is made at the end of the respective period (we will clarify this shortly with an example). On the other hand, the fixed payment can take place with a different frequency to the floating payment. Annual fixed payments are relatively common (even if, in general, these features are easy to customize) with payments taking place at the end of each period. This kind of swap is also called a *vanilla* interest rate swap, being the simplest example of a multi-period swap that can be negotiated. It is also worth mentioning that, in a vanilla interest rate swap, the notionals are never exchanged between the two counterparties. Only the interest payments are exchanged.

Let us clarify with an example. Assume a corporation has borrowed a certain amount of money (EUR 100 for simplicity) from a bank and is paying a floating interest rate on this borrowing linked to the 6-month Euribor rate.[24] Let us assume that the corporation borrowed the money for 5 years. Furthermore, let us also assume that the corporation is concerned with

---

[24] For simplicity, we are assuming that there is no spread over the Euribor rate that the corporation has to pay (i.e., the corporation is borrowing at Euribor "flat"). In practice, a spread over the interbank lending rate is likely to be paid; such a spread will typically depend on the creditworthiness of the corporation undertaking the borrowing and on the general financial conditions prevailing when the borrowing is agreed.

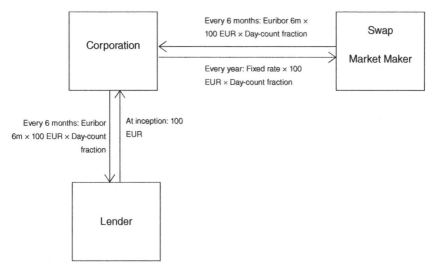

Figure 2.5   Interest rate swap payments

the potential volatility of interest cash flows arising from the variability of the Euribor rate. An interest rate swap will allow the corporation to "fix" the level of interest rate such that it will not be exposed to future fluctuations of the Euribor rate. This will obviously mean that the corporation will give up any potential benefit of a reduction in Euribor rates but it will be protected in case the Euribor rate increases over its 5-year borrowing timeframe.

Let us see how this will work in practice. The corporation would contact a swap bank and enter into a 5-year swap whereby the corporation pays a fixed rate on the notional (EUR 100) and receives a floating rate (6-month Euribor) on the same notional. We will assume that the fixed payments are taking place annually whereas the floating payments have semi-annual frequency (since they are linked to the 6-month Euribor rate). This will match the schedule of the existing borrowing contract that the corporation is looking to hedge. The net result is that the corporation will receive floating payments from the swap bank that match the floating payments payable to the financial institution who lent the money to the corporation in the first place.

These two streams of floating payments will offset each other (as Figure 2.5 shows) and the only net payment for the corporation is the fixed leg on the swap that the corporation must pay to the swap bank. The end result is, therefore, a "transformation" of floating interest payments into fixed interest payments. This allows the corporation to offset the risk of fluctuations of interest payments linked to fluctuations in the 6-month Euribor rate.

Now, say that, given the prevailing market conditions at the time of the negotiations around the swap, the fixed rate turned out to be 4.50% (we will get back to how this level is determined). What this means is that from a financial point of view, a stream of five annual fixed payments of 4.50% of the notional has the same expected present value of a stream of 10 semi-annual floating payments of 6-month Euribor on the same notional.[25]

As noted previously, the payments related to the floating leg are made at the end of each semi-annual period based on the 6-month Euribor rate prevailing at the beginning of

---

[25] For the time being, we are ignoring the impact of the day-count fraction and payment conventions.

Table 2.3   Cash flows of the interest rate swap

Time	Floating rate observation	Net cash flow
0 (swap is traded)	FR1	None
Month 6	FR2	FR1 × DCFloat × NA
Month 12	FR3	(FR2 × DCFloat − FIX × DCFix) × NA
Month 18	FR4	FR3 × DCFloat × NA
Month 24	FR5	(FR4 × DCFloat − FIX × DCFix) × NA
Month 30	FR6	FR5 × DCFloat × NA
Month 36	FR7	(FR6 × DCFloat − FIX × DCFix) × NA
Month 42	FR8	FR7 × DCFloat × NA
Month 48	FR9	(FR8 × DCFloat − FIX × DCFix) × NA
Month 54	FR10	FR9 × DCFloat × NA
Month 60	–	(FR10 × DCFloat − FIX × DCFix) × NA

each respective period; the payments related to the fixed leg are made at the end of each annual period. To sum up, the cash flows for this interest rate swap can be expressed according to the timeline in Table 2.3.

In the table, the term *NA* is the swap notional. The floating rates *FR1, FR2, . . . , FR10* and the fixed rate *FIX* should be adjusted by the appropriate day-count fraction (*DCFloat* and *DCFix* respectively) because the interest rate is always expressed in annualized form but the actual payments are based on the number of days in each interest period. At inception of the trade, the net present value of the five fixed annual payments would equal the net present value of the 10 floating payments.

And, as a reminder, notionals are not exchanged; interest rate swaps are not a way for either party to borrow or lend money!

So far in our example we took for granted the level of the 5-year swap rate; we said that this can be seen as the fixed rate that makes the present value the stream of fixed payments equal to the present value of the stream of floating payments. In our example, if we assume that the level of 5-year swap is 4.5%, we mean that a stream of fixed payments of 4.5% (on the notional) is equal (on a forward-looking basis in present value terms) to a stream of floating payments (Euribor 6 month) on the same notional.

In other words, 4.5% is the level of equilibrium prevailing in the market when we assumed our swap is traded. Obviously this level is subject to change continuously given the demand and supply dynamics prevailing in the market and/or the general perception about the level of interest rates.

A thorough discussion about pricing and valuation of an interest rate swap is outside the scope of this book but we will try to give an intuitive idea on how an interest rate swap can be priced and how to value an existing interest rate swap exposure.[26]

A highly simplified (but useful for developing intuition) approach to pricing an interest rate swap is to assume that we have full knowledge of the price of (risk-free) zero coupon bonds for all maturities. As the price of a risk-free zero coupon bond is nothing but the present value of its notional redeemed as a point in the future, knowing the prices of the zero coupon bonds

---

[26] Readers interested in more detail may wish to look at the book by Schofield and Bowler (2011).

for each maturity is equivalent to knowing all the discount factors prevailing at any given time. Therefore, the standard theoretical assumption that is made when presenting pricing and valuation of an interest rate swap is that we know how to discount any future cash flow or, another way of saying this, we know the price of all risk-free zero coupon bonds for all maturities. Needless to say, the term structure of zero coupon bond prices (or discount factors) will identify a term structure of zero interest rates, so that we can discount any future cash flow using the appropriate zero rate.

Given the idea of no-arbitrage, once a term structure of zero coupon interest rates is specified (or a term structure of discount factors, which is the same concept) it is possible to deduce all forward interest rates. Let us show this with an example. If a zero coupon bond with EUR 100 notional and 6 months' maturity is traded in the market at EUR 99 and another zero coupon bond with same notional and 1 year's maturity is traded at EUR 97.5 we can deduce that:[27]

1. The 6-month discount factor is 0.99 and the 6-month zero rate (expressed in annual terms) is equal to 2.03%.[28]
2. The 1-year discount factor is 0.975, corresponding to a 1-year zero rate (expressed again in annual terms) equal to 2.56%.
3. The 6-month discount factor 6-month forward is equal to $0.975/0.99 = 0.9848$. This is the result of a very simple no-arbitrage argument, such that discounting from year 1 to today has to be equal to discounting from year 1 to month 6 and then from month 6 to today. In other words, if we break the discounting horizon into two or more parts, the overall discounting cannot be affected. Hence we have that:
   (a) DF(0, 1-year) = DF(0, 6-month) × DF(6-month, 6-month) that can be rearranged as
   (b) DF(6-month, 6-month) = DF(0, 1-year)/DF(0, 6-month). The 6-month zero rate applicable in 6 months' time will therefore be equal to 3.1% (in annualized terms).

This example shows us that, once the term structure of the prices of zero coupon bonds is defined, one can deduce the term structure of zero interest rates, the term structure of forward prices of all zero coupon bonds and the term structure of forward interest rates.

This is extremely important since the forward interest rate that we are able to calculate in this way includes also the implied forwards for the floating rates that are part of an interest rate swap.[29] Therefore, even if today we cannot know what will be the exact realization of the floating leg of the interest rate swap, we can calculate the forward prices of each individual floating rate and discount its value to today. This is not too different from what we have already done for other forwards (say in equity or FX).

So, let us calculate the forward floating rates (i.e., the forward rate of each floating leg of an interest rate swap) and the respective present values of the cash flows from a 5-year EUR swap. We will assume that our floating leg is based on 6-month Euribor rates and so we will find it easier to work with semi-annual compounding on the floating leg of the swap. However, we should note that all rates are generally published in annualized terms, and therefore a conversion would generally be required.

---

[27] We are again assuming these are risk-free rates, i.e., the probability of the issuer defaulting is zero.

[28] To calculate the discount factor at time T given the interest rate i, DF = $(1 + i)^{-T} = (1 + 0.0203)^{-0.5} = 0.99$.

[29] As an aside, this particular approach to swap pricing assumes that the forward interest rate is equal to the expected future spot interest rate to which the floating leg of the swap settles.

First, note that the notation $DF(t_1, t_2)$ means the discount factor applicable when discounting to t_1 a cash flow payable in t_2 (i.e., this is the present value in t_1 of a cash flow paid in t_2).

- Given the discount factor $DF(0, t_n)$, where t_n is the end of the n period, the corresponding zero rate expressed with semi-annual compounding is equal to:

$$\left(\frac{1}{DF(0,t_n)}\right)^{0.5/t_n} - 1$$

- Given the discount factors $DF(0, t_n)$ and $DF(0, t_{n-1})$, the corresponding implied forward zero rate expressed with semi-annual compounding is equal to:

$$\frac{DF(0,t_{n-1})}{DF(0,t_n)} - 1$$

- This rate can be applied directly to the notional to calculate the forward cash flow payable at the end of the n period.
- Given the discount factors calculated in the previous bullet point, the corresponding present value of the cash flow determined according to the forward zero rate (expressed with semi-annual compounding) is equal to:

$$\left(\frac{DF(0, t_{n-1})}{DF(0, t_n)} - 1\right) \times DF(0, t_n) \times NA = [DF(0, t_{n-1}) - DF(0, t_n)] \times NA$$

Therefore the present value of the floating cash flow payable at the end of the period n is nothing but the notional multiplied for the difference of the discount factors applicable at the beginning of the period, i.e., $DF(0, t_{n-1})$, and the discount factors applicable at the end of the period, i.e., $DF(0, t_n)$.

- Given the term structure of discount factors, one can calculate the present value of the whole floating leg (expressed as the sum of the present value of each payment. This is going to be equal to (for $n = 0.5$ to $n = 5$):

$$NA \times [DF(0, t_{0.5-0.5}) - DF(0, t_{0.5})] +$$
$$NA \times [DF(0, t_{1-0.5}) - DF(0, t_1)] +$$
$$NA \times [DF(0, t_{1.5-0.5}) - DF(0, t_{1.5})] +$$
$$\ldots$$
$$NA \times [DF(0, t_{4.5-0.5}) - DF(0, t_{4.5})] +$$
$$NA \times [DF(0, t_{5-0.5}) - DF(0, t_5)]$$

At this point, we can see that $DF(0, t_{0.5-0.5}) = DF(0, 0) = 1$ and all the remaining discount factors except the last one, $DF(0, t_5)$, can be cancelled out. Consequently, the previous calculation can be simplified to:

$$NA \times [1 - DF(0, t_5)]$$

This result is extremely important. It basically tells us that the present value of a floating leg of an interest rates swap maturing in T and with effective date equal to $t = 0$ and valued in $t = 0$ is simply equal to the notional of the swap multiplied by $1 - DF(0, T)$, i.e., for the discount factor applicable to cash flow payable when the swap terminates.

What about the fixed leg? Well, the present value of the fixed leg is extremely easy to calculate once we know the applicable discount factors for each period a fixed payment is expected to be made. Assuming annual fixed payments based on a fixed rate F (we will have five payments as we are working on a 5-year swap), the present value of a fixed leg of our interest rates swap maturing in t_5 and with effective date equal to $t = 0$ and valued at $t = 0$ is simply equal to the sum of the present value of the five annual cash flows, i.e., $NA \times F \times DF(0, t_1) + NA \times F \times DF(0, t_2) + \cdots + NA \times F \times DF(0, t_5)$ or, generalizing for a swap expiring in T years:

$$NA \times F \times \sum_{i=1}^{T} DF(0, t_i)$$

As the present value of the fixed leg has to be equal to the present value of the floating leg, we need to find that F such that:

$$NA \times [1 - DF(0, T)] = NA \times F \times \sum_{i=1}^{T} DF(0, t_i)$$

It follows that:

$$F = \frac{[1 - DF(0, T)]}{\sum_{i=1}^{T} DF(0, t_i)}$$

In our example of 5-year swap, we invite you, the reader, to verify that the fixed rate that ensures the swap is in equilibrium (the present value of the fixed leg is equal to the present value of the floating leg) is equal to approximately 4.50%. Details of this calculation can be found in the spreadsheet "Chapter 2 – Swap Pricing Example".

Having market prices for zero coupon bonds of all the necessary dates is quite unrealistic. In practice, practitioners use swap prices the other way around. Given the deep liquidity of the swap markets, the common practice is to take the swap market quotes and derive from them the discount factors applicable for each tenor. The procedure is as we described above but done in reverse, i.e., from the swap rates you can calculate the discount factors and hence calculate the floating rates.

2.6.3 Commodity swaps

If party A pays a fixed price to and receives a floating price from party B, then we say that A buys a swap from B. Conversely, B receives a fixed price and pays a floating price and is said to sell a swap to A.

For example, a refinery, TFG Inc., is willing to buy 1,000,000 barrels of crude oil 6 months and 12 months from today.[30] Let us say that we know the following:

- 6-month forward offer: $100/bbl
- 12-month forward offer: $120/bbl
- 6-month interest rate: 1% p.a.
- 12-month interest rate: 2% p.a.

---

[30] The example is deliberately simplified for illustrative purposes and, in reality, physically settled crude swaps are usually structured with deliveries occurring over the whole period.

TFG can enter into forward contracts to buy the crude oil at certain levels guaranteeing the cost of buying oil for the next year. In particular, TFG could enter into long forward contracts for 1,000,000 barrels for delivery in 6 and 12 months. The present value of this transaction is:

$$\frac{\$100/\text{bbl}}{1.005} + \frac{\$120/\text{bbl}}{1.020} = \$217.125/\text{bbl}$$

This is the present value of the transaction per barrel.

TFG could enter into the two forward contracts and invest the required amounts today ($100/1.005 per barrel for 6-month oil and $120/1.02 per barrel for 12-month oil) at the 6-month and 12-month interest rates respectively. At the end of the 6- and 12-month periods, TFG would have enough money to buy the oil, paying the prices agreed in the forward contracts. Alternatively, it could pay an oil supplier $217.125/bbl and the supplier would commit to deliver the same amount of oil after 6 and 12 months. A single payment today for multiple deliveries in the future is termed a *prepaid swap*.

Of course, rather than enter into a forward contract now and pay for the oil in the future, TFG could have made a single payment to the oil supplier today for a single delivery of oil in the future. This is a prepaid forward. Obviously, the payment for a prepaid forward will be less in nominal terms than a payment in the future since the oil supplier would have the benefit of the cash up-front (and presumably earn interest on it at the risk-free rate).

Although it is possible to enter into a prepaid swap, buyers may actually be concerned about the credit risk that such a transaction entails. They have fully paid for something that will only be delivered after 6 and 12 months. Clearly, the prepaid forward has the same issue. For the same reason, the swap counterparty would be concerned about a post-paid swap, i.e., where the first tranche of oil is delivered after 6 months but the full payment for the oil is received only after 1 year.

An alternative is to make payments when the oil is delivered, while still fixing the average price today. To calculate the fair value of the swap, we can calculate the following:

$$\frac{x}{1.005} + \frac{x}{1.020} = \$217.125/\text{bbl} \Rightarrow x = \$109.925/\text{bbl}$$

Swaps normally involve equal payments each period, although, in theory, any schedule of payments such that the present value equals $217.125/bbl should be acceptable.

Swaps can be cash settled or physically settled through actual deliveries. If the swap is physically settled, the seller will deliver barrels of oil to TFG after 6 and 12 months. If the swap is cash settled, one party to the transaction pays any difference between $109.925/bbl and the then prevailing spot price, i.e., if the spot price is lower than the swap level; the swap counterparty pays TFG the difference between spot price and $109.925/bbl.

Figure 2.6 illustrates the flows if the swap is settled physically. These flows are the same for both 6 and 12 months:

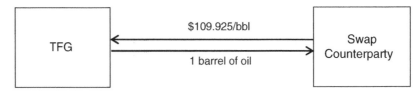

Figure 2.6   Commodity swap settled physically

Figure 2.7 illustrates the flows if the swap is settled financially. These flows are the same after 6 and 12 months:

Figure 2.7   Commodity swap settled financially

The cash flows in the figures above are on a per-barrel basis. For a swap on 1,000,000 barrels, we would need to multiply all the cash flows by 1,000,000.

Let us return to the cash flows for the physically settled swap. After 6 months, TFG pays $109.925/bbl but the 6-month and 12-month forward levels are $100/bbl and $120/bbl. Therefore, relative to the 6-month forward level, TFG, the swap buyer, is overpaying by $9.925/bbl and, relative to the 12-month forward level, TFG is underpaying by $10.075/bbl. The swap is equivalent to buying two forward contracts, involving a loan agreement to lend $9.925/bbl to the swap counterparty after 6 months and getting back $10.075/bbl 6 months after that.

The interest rate on the loan can be calculated easily and is approximately 3%, 2 × ($10.075/$9.925 − 1). This 3% is the 6-month implied forward interest rate. So, if the oil swap is priced fairly, the implied interest rate on the loan that is made for 6 months (in 6 months' time) should be the same as implied forward interest rate determined from market interest rates.

The swap counterparty receives the fixed payment from TFG and delivers the oil. If the oil price were to rally significantly, the swap counterparty delivering the oil would obviously incur losses. In order to avoid such losses, the swap counterparty may try to hedge the oil price risk that results from the swap.

This hedge can be executed in several ways. For instance, the swap counterparty could act as a "middleman" between TFG, the swap buyer, and a swap seller (Figure 2.8).

The fixed price paid by TFG exceeds the fixed price received by the oil seller. This price difference is the swap counterparty's bid–ask spread and represents the fee on this transaction. This situation, where the dealer matches a buyer and seller, is called a back-to-back transaction or a matched book transaction. Although the swap counterparty does not have to deal with price risk anymore, it may still be exposed to the credit risk of both parties.[31]

Another way of hedging the price risk would be to use forward contracts. After entering the swap with TFG, the swap counterparty has a short position in 6 months' and 12 months' oil. It could then enter into long forward contracts to hedge the exposure. Of course, if the swap counterparty wishes to make a profit on this transaction, it needs to sell the swap to TFG at a price above the level where it can hedge its exposure.

---

[31] Financial entities tend to make margin payments to each other to cover the associated credit risk from the transactions that take place between them. Many corporates do not, however. Any mark-to-market losses that a financial entity faces when dealing with a corporate are essentially an uncollateralized loan.

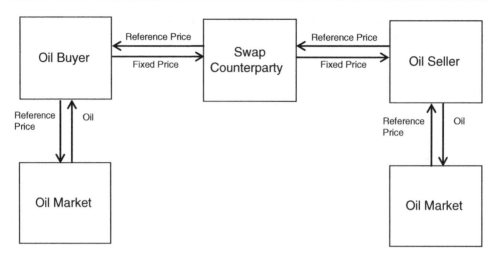

Figure 2.8   Example of swap counterparty acting as a "middleman"

2.6.4   Commodity swap valuation

As is the case with interest rate swaps discussed earlier, the market value of an at-market swap is generally zero at inception. This means that, in theory, either party could enter or exit the swap without having to pay anything to the other party. In practice, there will be some transaction costs, such as the bid–offer spreads. Let us ignore these for now and assume the swap is priced at mid.

In the previous example, we discussed an oil swap where $109.925 was the fair value. Of course, it is possible that a swap is agreed with an oil price that is different to this fair value level. In this case, however, the market value of the swap will not be zero and there will be an up-front payment. If the price of the swap were above $109.925, then the swap counterparty would be expected to pay TFG up-front. If the price of the swap were below $109.925 then TFG would be expected to pay the swap counterparty. In both cases, the up-front payment should be equal to the present value of the swap so that the combined value of the swap and the up-front payment sum to zero. Anything else would not be a "fair" transaction.

So, we know that the value of a swap (and any up-front payment) at inception is zero. As we know, the swap in the previous example is just two forward contracts and two loans at the 6-month and 12-month interest rates. Once the swap is agreed, however, its market value can change due to the following:

1. The forward prices of oil can change. For example, suppose that just after the buyer enters into the swap, the 6-month and 12-month forward prices rise by $3/bbl and $2/bbl respectively. The swap value will no longer be zero. Assuming interest rates had not changed, the new market value of the swap would be $222.1/bbl. So, higher market prices lead to a rise in the value of the swap:

$$\frac{\$103/\text{bbl}}{1.005} + \frac{\$122/\text{bbl}}{1.020} = \$222.1/\text{bbl}$$

2. Likewise, interest rates can change. In the example above, if interest rates fall, the fair value of the swap would rise.

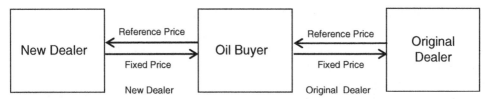

Figure 2.9 Commodity swap cash flows

3. Even if the oil and interest rates did not change, the value of the swap will remain zero until the first exchange of money is made. Once this happens, the buyer would have overpaid $9.9/bbl relative to the forward curve, and if the swap were unwound, the counterparty would have to pay the oil buyer that amount back. Therefore, even if the forward and interest rate prices do not change, the market value of swaps can change over time given the implicit borrowing and lending in the transaction.

Thus, if a buyer wants to exit the swap, he or she will have to reach an agreement with the counterparty – a standard feature of swaps documentation requires the permission of the counterparty either to unwind or assign/novate the swap. Alternatively, the buyer may enter into an offsetting swap either with the same counterparty (which is unlikely – in that case the two firms would simply unwind the original swap because the bilateral netting provisions of standard master agreements would render the original and offsetting swap economically identical to the offset of the original swap) or another one (which would expose the buyer to counterparty risk on both transactions). With the original swap, the buyer has to pay a fixed price and receive a floating price; with the offsetting one, the buyer would be receiving a fixed price and paying a floating one. The original obligation to pay a fixed price could even disappear if both the fixed price paid and the received one are the same. If this is not the case, the buyer would have to pay the difference between both, but this difference would be already known, eliminating the oil price risk. However, the credit risk still persists with the original counterparty and with the potential new one.

The cash flows would be as shown in Figure 2.9.

The closer the new dealer's offer and the original dealer's bid are, the less the oil buyer would have to pay. The oil buyer would have to pay: original dealer bid – new dealer offer. For example, suppose that, when the buyer wants to enter into an offsetting swap, the 6-month and 12-month forward bids are $98/bbl and $118/bbl. Assuming interest rates had not changed, the market value bid of the offsetting swap would be:

$$\frac{\$98/\text{bbl}}{1.005} + \frac{\$118/\text{bbl}}{1.020} = \$213.2/\text{bbl}$$

$$\frac{x}{1.005} + \frac{x}{1.020} = \$213.2/\text{bbl} => x = \$107.9/\text{bbl}$$

Therefore, the oil buyer would have to pay $109.9/bbl – $107.9/bbl = $2/bbl.
The present value of this difference is:

$$\frac{\$2/\text{bbl}}{1.005} + \frac{\$2/\text{bbl}}{1.020} = \$3.95/\text{bbl}$$

The buyer will then have to make a strip of payments with a present value of $3.95/bbl.

2.6.5 Commodity swaps with variable notional and price

It is quite common for a commodity buyer or seller to enter into a swap in which quantities vary over time. For example, a commodity buyer may wish to hedge a variable demand schedule. The buyer may also want to fix different prices in different periods. How does one determine the swap price for varying quantities?

Revisiting the previous example: a refinery, TFG Inc., is willing to buy 200,000 barrels of crude oil in 6 months and 500,000 barrels 12 months from today. Let us keep the same assumptions:

- 6-month forward offer: \$100/bbl
- 12-month forward offer: \$120/bbl
- 6-month interest rate (i.e., 6-month zero coupon yield): 1% p.a.
- 12-month interest rate (i.e., 12-month zero coupon yield): 2% p.a.

TFG can enter into forward contracts to buy the crude at certain levels and guarantee the cost of buying oil for the next year. In particular, TFG could enter into long forward contracts for 200,000 barrels after 6 months and 500,000 barrels after 12 months. The present value of this transaction is:

$$\text{Total barrels: } 200{,}000 \text{ bbls} + 500{,}000 \text{ bbls} = 700{,}000 \text{ bbls}$$

$$\frac{200{,}000 \text{ bbls}}{700{,}000 \text{ bbls}} \times \frac{\$100/\text{bbl}}{1.005} + \frac{500{,}000 \text{ bbls}}{700{,}000 \text{ bbls}} \times \frac{\$120/\text{bbl}}{1.020} = \$112.46/\text{bbl}$$

This is the present value of this weighted transaction per barrel.

TFG could invest this amount today, in the right proportions, at the 6-month and 12-month interest rates and make sure it will have enough money to buy oil in 6 and 12 months. Or, it could pay an oil supplier \$112.46/bbl for 200,000 bbls after 6 months and for 500,000 bbls after 12 months, and the supplier would commit to deliver the oil after 6 and 12 months.

To calculate the fair value of the swap, we can do the following:

$$\frac{200{,}000 \text{ bbls}}{700{,}000 \text{ bbls}} \times \frac{y}{1.005} + \frac{500{,}000 \text{ bbls}}{700{,}000 \text{ bbls}} \times \frac{y}{1.020} = \$112.46/\text{bbl}$$

$$\Rightarrow y = \$114.2/\text{bbl}$$

If, instead, we want to fix two different swap prices for each period:

$$\frac{200{,}000 \text{ bbls}}{700{,}000 \text{ bbls}} \times \frac{a}{1.005} + \frac{500{,}000 \text{ bbls}}{700{,}000 \text{ bbls}} \times \frac{b}{1.020} = \$112.46/\text{bbl}$$

$\Rightarrow$ it is enough that we fix one of them and solve for the other variable, i.e., if $a = \$116/\text{bbl}$ then $b = \$113.5/\text{bbl}$

2.6.6 Currency swaps

Suppose a dollar-based firm has issued a GBP-denominated 2-year fixed rate bond. The firm is obligated to make a strip of payments that are fixed in GBP terms but variable in dollar terms (as the exchange rate can fluctuate). We assume the following:

Table 2.4 Cash flows of the currency swap

Year	Un-hedged GBP cash flow	Forward exchange rate	Hedged dollar cash flow
1	−£3.0	$1.473	−$4.420
2	−£103.0	$1.523	−$156.919

- Effective annual GBP-denominated interest rate: 3%
- Effective annual USD-denominated interest rate: 6.5%
- Price of the bond: £100 i.e., we are assuming that the coupon rate of the bond is equal to the GBP-denominated interest rate of 3%, causing the bond to be worth £100 when issued
- Spot exchange rate bid: $1.42, i.e., the firm can sell £ and buy $ at $1.42 for each £
- Spot exchange rate offer: $1.425, i.e., the firm can buy £ and sell $ at $1.425 for each £. Keep in mind that it is a dollar-based firm so it has dollars, not pounds.
- 1-year forward exchange rate offer: $1.425 × (1 + 6.5%)/(1 + 3%) = $1.473
- 2-year forward exchange rate offer $1.425 × (1 + 6.5%)²/(1 + 3%)² = $1.523

Let's assume now that the firm wants to eliminate the risk exposure to GBP and therefore "to know in advance" the dollar value of the future payments. Since these payments are in GBP, the firm will buy GBP forward to hedge that exposure, and hence to eliminate the currency risk (Table 2.4).

The present value of the hedged cash flows is:

$$\frac{\$4.420}{1.065} + \frac{\$156.919}{1.065^2} = \$142.5$$

However, the dollar value of the debt at inception (i.e., the $ amount that the firm can receive after selling the £100 received from the issue of the bond at the spot exchange rate of 1.42) is £100 × $1.42 = $142.0.

The difference between the present value of the hedged cash flows ($142.5) and dollar value of the debt at inception ($142) is $0.5. This is due to the bid – offer spread of the exchange rate.

We can also hedge the GBP exposure by entering into a currency swap, i.e., making debt payments in one currency and receiving debt payments in a different currency. There is normally an exchange of principal, at both the start and end of the swap. The currency swap generates a different cash flow stream compared to the one generated by hedging the cash flows via forward contracts. However, the valuation concepts are equivalent.

Following the previous example, suppose now that the dollar-based firm decides to enter into a currency swap to hedge its pound exposure.

The firm now enters into a swap where it pays 6.5% p.a. on a $142.5 amount and receives 3% on a £100 amount (Figure 2.10).

1. The dollar-based firm issues a GBP-denominated bond at a price of £100 (this is like receiving a loan of £100).
2. The dollar-based firm has to pay 3% coupon per annum on this bond.
3. The dollar-based firm needs to hedge the risk from the GBP exposure, i.e., it enters into a currency swap with a market maker: the firm will pay to the market maker the £100 received after issuing the bond and will receive the $ equivalent amount of $142. At maturity these cash flows will be reversed

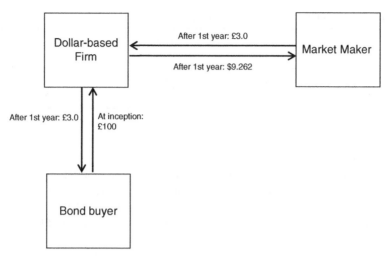

Figure 2.10   Currency swap cash flows

4. The market maker needs to pay pound interest to the firm and the firm pays dollar interest in exchange, i.e., the market maker pays 3% per annum on the £100 amount and the firm pays 6.5% on the $142 amount.
5. At the bond maturity date the dollar-based firm will receive the £100 back, that will be used as redemption amount to be paid to the bond-holder. At the same time the dollar-based firm will pay the $142 back to the market maker. Therefore the initial exchange of cash flows now gets reversed.

The currency swap ensures that the dollar-based firm has no GBP exposure (neither on the £100 bond notional, nor on the bond coupon); in practice the £-denominated bond that the dollar-based firm issues is "converted" into a $-denominated bond; we invite the reader to check the $-denominated cash flows to understand this point as far as the $-denominated cash-flows are concerned, the dollar-denominated firm will receive $142 at inception, pay $ interest on this amount of 6.5% and finally will pay back the $142 to the market maker.

2.6.7   Equity swaps

In the equity space, a total return swap is a swap where payments occur as follows:

- One party pays the realized total return, i.e., dividends plus capital gains, on a reference asset. This party is called the total return payer.
- The other counterparty pays a floating rate, i.e., USD Libor. This party is called the floating rate payer.[32]

The two parties exchange only the difference between the two rates.

The total return payer is simultaneously short the reference asset and long an asset paying the floating rate. The cash flows are described as follows as shown in Figure 2.11.

---

[32] This is generally true when total return swaps are structured in the so-called "unfunded" format, i.e., there is no exchange of notional; however, it is not unusual to observe "fully funded" total return swaps (this may occur in the case of total return swaps on bonds) where there is initial and final exchange of notional and therefore there is no floating rate payment.

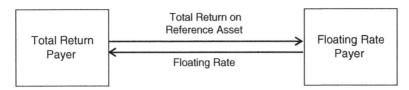

Figure 2.11   Equity swap cash flow

Table 2.5   Equity swap cash-flows table

Tenor	KYC pays: FTSE100 capital gain	KYC pays: FTSE100 dividend	KYC receives: floating rate: 6-month GBP Libor	Net payment to total return payer, i.e., KYC
6 months	2.5%	1.3%	1.0%	−2.8%
12 months	1.0%	1.4%	1.25%	−1.15%
18 months	3.5%	1.5%	1.0%	−4.0%
24 months	−2.0%	1.6%	1.5%	+1.9%

Consider the following situation. KYC is a European asset manager with £1bn invested in FTSE100 stocks. Whatever the reasons, the portfolio managers have become bearish about the prospects for the UK equity market and want to reduce their exposure to UK stocks from £1bn to £800m. One possible way to achieve this is to sell £200m of equities. A simpler way is to retain the underlying position and enter into a total return swap. The asset manager would then be obliged to pay the total return, i.e., the capital gain plus dividends, on £200m notional of the FTSE100 Index position they currently hold, but, in return, it would receive a floating rate return such as 6m GBP Libor. In this case, KYC will be able to avoid the myriad transaction costs of a sale of £200m of UK equities. Table 2.5 illustrates the expected cash flows over the next 2 years.

At the end of the first 6 months, assume that KYC earns 3.8% on the FTSE100 Index (2.5% capital gain and 1.3% dividend yield). It needs to pay this across to the counterparty on £200m notional, the portion it has swapped. It receives 1% in exchange as the floating rate (we have assumed an annual interest rate of 2%). Its net payment is 2.8% of £200m, i.e., £5.6m.

SUMMARY

In this chapter, we have introduced the standard derivative products of forwards, futures and swaps. We covered the most common jargon and we started discussing the pricing and hedging framework for derivatives, with examples taken from a variety of asset classes. In particular, we spent a lot of time on the concept of the forward contract. Our framework was based mainly on intuition rather than being theoretically rigorous although the conclusions that we draw are accurate. Those readers who wish to cover interest rate swaps more fully, for example, may wish to look at Das (1994), Miron and Swannell (1991) or Ungar (1996).[33] For a more thorough discussion of the differences between forward and futures prices, see the classic Cox, Ingersoll and Ross article in the December 1981 edition of the *Journal of Financial Economics*.

---

[33] The book by Ungar, in particular, looks at the swaps market but with very little mathematics. This is a good introduction.

3

Derivatives: Options and Related Strategies

The previous two chapters have set the general backdrop for the book as a whole. In this chapter, we move on to derivative instruments more explicitly. Options are at the core of the derivatives markets and most of this book will be focused on pricing options and assessing the risks arising from taking an option position. The concepts presented in this chapter will be crucial to the understanding of the remainder of the book. As options are certainly one of the most important products in the derivatives space, we will analyse the basics in some detail.

3.1 CALL OPTIONS

3.1.1 Definition

A *call option* is a contract between two parties (the buyer and the seller). It gives the buyer the right – but not the obligation – to buy a specific quantity of a certain asset at a point in the future at a known price determined today. The known price is called the *strike price* or the *exercise price*.

On the other hand, the seller of the call option has the obligation – not the right – to sell that quantity of the asset at the strike price if the buyer decides to exercise his or her right. The seller of the option is also known as the option *writer*.

So, as noted above, if you buy a call option, you acquire the right to buy something in the future. You are not under an obligation to buy that something, however. You will only buy it, assuming that you are rational, if it is economically sensible to do so. If you decide to buy the asset specified in the contract, it is known as *exercising* the option.

Assuming that you exercise the option, the asset that you buy is termed the *underlying* asset. In some cases, for example when it is not practical to take delivery of the underlying asset (perhaps it is an equity index representing a basket of many individual stocks), you will not be entitled to receive the underlying asset but you will receive, instead, a cash amount representing the profit due to you from buying the underlying asset at the strike price and selling it at its value when the option expires. This is called *cash settlement*. When it is possible to deliver the underlying asset, however, cash settlement is generally avoided. In this case, we have *physical delivery* of the underlying.

When can you exercise the option? Depending on the so-called *style* of the option, you will be able to exercise the option and buy the underlying asset either at a specified date in the future (*European* style) or at any time over a specified period (*American* style). The choice of the words European and American to describe when an option can be exercised is perhaps unfortunate. The choice has nothing to with whether they are traded in America or Europe since investors trade both American and European options in either geography. If the option can be exercised only during specific periods in the life of the option, i.e., on various exercise dates but not for the entire period, then the option is called Bermudan. Think about Bermuda

Table 3.1 Call option payoff and profit & loss

Value of S&P 500 Index at expiry	1,450	1,500	1,500.12	1,505
Buyer's payoff	0	0	12	500
Buyer's profit and loss	−12	−12	0	488
Seller's payoff	0	0	−12	−500
Seller's profit and loss	12	12	0	−488

sitting somewhere between Europe and America, but being closer to America, and you will get the picture.

Since the option gives the buyer the right to buy something, it is natural to expect that the buyer of the option will have to pay something to the seller since a service is being provided. This is the price of the option and is generally called the *option premium*. It is very important not to confuse option price with strike price. Remember, the option price is the price that the option buyer pays to the option seller in order to buy the option. The strike price (or exercise price) is the price that the option buyer will have to pay to the seller if he or she exercises the option, i.e., to buy the underlying asset. Consequently, the strike price will *only* be paid if the buyer exercises the option to buy.

For obvious reasons, it is natural to expect that the call option buyer will only exercise the right to buy if it makes sense to do so. He or she can decide whether or not to exercise. If the prevailing price of the underlying asset is higher than the strike price (when it is possible to exercise the option) then the call option buyer will find it more sensible to pay the strike price than the market price for the underlying asset.

3.1.2 Examples

1 – A trader buys a European call option on the S&P 500 Index with the strike price set at 1,500 points and an expiration date of Dec 2013. The standard convention for exchange-traded S&P index options is that they may only be exercised on the last business day before the expiration date. The expiration date is the Saturday following the third Friday of the expiration month.[1] Since the underlying asset is an equity index then, if the option is exercised, there will be no physical delivery of the underlying asset. Instead, there will be a cash amount paid to the option buyer. This amount represents the profit from buying the index at the strike price and selling it at the price prevailing at expiry, assuming a premium price paid of $12 (see Table 3.1).

2 – A corporation buys a European call option on the EUR/USD FX rate with a strike price at 1.35 and a life of 3 months, i.e., the option expires after 3 months. Note that FX options typically involve physical settlement.[2] This implies that, if the call option is exercised, the corporation will have the right to buy the agreed amount of EUR against selling a corresponding amount of USD using an exchange rate equal to the strike price (1.35 in this case).

3 – A fund manager buys an American call option on XYZ Incorporated with a strike price set at $100 and a maturity of 2 months. Options on individual stocks tend to be quoted American style so they can be exercised at any time before the expiry of the option contract. Like FX options, equity options typically involve physical settlement. So, if the call option is

---

[1] Obviously, if the option is traded in OTC format, there is full flexibility in the choice of the expiry date.
[2] Unless the underlying currency cannot be delivered because of restrictions imposed by the issuing country.

exercised, the buyer will have the right to buy the agreed amount of stock, paying the strike price, $100, for each stock bought.

3.1.3 Scenario analysis for the S&P 500 Index call option

In the following chapters we will describe ways to determine the prices of the options just described and to manage the market risk associated with options trading. At this stage, let us simply assume that the premium paid for the S&P option described above is $12.

At expiration, we can expect the following payoff and profit and loss profile for the buyer and the seller of the European call option on the S&P 500 that we just described. In Table 3.1, we assume that one option contract has been traded. Market convention in this case is cash settlement of $100 for each index point (all the amounts are in USD).

If the S&P 500 Index at expiry is at or below the strike price, then there is no need to exercise the option and the buyer gains nothing from the option but loses the up-front premium, in this case $12. If the index at expiry is above the strike price, then it makes sense to exercise since one is, in effect, simultaneously buying low and selling high. The net profit and loss to the buyer is the difference between the actual price and the strike price multiplied by $100 per index point less the premium. So, at 1,505, the option pays off $5 \times \$100$. The premium paid is $12 and, hence, the net gain (ignoring discounting) is $488. Breakeven occurs at 1,500.12. At this level, the payoff from exercising the option is $12 and this exactly compensates for the cost of the option in the first place. Note that the profit and loss of the buyer and of the seller match. There is no financial alchemy here.

Figure 3.1 depicts the payoff from the call option at the expiration date from the buyer's point of view. Since the option that we just analysed is a European-style option, the expiration date of the option is the same as the exercise date; European options can only be exercised on the final day. So, the payoff at expiration and the payoff at exercise are the same.

Adjusting for the premium that the buyer has paid to buy the option in the first place gives the profit and loss for the call option at the expiration date (again from the buyer's perspective). This is shown in Figure 3.2.

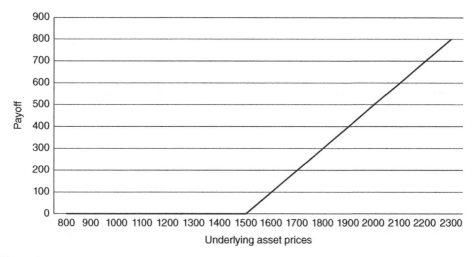

Figure 3.1   Buyer call payoff at expiration

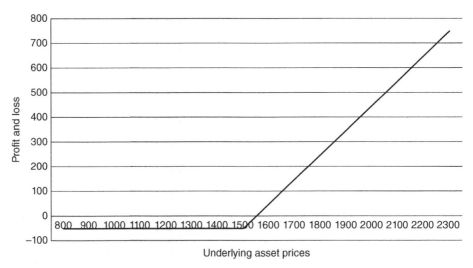

Figure 3.2 Buyer call profit and loss at expiration

From the seller's point of view, in Figures 3.3 and 3.4 we have the payoff and profit and loss for the call option at the expiration date shown.

When the option payoff (for the holder) is positive (i.e., when the price of the underlying asset is higher than the strike price), the call is said to be *in-the-money* (ITM). When the price of the underlying asset is the same as the strike price, 1,500 in the example, the call is said to be *at-the-money* (ATM). When the price of the underlying asset is below the strike price, the call is said to be *out-of-the-money* (OTM).

The approach above can be extended to the other two options. In the third case, however, the buyer is able to choose the exercise date. In deciding when to exercise, we assume that the buyer chooses an optimal time.

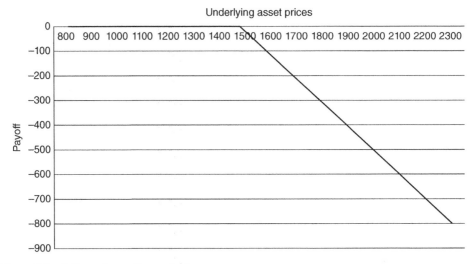

Figure 3.3 Seller call payoff at expiration

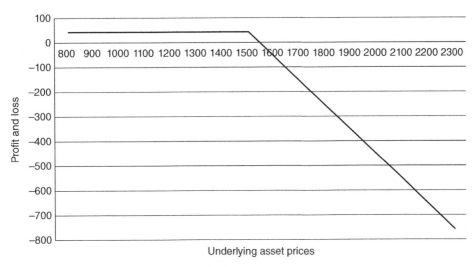

Figure 3.4   Seller call profit and loss at expiration

3.2   PUT OPTIONS

3.2.1   Definition

A put option is a contract that gives the buyer the right – again, the right but not the obligation – to sell a certain quantity of an underlying asset at the strike price. The seller of the option has the obligation – not the right – to buy the agreed quantity of the underlying asset at the strike price if the buyer exercises his or her right. As in the case of the call option, the seller of the option is also called the *writer*.

To reiterate, if you buy a put option, you acquire the right to sell the underlying asset at the strike price. You are not under an obligation to sell. This will depend upon whether it makes sense or not. As with the call option, the put option buyer will have to pay the option premium to the seller.

3.2.2   Examples

1 – A trader buys a European put option on the S&P 500 Index with a strike price at 1,500 points and an expiration date of Dec 2013. As discussed in section 3.1.1, since the underlying asset is an equity index, *cash settlement* will take place upon exercise of the option and a cash amount will be paid to the option buyer. This amount represents the profit that would accrue from selling the index at the strike price and buying it at the price prevailing (see Table 3.2).

Table 3.2   Put option payoff and profit & loss

Value of S&P 500 Index at expiry	1,200	1,499.86	1,500	1,505
Put buyer's payoff	30,000	14	0	0
Put buyer's profit and loss	29,986	0	−14	−14
Put seller's payoff	−30,000	−14	0	0
Put seller's profit and loss	−29,986	0	14	14

2 – A corporation buys a European put option on the EUR/USD FX rate with a strike price of 1.30 and an expiration date of 3 months. This option will be *physically settled* if the put option is exercised. The corporation will then sell the agreed amount of EUR against buying a corresponding amount of USD using an exchange rate equal to the strike price (1.30 in this case).

3 – A fund manager buys an American put option on XYZ Incorporated with a strike price set at $80 and an expiration date of 2 months. Again, there is physical settlement, which implies that, if the put option is exercised, the buyer will have the right to sell the agreed amount of stock and receive the strike price for each unit of stock sold.

3.2.3 Scenario analysis for put options

Assume that the premium paid for the S&P put option described above is $14. At the expiration date, we have the following payoff and profit and loss profiles for the buyer and the seller. As in section 3.1.2, we are assuming that one exchange traded option contract has been negotiated with a cash settlement amount of $100 for each index point (all the amounts in USD).

In this case, the breakeven index level is 1,499.86. At this index level, the buyer of the put would get a payoff of $14 from exercising the option and this is exactly offsetting the cost of the option. If the S&P 500 Index at expiry is at or above the strike price, then there is no need to exercise the option and the buyer gains nothing from the option but loses the up-front premium, in this case $14. If the index at expiry is below the strike price, then it makes sense to exercise since one is, in effect, simultaneously selling low and buying lower. The net profit and loss to the buyer is the difference between the actual price and the strike price multiplied by $100 per index point less the premium. So, at 1,200, for example, the option pays off $300 \times $100, i.e., $30,000. The premium paid is $14 and, hence, the net profit and loss gain (ignoring discounting) is $29,986. Again, the profit and loss of the buyer and of the seller match.

Figure 3.5 shows the payoff of the put option at the exercise date/expiration date from the buyer's point of view.

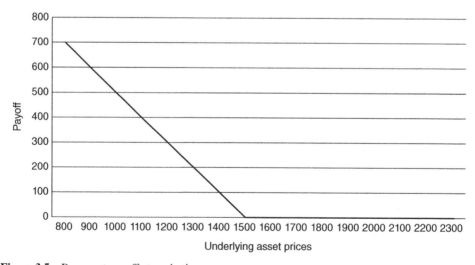

Figure 3.5   Buyer put payoff at expiration

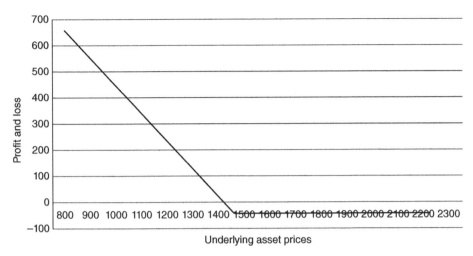

Figure 3.6   Buyer put profit and loss at expiration

Taking into account the premium that the buyer paid to buy the put option, we have the profit and loss for the put at the expiration date (again from the buyer's perspective) (Figure 3.6).

From the seller's point of view, Figures 3.7 and 3.8 show the payoff and profit and loss at exercise/expiry.

When the put option payoff (for the buyer) is positive (i.e., the price of the underlying asset is lower than the strike price), the put is said to be *in-the-money* (ITM). When the price of the underlying asset is the same as the strike price, 1,500 in this example, the put is said to be *at-the-money* (ATM) and, when the price of the underlying asset is above the strike price, the put is said to be *out-of-the-money* (OTM).

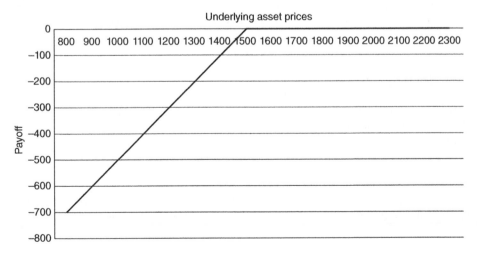

Figure 3.7   Seller put payoff at expiration

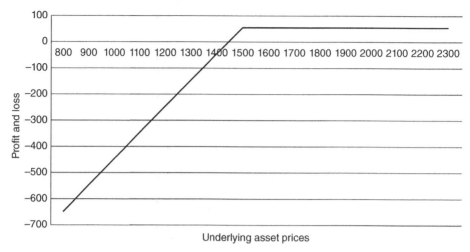

Figure 3.8   Seller put profit and loss at expiration

Of course, the approach above can be extended to the other two options, the FX option and the single stock option. Again, in the third case, the buyer is able to choose the exercise date. In deciding when to exercise, we assume that the buyer chooses an optimal time.

3.3 BOUNDARY CONDITIONS FOR CALL AND PUT OPTIONS PRICES

3.3.1 Introduction and basic notation

In the following section, we will focus on boundary conditions for option prices[3] and the parity relationships between the prices of similar call and put options. At this stage, we wish to stress that the boundary conditions and the parity relations that we will describe are based on no-arbitrage arguments. As such, they are valid irrespective of the future price behaviour of the underlying asset or of other market variables that can affect option prices.

As a first step, let us introduce some basic notation:

C will denote the call option price,
P will denote the put option price,
S will denote the spot price of the underlying asset,
K will denote the strike price,
T will denote the tenor of the option,
t will denote any given time before the expiry of the option, and
S_T will denote the spot price of the underlying asset at time T, i.e., when the option expires.

Based on simple no-arbitrage arguments, it is relatively straightforward to identify upper and lower bounds for option prices. The basic idea is that, whenever a no-arbitrage condition is violated, it would be possible to build a portfolio (of options and the underlying asset) such

---

[3] In other words, the upper and lower bounds for option prices.

that there is no possibility of incurring a loss and, under some circumstances, a net profit may be achieved.

Let us start from the basic boundary conditions showing how to build the riskless portfolio and calculating the amount of the "risk-free" profit. We will refer to a "long position" in a certain security whenever a market participant owns that security and a "short position" when this security has been sold short.

3.3.2 A call option cannot be worth more than the price of the underlying asset

Consider our first boundary condition. The price of a call option (either European or American) cannot be higher than the price of the underlying asset. Intuitively, since a call option is the right to buy the underlying, it is reasonable to expect that the price of this right (i.e., the option price) cannot be higher than the price of the underlying to which the right refers. Obvious?

Think about this, if the condition does not hold, then an arbitrage opportunity exists. Market participants would have a clear way to make a risk-less profit; sell the call option (at the price C, which is higher than the underlying asset) and buy the underlying asset at the price S. The profit and loss at the expiry of the resulting portfolio will clearly be equal to the combined sum of the profit and loss from the option and the profit and loss from the underlying asset position:

- Profit and loss on the short position in the option = premium received for selling the option, C, less the option payoff at exercise; $C - \text{Max}(S_T - K, 0)$.
- Profit and loss on the long position on the underlying = price of the underlying at exercise, S_T, less the purchase price of the underlying, S.

So, the total profit and loss (which we will indicate with P&L in the various formulae below) of the portfolio at expiry will be:

$$\text{P\&L} = S_T - S + C - \text{Max}(S_T - K, 0)$$

Now, if $S_T > K$, then the profit and loss above is:

$$\text{P\&L} = S_T - S + C - S_T + K$$
$$\text{P\&L} = C + K - S$$

Since, in this example, C is higher than S, then the total profit and loss >0, i.e., the arbitrage is profitable.

On the other hand, if $S_T \leq K$, then the option expires worthless and the profit and loss is equal to the option premium received from selling the option plus the profit and loss on the underlying position:

$$\text{P\&L} = S_T - S + C$$

But, of course, in this example, C is higher than S, and so the profit and loss >0, i.e., the arbitrage is profitable as long as S_T is non-negative.[4]

---

[4] It is perhaps rather trivial to note that the price of the underlying needs to be non-negative. How often do we see negative prices on assets?

3.3.3   The price of a put option cannot be higher than the present value of the strike price, K

The payoff from a European put option will be at its maximum when the price of the underlying asset is equal to zero.[5] In this case, the option payoff will be equal to K. So, if K is the maximum payoff, then the price of the put option cannot be higher than K. If the condition did not hold, then one would sell the put option in the knowledge that the premium received would more than compensate for any possible payoff at expiry. Since the European option payoff comes at the option expiry, however, we can refine this boundary condition further. *On any date before expiry, the price of a put option cannot be higher than the present value of the strike price, K.* If this condition did not hold, then one would sell the put option (and invest the proceeds in an interest-bearing asset) in the knowledge that the net present value of the premium received would more than compensate for any possible payoff at expiry.

What about for an American put option? In this case, there is never a requirement to wait until expiry to monetize the payoff. If the price of the underlying asset reaches zero, it will certainly be optimal for the holder to exercise the option immediately. The maximum payoff from the option will again be K.

3.3.4   Lower boundaries for call options on non-dividend paying stocks

At any time, t, the price of a European call option on a non-dividend paying stock cannot be lower than $\text{Max}(0, S_t - K\,\text{DF}(t, T))$, where $\text{DF}(t, T)$ is the discount factor prevailing at time t for cash flows payable at time T. If this were not the case, a straightforward arbitrage opportunity would exist.

We do not aim to prove this but we will illustrate the principle with a simple example.

Consider a European call option with 3 months until expiry, a strike price equal to 100 written on a non-dividend paying stock, whose price is equal to 110. For simplicity, we will assume a zero interest rate, i.e., $\text{DF}(t, T) = 1$. The lower boundary for this call option is equal to:

$$\text{Max}(S_t - K, 0) = \text{Max}(110 - 100, 0) = 10$$

Now assume that the option price available in the market is 5, i.e., it is lower than its lower bound value of 10. Market participants could easily buy this option for 5 and sell the underlying at 110. The profit and loss at the expiry of the option is going to be equal to the sum of the option profit and loss and the profit and loss on the underlying asset.

- Profit and loss on the long position in the option = option payoff – premium paid for the option = $\text{Max}(S_T - 100, 0) - 5$.
- Profit and loss on the short position in the underlying = sale price of the underlying – final price of the underlying = $110 - S_T$.

Therefore, the total profit and loss of the strategy is:

$$\text{P\&L} = \text{Max}(S_T - 100, 0) - 5 + 110 - S_T$$

If $S_T > 100$, i.e., the call expires in-the-money and the total profit and loss is:

$$\text{P\&L} = S_T - 100 - 5 + 110 - S_T = 5$$

---

[5] Again, assuming that asset prices cannot be negative.

On the other hand, if $S_T \leq 100$, i.e., the call expires worthless and the total profit and loss is:

$$P\&L = -5 + 110 - S_T = 105 - S_T \geq 5$$

Therefore, irrespective of the final price of the underlying, one can easily lock in a profit of at least 5.

3.3.5 Lower boundaries for put options on non-dividend paying stocks

At any time, t, the price of a European put option on a non-dividend paying stock cannot be lower than $\text{Max}(0, K\,\text{DF}(t, T) - S_t)$, where $\text{DF}(t, T)$ is the discount factor prevailing at time t for cash flows payable at time T. Again, if this is not the case, a straightforward arbitrage opportunity arises.

Consider a similar example to the one above, i.e., a European put option with 3 months until expiry, a strike price equal to 100 written on an underlying (non-dividend paying stock) whose price is equal to 90. For simplicity, we will again assume a zero interest rate, i.e., $\text{DF}(t, T) = 1$. As above, the lower boundary for the put option is equal to:

$$\text{Max}(K - S_t, 0) = \text{Max}(100 - 90, 0) = 10$$

Now, assume that the option price available in the market is 5, i.e., it is lower than its lower bound value of 10. Market participants could buy this option for 5 and buy the underlying at 90. The profit and loss in this case is:

- Profit and loss on the long position in the option = option payoff – premium paid for the option = $\text{Max}(100 - S_T, 0) - 5$.
- Profit and loss on the long position in the underlying = final price of the underlying – purchase price of the underlying = $S_T - 90$.

Therefore, the total profit and loss of the strategy is:

$$P\&L = \text{Max}(100 - S_T, 0) - 5 - 90 + S_T$$

If $S_T \geq 100$, i.e., the put expires worthless, the profit and loss is:

$$P\&L = -5 - 90 + S_T \geq 5$$

On the other hand, if $S_T < 100$, i.e., the put expires in-the-money:

$$P\&L = 100 - S_T - 5 - 90 + S_T = 5$$

As in the case of call options, and irrespective of the future dynamic of the underlying price, there is a straightforward strategy that allows one to lock in a profit of at least 5.

3.4 PUT–CALL PARITY

So far we have looked at the upper and lower bound for individual puts and calls. We will now introduce a very important relationship between call and put options, known as the *put–call parity*. The put–call parity allows us to express the price of a put relative to the price of the call and vice versa.

The intuition behind the put–call parity stems from the fact that it is possible to combine a long position in a call option and a short position in a put option with the same strike and expiry (and, obviously, the same underlying asset) to replicate a long position in the underlying asset itself. Symmetrically, it is possible to combine a short position in a call option and a long position in a put option with the same strike and expiry (and, obviously, the same underlying asset) to replicate a short position in the underlying asset itself.

For simplicity, assume the case of a European call and put option on a generic underlying asset, both expiring in T with strike price $K = 100$. Also, assume that a trader has bought the call option and sold the put option. Since the strikes are identical then, at expiry, it will be optimal to exercise the call option (if the price of the underlying asset is higher than K) or the put option (if the price of the underlying asset is lower than K). Under no circumstances will it be optimal to exercise both, since the price of the underlying asset cannot simultaneously be both higher and lower than the strike price K.

If the call option is exercised, the trader (who owns the call option) will have to pay to strike price K to enter a long position in the underlying price (worth $S_T > K$ at expiry). If, however, the put option is exercised, the trader's counterparty (who bought the put option) will exercise the put option and, as such, the trader will have to buy the underlying asset (worth $S_T < K$ at expiry) paying an amount equal to the strike price K. This is summarized in Table 3.3.

As can be seen from the table, irrespective of the price of the underlying asset, the payoff is equal to $S_T - K$. Obviously, $S_T - K$ can take many different values depending on the price of the underlying asset at expiry, S_T, but the payoff of the overall strategy can, nevertheless, be described simply by the difference between the price S_T and the fixed quantity K.

At this point, we would note that a strategy consisting of a long position in the underlying asset and a short cash position in the present value of the strike price K will produce the same outcome. At expiry, the long position in the underlying asset will be worth S_T and the short cash position in the present value of the strike price K will be worth K. So, the combined position will be worth $S_T - K$.

But if the two strategies have the same payoff at expiry, they should also have the same price at any time before the expiry. We can summarize this as: at any time, t, a portfolio composed of a long position in a call option and a short position in a put option with the same strike K,

Table 3.3 Put–call parity

Price of the underlying asset	Action	Position in the underlying asset after the expiry	Cash position after expiry	Trader's payout
$S_T > K$	The trader exercises the call option	The trader buys the underlying asset from the counterparty who sold him the call option	The trader pays an amount = K to buy the underlying asset at the strike price	$S_T - K$
$S_T < K$	The trader's counterparty exercises the put option	The trader buys the underlying asset from the counterparty who exercised the put option	The trader pays an amount = K to buy the underlying asset at the strike price	$S_T - K$

expiry T and underlying asset is equivalent to a long position in that underlying asset and a short cash position equal to the present value of the strike price K, i.e.:

$$\text{Call price}\,(t) - \text{Put price}\,(t) = S_t - K\,DF(t, T)$$

This is put–call parity.

3.5 SWAPTIONS

A swaption is an option that gives the buyer the right but not the obligation to enter into a swap. A payer swaption allows the buyer to pay fixed in a swap with a predetermined maturity and receive the floating leg. Conversely, a receiver swaption allows the buyer to receive fixed in the swap and pay the floating leg. If the buyer exercises the payer swaption, then the two parties (buyer and seller of the swaption) will enter the underlying swap (with the swaption buyer paying the fixed rate or fixed price and the swaption seller receiving it). Note that the fixed level specified for the swaption plays a role similar to that of a strike price.

Swaptions are generally quoted with the maturity of the option followed by the maturity of the associated swap. So, a swaption that had a maturity of 1 year but which, upon exercise, became a 10-year swap would be quoted as a 1 year into 10-year swaption. Typically the underlying swap will be a vanilla interest rate swap or a commodity swap but "swaption" can actually be used to refer to an option on any type of swap. Like any option, swaptions can be American, European or Bermudan. When swaptions are traded, market participants have to specify not only the expiry and the strike price of the swaption, but they also have to describe in detail all the features of the underlying swap (such as settlement frequency, fixed price, floating index and tenor, time to maturity at exercise of the option). The buyer of a swaption will have to pay an up-front premium to the seller.

In the interest rate world, the buyer of a payer swaption will tend to benefit if swap rates subsequently rise faster (or fall slower) than is discounted in the interest rate swap curve while the buyer of a receiver swaption will tend to benefit if swap rates subsequently fall faster (or rise less) than is discounted.[6] Although many swaptions are physically settled at expiry, most are cash settled. This means that the buyer of the swaption, upon exercising, does not necessarily enter into a swap agreement. Instead, he or she will receive a cash amount equivalent to the current market value of a swap that has the same terms as the swap defined in the swaption contract.

We can see how a payer swaption works by returning to the two-date oil swap examples (introduced in Chapter 2). The 1-year oil swap price was $109.9/bbl, but TFG would like to speculate on the swap price being even lower over the next 2 months.

Suppose the following: if in 2 months the fixed price for a swap commencing in 4 months, i.e., 6 months from today, is $109.9/bbl or above, TFG will enter into a swap agreeing to pay $109.9/bbl after 4 months and after 10 months. If, on the other hand, the market swap price is below $109.9/bbl, TFG will not have the obligation to enter into the swap; TFG only has the right to do so. If, for instance, the market swap level is at $108/bbl, TFG may be

---

[6] In fact, interest rates will need to move past the strike interest rate on the swaption in order for the investor to break even and begin making money since, presumably, the swaption premium is a non-zero amount. The amount by which the interest rate needs to move past the strike interest rate on the swaption (above in the case of the payer and below in the case of the receiver) is the interest rate move that would be required to increase the net present value of the swap by an amount equal to the initial cost of the swaption.

Figure 3.9   Cash flows chart

interested in entering into the swap at that level and certainly leave the swaption to expire without exercising. Through the swaption, TFG has the possibility to enter into a swap at a level which is below the market price; therefore it will have to pay a premium. TFG purchases a payer swaption: it has the right, not the obligation to pay a fixed price of $109.9/bbl for 1 year of oil. The swap counterparty has sold this swaption.

When the swaption is exercised, TFG commits to buy oil at a fixed level after 6 and 12 months. TFG can exercise the option and simultaneously hedge the swap with another swap, converting the stream of swap payments into a stream of fixed payments, with a fixed present value. Suppose that TFG can enter into another swap where it receives $111/bbl (which is the bid of the new swap counterparty) and pays variable. The stream can be illustrated as shown in Figure 3.9.

The swaption, once exercised, is equivalent to an ordinary option, with the present value of the swap of obligations as the underlying asset, i.e., at the moment of exercise, the premium of that option would be:

$$\frac{(\$111/bbl - \$109.9/bbl)}{(e^{1\% \times 0.5})} + \frac{(\$111/bbl - \$109.9/bbl)}{(e^{2\% \times 1})} = \$2.17/bbl$$

3.6   OPTIONS STRATEGIES

3.6.1   Introduction to option strategies

So far we analysed the payoff from individual options. In the following sections, we will present the most common payoff profiles obtained by combining several options. We will start from combinations of option of the same type (i.e., call or put options) and then show some typical combinations of option of different types (i.e., both call and put options used within the same strategy). In Chapter 7, we will analyse the risk profile of each option strategy presented in the following sections.

Before discussing each strategy, however, we would just make a quick remark. Given the put–call parity, any call can, in theory, be decomposed into a combination of a put and a forward contract. Also, any put can be obtained by trading a call and a forward contract. Therefore, at least in theory, put and call options can be considered interchangeable. In practice, however, it is uncommon to trade options that are already in-the-money; deeply in-the-money options are definitely not common and they tend to be replaced by options of a different type (i.e., a call will be replaced by a put and a put will be replaced by a call). In this case, for the same strike, the option will now be out-of-the-money. An example should clarify this concept: say the EUR/USD FX rate is currently trading at 1.30; a trader who wants to protect him- or herself from a fall in this rate below, say, 1.28 could technically buy an in-the-money call with strike equal to 1.28 and sell EUR/USD forward. In practice, the trader would buy a 1.28 put since this is easier.

In the following examples, we will assume that the options being discussed are either close to at-the-money or out-of-the-money.

3.6.2   Option spreads

An *option spread* is simply a position containing calls and puts, where some options are bought and some are sold.

Option spreads are a relatively common strategy and when constructed either with just calls or just puts are sometimes called *vertical spreads*.[7] Of course, it is possible to have option spread trades constructed using both puts and calls (e.g., *ratio spreads* and *risk reversals*) or more exotic options but it is worth noting that adding more and more complexity into a spread trade does not necessarily make it any more useful (or cheap to trade). Certainly, adding complexity makes them more difficult to understand intuitively and to manage the implied risks.

In the following analysis, we will look at the most common option spread strategies, assuming European options.

3.6.3   Directional strategies using vertical spreads

Directional strategies can be effected using single options (i.e., a single put or a call) or by simple combinations of puts and calls. Generally, bullish strategies are constructed buying calls while bearish strategies are constructed buying puts. However, this need not always be the case.

1. Purchase of a call spread

Buy a low-strike call and sell a high-strike call with the same expiration date
Note that, in this strategy, the same number of contracts of each option[8] are bought and sold.

The low-strike call will cost more than the high-strike call and so this trade will imply the need to pay premium. In time, the rationale behind which strategies cost money or earn premiums at the outset will become intuitive, if not now. The low-strike call option has a greater chance of expiring in-the-money than does the high-strike call option. Since there is a greater chance of making money on the trade, the price of the low-strike option has to be higher. If it were otherwise, it would imply the existence of arbitrage opportunities.

The premium paid for the call spread represents the maximum possible loss for this strategy. The purchase of a call spread is a "lower-cost" alternative to buying just the low-strike call option (since the total cost is offset partly by the premium received from selling the high-strike option) although the trade-off is clearly that the upside potential is thereby limited. A glance at the payoff diagrams for the purchase of a call and a call spread may make this a little more obvious (Figure 3.10).

---

[7] This stems from the way in which option prices are generally presented in newspapers, with strikes for the calls and the puts arranged vertically.

[8] In some cases, investors will buy and sell different numbers of contracts. In this case, the strategies are termed *ratio spreads*. Again, there will be a low-strike and a high-strike and the expiration dates will be the same. Since ratio spreads involve buying and selling unequal numbers of contracts, it is possible to construct ratio spreads for zero premia. Ratio spreads will obviously have very different risk–return profiles compared with vertical spreads.

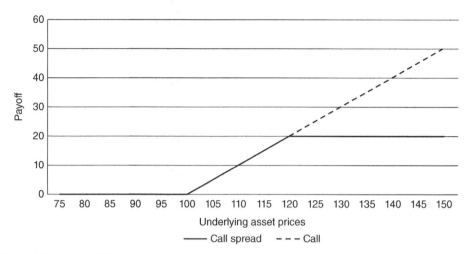

Figure 3.10   Long call spread vs. long call payoffs

Table 3.4   Comparison between being long a call and being long a call spread

	Long call	Long call spread
Maximum loss	Call premium paid	Net premium paid
Maximum gain	Unlimited	Difference between the strike prices less the net premium paid
Breakeven	Strike price plus the premium paid	Lower strike price plus the net premium paid

Note that, *while the maximum loss is lower in absolute terms for the call spread than the outright call, the percentage loss is the same, i.e., 100% of the premium paid.* Such an insight is often overlooked. So, if an investor spends the same amount of money on buying bull call spreads that he or she would have spent on buying calls outright, then the maximum loss is exactly the same in cash terms.

So, for example, if a call costs twice as much as a call spread then an investor willing to risk a fixed cash amount in options could buy twice as many call spreads as outright calls. Consequently, while payoff diagrams are relevant for understanding the risk and reward for a single unit of a strategy (e.g., one single call option or one bull call spread), they can be misleading when thinking about actual cash flows from competing strategies.

Notwithstanding the previous comment, Table 3.4 describes briefly the risk and rewards of buying an outright call and a call spread. As can be seen, the call spread breaks even before the outright call. This should also be clear from the payoff diagrams above.

Why buy a call spread? When used as a directional strategy,[9] the buyer clearly has to believe that the price of the underlying asset will rise but that is also true of buying an outright call. So, there must be something else. The difference is in the degree of price bullishness. Returning to Figure 3.10, one can see that the maximum profit on the call spread occurs at the higher strike price.[10]

---

[9] In Chapter 7 we will present non-directional ways to trade an option spread.
[10] In addition, the maximum loss occurs at (or below) the lowest strike price.

Consequently, if somebody expects the underlying asset price to rise to a certain point but not much further, he or she may be willing to give up the implied upside potential past this point by selling a call struck at that level. So, if you are bullish but do not have a clear ceiling on the price potential, then perhaps buy calls. On the other hand, if you are bullish but think that the upside is limited to a ceiling, buy a bull call spread with the high-strike set at the ceiling.

Choosing the strike prices is, thus, an art rather than a science especially for the higher-strike call. The higher strike needs to be set high enough to provide a reasonable upside potential (or the investor fails to participate in a sufficient portion of the upward move) but low enough to generate enough premium received to make the sale of the call worthwhile. When introducing the concept of volatility and volatility smiles in Chapters 6 and 7, we will again discuss option spreads and we will show additional factors affecting the risk–reward of trading these kinds of strategies.

2. Purchase of a put spread

Buy a high-strike put and sell a low-strike put with the same expiration date

This is basically the symmetric version of the previous case. Again, the same number of contracts will be bought and sold.

The high-strike put will cost more than the low-strike put and so this trade will imply the need to pay premium. This represents the maximum possible loss. The purchase of a put spread is a lower-risk alternative to buying a straight put although the trade-off is clearly that the upside potential is limited.

Note again that, while the maximum loss is lower in absolute terms for the put spread than the outright put, the percentage loss is the same, i.e., 100% of the premium paid (Table 3.5).

Why buy a put spread? As in the call spread, when used as a directional strategy, the buyer has to believe that the price of the underlying asset will fall. The maximum profit occurs at the lower strike price and the maximum loss occurs at (or above) the higher strike price. Again, choosing the strike prices is an art rather than a science especially for the lower-strike put. The lower-strike needs to be low enough to provide a reasonable potential profit but high enough to generate sufficient premium received to make the sale worthwhile.

3. Sale of a call spread

Sell a low-strike call and buy a high-strike call with the same expiration date

This is exactly the opposite as case 1. Again the same number of contracts will be bought and sold.

Table 3.5   Comparison between being long a put and being long a put spread

	Long put	Long put spread
Maximum loss	Put premium paid	Net premium paid
Maximum gain	Strike price	Difference between the strike prices less the net premium paid
Breakeven	Strike price less the premium paid	Higher strike price less the net premium paid

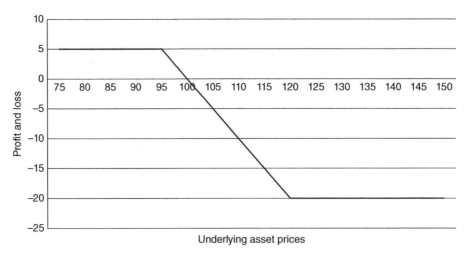

Figure 3.11   Short call spread profit and loss

The high-strike call will cost less than the low-strike call and so this trade will imply a positive net premium for the seller.

A sale of a call spread strategy might be employed by somebody believing that the price of the underlying asset will go down in future but only moderately (or at least it will not go up) and is willing to collect some premium to face a limited liability. It is a less risky alternative compared with the sale of an outright call option but obviously the premium received is lower; the potential liability for an outright call is obviously unlimited, whereas, in the case of a call spread, it is limited to the difference between the two strikes.

The maximum gain from this strategy is the net premium received at the inception of the trade (see the profit and loss diagram, Figure 3.11). To achieve this gain, the stock price needs to close at or below the strike price of the low-strike call. In this case, both options would expire worthless.

The maximum loss occurs if the underlying asset price rises to (or above) the strike of the high-strike option. At this point, the loss is the difference between the strike prices of the two options less the net premium received at the inception of the trade.

In Table 3.6, we compare two different bearish strategies, selling a call spread and buying a put option to highlight the differences between the two.

Table 3.6   Comparison between being short a call spread and being long a put

	Short call spread	Long put
Maximum loss	Difference between the strike prices less the net premium received	Put premium paid
Maximum gain	Net premium received	Strike price
Breakeven	Lower strike price plus the net premium received	Strike price less the premium paid

Table 3.7 Comparison between being short a call spread and being long a put spread

	Short call spread	Long put spread
Maximum loss	Difference between the strike prices less the net premium received	Net premium paid
Maximum gain	Net premium received	Difference between the strike prices less the net premium paid
Breakeven	Lower strike price plus the net premium received	Higher strike price less the net premium paid

By widening the difference between the two strikes, the maximum gain can be increased (i.e., the premium received will be higher), although, as should be clear, this would mean that the potential liability is larger.

Table 3.7 compares the payoff from selling a call spread with the payoff from buying a put spread.

4. Sale of a put spread

Sell a high-strike put and buy a low-strike put with the same expiration date

This is exactly the opposite strategy as case 2. As before, the same number of contracts will be bought and sold.

The low-strike put will cost less than the high-strike put and so this trade implies a net premium received. Some investors consider selling put spreads to be "income generating". As one can see from Table 3.8, buying a call spread and selling a put spread are fundamentally different strategies.

Why sell a put spread? Clearly the seller has to believe that the price of the underlying asset will rise or, at the very least, not fall below the level of the higher strike price and he or she is willing to collect some premium to face a limited liability. This may be the case when the asset price is very near to strong support levels. It is a less risky alternative to the sale of an outright put option but obviously the premium received is lower.

3.6.4   Risk reversal and collars

In practice, it is common to use "risk reversal" to describe a strategy where a high-strike call is sold against the purchase of a low-strike put or, vice versa, a high-strike call is bought against the sale of a low-strike put. Again, the underlying asset is the same, as is the expiration date.

Table 3.8 Comparison between being short a put spread and being long a call spread

	Short put spread	Long call spread
Maximum loss	Difference between the strike prices less the net premium received	Net premium paid
Maximum gain	Net premium received	Difference between the strike prices less the net premium paid
Breakeven	Higher strike price less the net premium received	Lower strike price plus the net premium paid

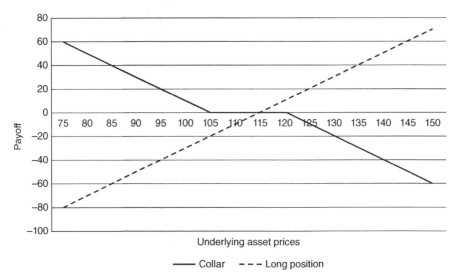

Figure 3.12   Collar vs. long position payoffs

The difference between the two strike prices is called the *width*. When this structure is used to hedge long or short positions of a certain underlying, in general in the commodity or interest rate spaces it is referred to as a collar. Normally, the low strike is called the floor and the high strike is the cap or ceiling.

As should be clear from the payoff diagram (Figure 3.12), a collar position consisting of long a put and short a call is a bearish position in the underlying; this is why they can act as hedges against a long position. An investor who holds this exposure will make money when the market falls but lose money when it rises. The difference between this collar and a short position in the underlying is that the payoff at expiration of the collar does not change for prices on the underlying asset between the strike prices, i.e., the width.

Option purists may argue that risk reversals/collars require equal numbers of puts and calls; however, it is also possible to think of this structure using fractional amounts of options. For example, consider a situation where an investor who is long an asset buys a put option (which provides full downside protection) but sells more call options to raise the absolute amount of premium earned. This will reduce the net cost of the structure but, of course, the trade-off is that the investor now has a short position if the underlying asset rises above the call strike price.

Although both concepts refer to the same structure, collars, as mentioned above, are used to hedge a certain long or short position, but risk reversals are mainly used to express views on volatility skew.[11]

3.6.5   Volatility[12] strategies with puts and calls

1. Straddles

A *straddle* is a long call and put position with the same strike and time to expiration. The rationale behind a straddle is relatively simple. If the price of the underlying asset price goes

---

[11] We will discuss volatility skew in much more detail in Chapter 7.
[12] The reason why these are described as volatility strategies will be clear in Chapters 6 and 7.

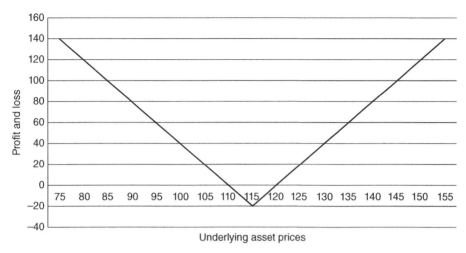

Figure 3.13   Long straddle profit and loss

up, the long call position will benefit. On the other hand, if the underlying asset price goes down then the long put position will benefit. Thus, a long straddle position benefits from asset price moves in both directions. The disadvantage of the straddle is that the absolute premium will be "high" since it implies buying two options (Figure 3.13).

As we will discuss in Chapters 6 and 7, we anticipate that a buyer of a straddle is taking a bet on the volatility of the price of the underlying asset. The buyer of an at-the-money straddle, for example, hopes that the asset price is going to move sharply irrespective of the direction (hence the exposure to volatility). Conversely, selling a straddle would suggest a bet that actual volatility in the future will be relatively low.[13] Imagine a biotech company developing a drug that will either cure a specific type of cancer, or go bankrupt. Here, buying a straddle might be precisely the position to take. We do not know which of the two scenarios will occur, but it will be one or the other.

Of course, the short position in the straddle has a very different risk–reward profile to a long position. In this case, the maximum profit is the premium received while the maximum loss is technically unlimited (Figure 3.14).

2. Strangles

A "disadvantage" of straddles is generally said to be the high absolute cost. Of course, in a relative value sense, a high-cost option is not necessarily expensive. Whether a straddle is rich or cheap depends not on the absolute amount of premium paid but on the cost versus the expected payoff. Nevertheless, some market participants may wish to reduce the absolute amount of premium paid by buying out-of-the-money options rather than options with the same strike. This is called a *strangle*. Such strategies reduce the maximum loss if the options expire worthless but, of course, they increase the price moves required to break even and they reduce the upside gain for any given price move (Figure 3.15).

---

[13] As it will become clearer in Chapters 6 and 7, the bet is not on a high or low volatility in absolute terms but relative to the volatility that has been used to price the straddle.

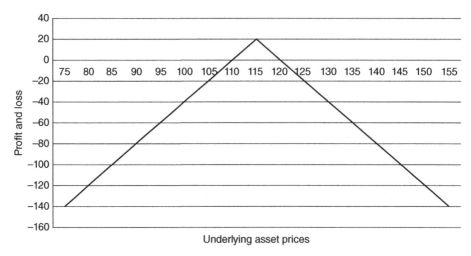

Figure 3.14   Short straddle profit and loss

Again, as with the straddle, buying a strangle is really a bet that the underlying volatility will be high, whereas selling a strangle suggests a bet that underlying volatility will be relatively contained. Also, as with straddles, the short position in a strangle has a very different risk–reward profile to that of the long position; the maximum profit is the premium received while the maximum loss is technically unlimited (Figure 3.16).

When comparing fairly priced straddles and strangles, there will be a region for the underlying asset price where each strategy outperforms the other; see the payoff diagram, Figure 3.17. For small price moves away from the strike price, the strangle outperforms the straddle (since the premium paid for the strangle can be significantly lower). However, for large price moves away from the strike price, the straddle will outperform. The decision to use a straddle or a

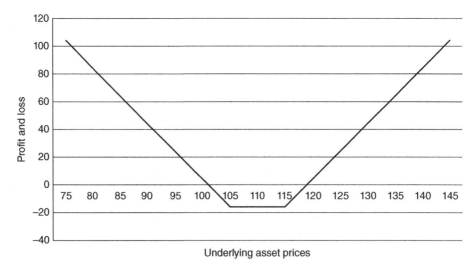

Figure 3.15   Long strangle profit and loss

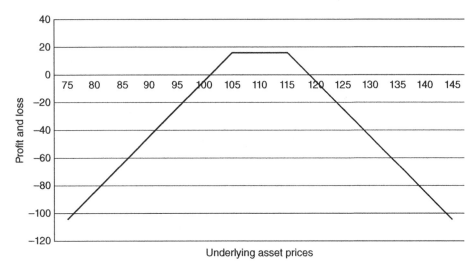

Figure 3.16   Short strangle profit and loss

strangle will depend very much on the investor's expectation for the asset price movements. This does not mean that one strategy is "better" than the other, however. Typically the options market will price the straddle and the strangle assuming that they are equivalently fair bets. If an investor has a preference for one strategy relative to the other it is because his expectations for the asset price movements are different to that which is expected by the market.

To mitigate the unlimited downside that can arise from the short straddle position, an investor could buy out-of-the-money puts (to eliminate the extreme losses on the downside) or out-of-the-money calls (to eliminate the extreme losses on the upside). Such a position is sometimes called an *insured written straddle*. It is also a type of *butterfly spread*, a set of option strategies that we discuss next. Since the purchase of the out-of-the-money options will imply

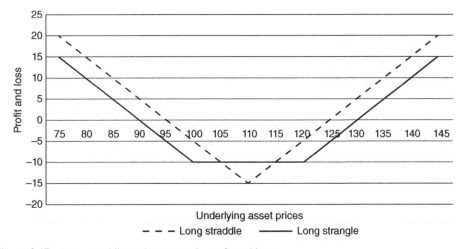

Figure 3.17   Long straddle vs. long strangle profit and loss

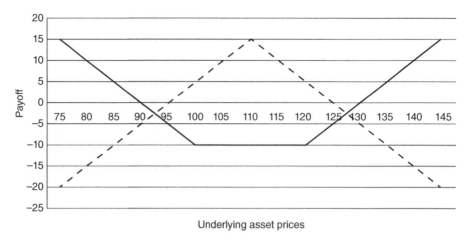

Figure 3.18   Short straddle vs. long strangle payoffs

a payment of premium, the maximum profit from an insured written straddle will obviously be less than that of the straddle. On the other hand, the potential losses will be reduced.

A special case of the insured written straddle arises from a short position in a straddle and a long position in a strangle. In this case, the payoff will be symmetric, as in Figure 3.18.

3. Butterfly spreads

Earlier, we suggested that a short position in a straddle and a long position in a strangle is a butterfly spread. Option purists would, at this point, pull out their hair. Technically, a butterfly spread involves only calls or only puts. Since the name "butterfly" comes from the shape of the payoff diagram, however, rather than anything to do with the animal kingdom, it does seem a little pointless to get too bothered about this distinction and most people do not.

The most traditional butterfly spread is one created by buying a call, selling two higher-strike calls and then buying an even higher-strike call. Alternatively, one could use puts. Assuming that the distances between the strike prices are equal, then the payoff will be symmetrical; see the following diagrams. Again, at this point, option purists would say that "true" butterfly spreads require the distances between the strikes to be equal. Sure, but then what do we call all the other strategies where the payoff diagrams look a bit like butterflies but not exactly?

For example, what if the distances between the strike prices are not symmetrical? And, what if the number of contacts does not follow the 1-2-1 pattern in Figure 3.19? For example, imagine a structure where the investor buys two at-the-money calls, sells six higher-strike calls and buys four even higher-strike calls. This would seem to constitute a butterfly spread, although the payoff would not be symmetric.

Assume, for example, that an investor buys a $75 call, sells five $91 calls and buys four $95 calls. The payoff diagram for this exposure would be as shown in Figure 3.20.

This looks like a butterfly.

What about the following strategy? An investor buys a $75 put, sells five $91 puts and buys four $95 puts, i.e., the strategy as above but with the calls replaced by puts. The payoff diagram for this exposure would be as shown in Figure 3.21.

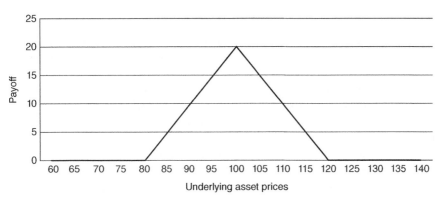

Figure 3.19 Butterfly payoff

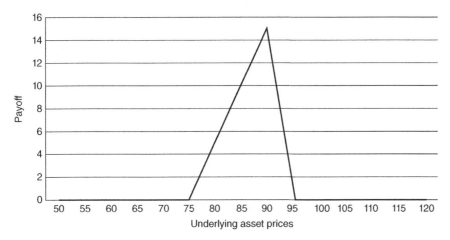

Figure 3.20 Butterfly payoff with calls

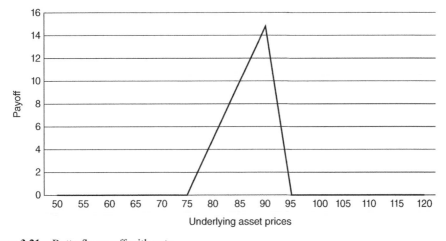

Figure 3.21 Butterfly payoff with puts

SUMMARY

In some sense, views on how the price of an option will change are a function of how the price of the underlying asset is expected to change and how implied volatility is thought to change (as we will see in Chapters 6 and 7). The scope of this book was not to discuss the entire range of option strategies and one may argue that the chapter is incomplete. For example, we have not included ladders, strips and straps, ratio spreads, ratio back spreads, condors, synthetic straddles and calendar spreads. If we had, however, this would be a book on option strategies, which was not our intention.

It should be clear that, in some instances, there are competing strategies for a particular scenario. As long as the competing option strategies are priced "fairly", a choice between them will depend upon the investors' set of expectations relative to those implied by the market and their degree of risk aversion. One strategy may cost premium and another may earn it but one certainly cannot argue that the first strategy is more expensive than the other in a relative value sense. Instead, each option strategy has its own risk and reward characteristics and may be appropriate for one market participant but not another.

4

Binomial Option Pricing

In this chapter, we will discuss the binomial model. Although the use of binomial tree has been superseded by other numerical techniques in recent years, they remain a good way to understand certain option structures. Regardless of whether the binomial model is still used in practice to price options and other derivatives, it is still very worthwhile to understand the approach.[1]

The binomial model is useful in that it demonstrates clearly, in discrete time, a concept that we will introduce in Chapter 5, i.e., option replication and risk-neutral valuation. In particular, the binomial model provides a link between risk-neutral probability and payoff replication.[2] A key message is that there will only be one price generated for a given option specification since any other price would offer arbitrage opportunities. This unique price is independent of the risk aversion of market participants and the distribution of future price movements of the underlying asset.

We will see how the binomial model can be used to price both European and American call and put options, with examples that will reference a variety of different underlying asset classes. In these examples, we will generally assume that we are working with mid prices but this is just for simplicity and, in reality, one will almost always have to deal with a bid or an offer price. We should note that prices for vanilla European calls and puts can be calculated as a closed-form solution from, say, the Black–Scholes model, and that we do not need to use a numerical technique to price these. However, apparently minor changes to the specification of the option can require a numerical solution. The most obvious example is an American put. There are no closed-form solutions for American puts and prices must be found numerically.

4.1 ONE-PERIOD BINOMIAL TREE: REPLICATION APPROACH

Let us start with the simplest possible binomial tree, where there is just one time step (a one-period tree). Given the price of the underlying asset at inception, we will assume that the price at the end of the period can move either up or down. The reason the model is called "binomial" is that there are only two possible outcomes. The binomial model is also often referred to as the Cox–Ross–Rubinstein pricing model.

Consider a European call option on gold, with a \$1,700/oz strike and a maturity of 2 years. Our aim is to price this option. The spot price of gold is also currently \$1,700/oz; in other words, we have taken an option that is struck at-the-money spot. We will assume that each option is written on one ounce of gold only. The continuously compounded risk-free interest rate is 6% per annum.

---

[1] In the second edition of *Frequently Asked Questions in Quantitative Finance*, Paul Wilmott says that "the Binomial Method is Rubbish". What he really means is that it has been superseded by other numerical techniques and he goes on to say, "I really like the binomial method. But only as a teaching aid. It is the easiest way to explain (1) hedging to eliminate risk, (2) no arbitrage and (3) risk neutrality."

[2] The price of an option is linked to the payoff replication via the use of delta hedging, as we will see in sections 5.5 and 5.6.

Table 4.1   One-period binomial tree for a call option

Gold price after 2 years ($/oz)	$1,600/oz	$2,000/oz
Payoff/value of the call at maturity	$0/oz	$300/oz

We will assume that gold at the end of the first (and only) step can take one of two values, $1,600/oz or $2,000/oz. At expiry, therefore, the option can be either in-the-money or out-of-the-money, depending on whether the future gold price is above or below $1,700/oz. If the option expires out-of-the-money, its value is zero. If the option expires in-the-money, however, its value will be equal to the difference between the spot price of gold observed at expiry and the strike price, here $300. The payoff of the European call option at the end of 2 years is $Max(0, \text{Asset price}_{2Y} - \$1,700/oz)$, where Asset price_{2Y} is the price of gold after 2 years. This is summarized in Table 4.1.

In order to price this call option, we need to hedge the exposure, creating a replicating portfolio whose value matches the payoff of the option.

This is achieved by buying or selling a particular amount of the underlying asset. The ratio is determined by considering how the price of the option moves over the life of the transaction relative to the movement in the price of the underlying asset. It is given by the following formula, where Option value_{up} is the value of the option at expiry in the "up" world, $\text{Option value}_{down}$ is the value of the option at expiry in the "down" world, Asset price_{up} is the price of the asset in the "up" world and $\text{Asset price}_{down}$ is the price of the asset in the "down" world.

$$\frac{\text{Option value}_{up} - \text{Option value}_{down}}{\text{Asset price}_{up} - \text{Asset price}_{down}}$$

$$\frac{\$300 - \$0}{\$2,000 - \$1,600} = \frac{\$300}{\$400} = 0.75$$

From this, we can see that the value of the option moves by only 75% of the movement in the underlying price. This suggests that, in order to replicate the payoff from the option position, the appropriate hedge is to purchase three quarters of the amount of the underlying asset, in this case $\frac{3}{4}$ ounce of gold.

This "hedge ratio" means that, for example, if a trader sells four options, he or she would only need to buy (and hold) 3 ounces of gold to hedge the option exposure. Figure 4.1 depicts the payoff from holding 3 ounces of gold assuming our two-state world, where we represent a buy by a "positive amount" and a sell by a "negative amount".

Figure 4.2 shows the value of the option portfolio over the same period. It indicates that, having sold four options and received a premium inflow, the option trader could be faced with a possible payoff at the option's expiry. At expiry, we can see the total payoff if the four options are exercised. This would happen only if the strike, in this case $1,700/oz, were lower than the price of the underlying asset at expiry.

Figure 4.3 combines the previous two and shows that, having sold four options and bought 3 ounces of gold at maturity, the trader has created a portfolio that has a value of $4,800 at expiry in both future states of the world, the "up" state and the "down" state. In other words, the exposure is hedged. There is no risk. The trader is guaranteed the $4,800 at maturity regardless of the behaviour of the underlying asset.

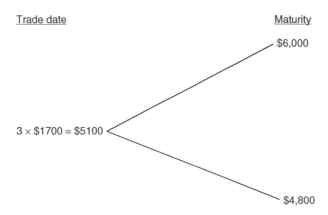

Figure 4.1   The value of the replicating portfolio

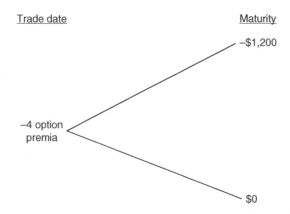

Figure 4.2   The option exposure

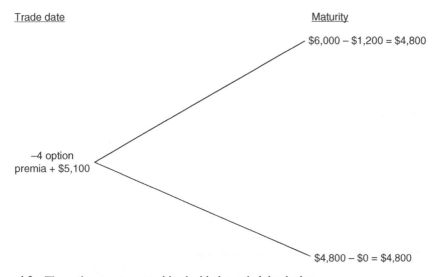

Figure 4.3   The option exposure combined with the underlying hedge

The portfolio is worth $4,800 after 2 years but the present value of the portfolio, given interest rates at 6%, is $4,257 (i.e., $4,800 \times e^{-2\times6\%}$).

Since the trader bought 3 ounces of gold at a spot price of $5,100 ($1,700/oz), the value of the short option position needs to be worth –$843 ($4,257 less $5,100). Any other value would imply an arbitrage opportunity. So, if the short option position is worth –$843, then the value of a long position in just one option would be $210.75. The arbitrage-free price for the option is $210.75.

To be clear, at the trade date the option trader will experience a net outflow of funds. The trader must buy the asset, 3 ounces of gold costing $5,100, to hedge the portfolio but he or she will receive $843 from the sale of the four options. The difference between these two cash flows ($4,257) will have to be borrowed and this is financed at the current rate of interest, i.e., 6%. In other words, $4,800 needs to be repaid at maturity, i.e., $4,257 \times e^{2\times6\%}$. The repayment is equal to the value of the portfolio at maturity, irrespective of whether the underlying asset price rises or falls.

This can be shown another way. Consider the trader's cash flows at maturity.

1. Gold rises to $2,000/oz:
   - The option holder exercises the call options. The trader receives $1,700 \times 4, i.e., $6,800, from the holder of the option.
   - The trader delivers the 3 ounces of gold held as the hedge but must buy one more ounce of gold at the prevailing market price of $2,000.
   - The trader repays the $4,257 principal and interest due on the loan, i.e., $4,800.
   - The net cash flow for the trader is zero. The total paid out is $6,800 and this is exactly matched by what is received from the option exercise.
2. Gold drops to $1,600/oz:
   - The option holder does not exercise the call options.
   - The trader sells the 3 ounces of gold held as a hedge at the prevailing market price of $1,600/oz. Total received $4,800.
   - The trader repays the $4,257 principal and interest due on the loan, i.e., $4,800.
   - The net cash flow is zero, i.e., $4,800 received and $4,800 paid out.

The net cash flows are zero, demonstrating again that, in both scenarios, the trader's exposure is fully hedged.

Now, at this point, we have calculated the price of the option using the interest rate, the strike price, the size of the up and down moves and the time step. Note that the price of the option does *not depend* on the probability of the up or down move. This never comes into the calculation. This is counterintuitive and probably should be stressed. The value of the option does not depend on whether the asset is likely to go up or down in price. We are just interested in asking, if it does move, how far will it move?

So, with this in mind, let us now consider a European put option on gold, with a $1,700/oz strike as before and the same tenor of 2 years. The spot price is again $1,700/oz, each option is written on 1 ounce of gold only and the continuously compounded risk-free interest rate is 6%. We have an at-the-money spot European put option.

As before, the underlying asset can only take one of two values at expiry, namely $1,600/oz or $2,000/oz. At expiry, the option can end up either out-of-the-money or in-the-money,

Table 4.2   One-period binomial tree for a put option

Gold price after 2 years ($/oz)	$1,600/oz	$2,000/oz
Payoff/value of the put at maturity	$100/oz	$0/oz

depending on whether the gold price is above or below $1,700/oz. The payoff of the European put option after 2 years is Max(0, $1,700/oz − Asset price$_{2Y}$). This is summarized in Table 4.2.

Again, the option can be hedged by buying or selling a particular amount of the underlying asset. This ratio can be calculated by determining how the price of the option moves over the life of the transaction relative to the movement in the price of the underlying asset. This is given by the following formula, defined in section 4.1.

$$\frac{\text{Option value}_{\text{down}} - \text{Option value}_{\text{up}}}{\text{Asset price}_{\text{down}} - \text{Asset price}_{\text{up}}}$$

$$\frac{\$100 - \$0}{\$1,600 - \$2,000} = \frac{\$100}{-\$400} = -0.25$$

Note here that the amount of gold that needs to be used for hedging purposes is negative. This indicates that the trader has to sell the underlying asset in order to hedge a long position in a put. Note that the value of the option moves by only −25% of the movement in the underlying asset price, i.e., if the price of gold rises by $1 then the price of the put option decreases by $0.25 and vice versa. To replicate the payoff of the option position, the appropriate hedge is to sell one quarter of the position in the underlying asset, in this case one quarter of 1 ounce of gold. So, for every four options sold, a trader would only need to sell (or go short) 1 ounce of gold.

Figure 4.4 shows the value of the replicating portfolio in the underlying alone assuming the trader sells four put options and hedges the exposure by selling 1 ounce of gold. On the trade date, each ounce costs $1,700 and, therefore, the trader receives $1,700 on that date. We represent this outflow as a negative number.

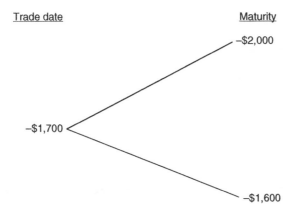

Figure 4.4   The value of the replicating portfolio

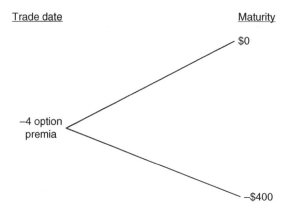

Figure 4.5 The option exposure

Note that the value of the underlying asset is represented as negative at maturity. The trader is short 1 ounce of gold on the trade date and needs to buy that ounce of gold in order to deliver it to the option holder, i.e., it is an expense. Figure 4.5 shows the value of the option portfolio over the same period. It indicates that, having sold four options and received a premium inflow, the trader could be faced with a possible payoff at the option expiry. At maturity, we can see the total payoff assuming that the four options are exercised. This will only happen if the strike, in this case $1,700/oz, is higher than the price of the underlying asset at expiry, i.e., the put option is in-the-money.

Figure 4.6 combines the previous two to show that, having sold four options and sold 1 ounce of gold at maturity, the trader has created a portfolio that has a value of –$2,000 in both future states of the world, the "up" state and the "down" state. In other words, the exposure is hedged. As before, there is no risk.

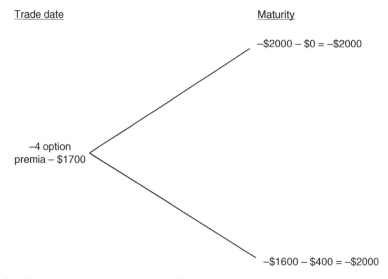

Figure 4.6 The option exposure combined with the underlying hedge

The portfolio is worth –$2,000 after 2 years but the present value, with interest rates at 6%, is –$1,774 (i.e., –$2,000 × e$^{-2\times6\%}$).

Given that the short position in 1 ounce of gold at a spot price of $1,700 is worth –$1,700, the value of the short position in the four options would need to be –$74 to ensure that the current value of the portfolio is –$1,774. In other words, the value of a long position in one put option is $18.50. This is the price of the put.

Note that, on the trade date, there is a net inflow of funds to the trader. The trader sells the asset, 1 ounce of gold in this case, at $1,700 to hedge the portfolio and receives $74 from the sale of the four options. The trader will lend it at current rates of interest, i.e., 6%, and receive $2,000 at maturity. The repayment on this loan is equal to the value of the portfolio at maturity, irrespective of whether the underlying asset price rises or falls.

Again, consider the cash flows at maturity.

1. Gold rises to $2,000/oz:
    *   The option holder does not exercise the put options. The trader buys 1 ounce of gold at the prevailing market price of $2,000 and delivers it against the short gold position held as a hedge.
    *   The trader receives the $1,774 principal and interest due on the loan, i.e., $2,000.
    *   The net cash flow to the trader is zero, $2,000 received and $2,000 paid out.
2. Gold drops to $1,600/oz:
    *   The option holder exercises the put options. The trader buys 4 ounces of gold at $1,700 × 4 = $6,800 from the holder of the options.
    *   The trader uses 1 of the 4 ounces to deliver against the short gold position held as a hedge and sells the remaining 3 ounces at the prevailing market price of $1,600/oz, i.e., the trader receives $4,800.
    *   The trader receives the $1,774 principal and interest due on the loan, i.e., $2,000.
    *   The net cash flow to the trader is zero – $6,800 is paid out buying the gold from the option holder and $6,800 is received.

Again, the net cash flow is zero in both cases illustrating that, in both the "up" world and the "down" world, the trader's exposure is fully hedged.

4.2 RISK-NEUTRAL VALUATION

4.2.1 Introduction to risk-neutral valuation

The pricing framework just described is the "risk-neutral valuation". Regardless of whether a market participant believes that the underlying price is more likely to rise than to fall, there can only be one solution for the fair value of each option given the option's specification, the prevailing interest rate and the sizes of the up and down moves. If this were not the case and there were multiple equilibrium prices then it would be possible to exploit a potential arbitrage opportunity.

In the two previous examples, if the call or put options were trading higher than their fair values, they should be sold and the duplicating portfolio purchased. Conversely, if the options are trading below their fair values, they should be purchased and the duplicating portfolio sold.

Clearly, the model presented so far is very simplistic. In particular, it is only a one-period model (prices are assumed to move only once), the movement in the underlying asset price is known with certainty and no account has been taken of any possible income or cost of storage accruing to the asset over the life of the trade. Nonetheless, one key message from the analysis should be clear: the price of the option does *not depend* on the probability of the up or down move. We are just interested in asking, when it moves, how far will it move? If there is just one take-away from this chapter, it should be this point.

Finally, in the examples, we discounted all of the cash flows using the risk-free interest rate. Why? Well, since the trader was operating in a risk-free environment (he or she was able to create a portfolio that had precisely equivalent outcomes in both up or down economic scenarios, which makes it risk free) this seems appropriate. Regardless of whether the price of the underlying asset rose or fell, the trader's net exposure was zero. The trader was hedged. So, if a trader's position has no risk, it is reasonable to discount those cash flows at a risk-free rate.

4.2.2   An alternative way to think of the option price

If we return to the example of the call option, we can look at the problem in a slightly different way. Consider the following equation, where the left-hand side is the value of the trader's combined portfolio when the gold price is $2,000 and the right-hand side is the value of the portfolio when the gold price is $1,600 (and the call option is worthless). We are implicitly assuming that we are considering just one option contract but the analysis can easily be extended to N contracts by multiplying both sides of the equation by N. So:

$$2,000 \times \Delta - 300 = 1,600 \times \Delta$$

The quantity Δ is our delta. This is the hedge ratio that we defined above and measures the change in the value of the option given a change in the underlying asset price. We know that the value of the hedged portfolio must be the same in both worlds; otherwise it would not be hedged. The hedge ensures that the value of the combined portfolio (the option and the hedge) is equal in both scenarios at the time of the option expiry.

We also know, however, that the value of the combined portfolio at inception is equal to:

$$1,700 \times \Delta - 210.75$$

where $210.75 is the price of the call option and $1,700 is the price of gold at inception. Under the no-arbitrage condition, the present value of the portfolio at expiry has to be equal to its value at inception.

Therefore, we can write that:

$$(2,000 \times \Delta - 300) \times e^{(-2 \times 0.06)} = 1,700 \times \Delta - 210.75$$

One can easily verify that this equation holds when Δ is equal to 0.75, the hedge ratio that we calculated previously.

Rearranging the equation above we get:

$$210.75 = 1,700 \times \Delta - (2,000 \times \Delta - 300) \times e^{(-2 \times 0.06)}$$

Generalizing:

Option price = Strike price at inception $\times \Delta$ − present value of the portfolio measured when the call is in-the-money.

4.2.3   Risk-neutral probabilities

At this point, there may be some lingering scepticism regarding our contention that the probabilities of the up and down moves do not matter. This is understandable since it is very counterintuitive. Unfortunately, some market participants, especially academics, will talk about risk-neutral probabilities. For those people who wish to understand the intuition of options, such a concept is probably irrelevant. For those people who wish to know what are risk-neutral probabilities, however, we hope the following helps.

In our example world, there are two possibilities for the gold price. From the current spot price of \$1,700, it can rise to \$2,000 or fall to \$1,600. At this point, let us define a probability P_u of gold reaching \$2,000 and a probability P_d of gold reaching \$1,600. Clearly, P_d has to be equal to $1 - P_u$ since there are only two possible states of the world.

Let us now express the option price as a discounted *expected value* of the option payoff at maturity. We can write this as:

$$\text{Option price} = [300 \times P_u + 0 \times P_d] \times e^{(-2\times0.06)}$$

Or:

$$210.75 = [300 \times P_u + 0 \times P_d] \times e^{(-2\times0.06)}$$

Solving, we get that $P_u = 0.792$ (or 79.2%) and $P_d = 20.8\%$.

Mathematically, it can be shown that the implied risk-free probability of an up move is given by:

$$P = \frac{e^{rT} - d}{u - d}$$

where u measures the ratio of the underlying price in the up scenario divided by the underlying price at inception and d is the ratio of the underlying price in the down scenario divided by the underlying price at inception. The two values u and d are often call state prices. Note that since they are ratios, if $u = 1.1$, then this implies a 10% move higher in the underlying asset price. Likewise, if $d = 0.9$, then this implies a 10% drop in the underlying asset price.

What do these probabilities measure? Well, we did not use them to calculate the option price. In fact, we did not need to make any assumption about the probability of up or down moves. The trader's portfolio was hedged regardless of whether the market price of the underlying asset went up or down. All we needed to know was, assuming that the price changed, how far would it go? Intuitively, however, surely we should want to be able to express the option's price as a discounted *expected value* of the option's payoff at maturity?

The "probabilities" that we found allow us to describe the option price as an expected value of the option payoff (with the appropriate discounting). P_u and P_d are the implied probabilities of an upward or downward movement in what we have already defined as a "risk-free world", however. They have nothing to do with the actual expectations held by market participants of the relative likelihood of upward or downward price movements.

4.3   TWO-PERIOD BINOMIAL TREE: VALUING BACK DOWN THE TREE

Before, we assumed that the underlying asset could only have one of two values at expiry, namely \$1,600/oz or \$2,000/oz. Let us extend this model and consider two periods. We will

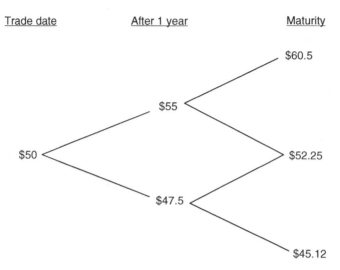

Trade date	After 1 year	Maturity

Figure 4.7   The possible values of the stock

assume that we have a stock whose value can go up 10% or down 5% in two consecutive periods.

The current value of the stock is $50 and the risk-free interest rate is 6% per annum. We will now price a call option on the stock with a strike $50 and expiration date of 2 years. For simplicity, we will assume that the stock does not pay dividends.

The possible values for the stock are as shown in Figure 4.7.

In this example we will assume that the option is written on one unit of stock only. The payoff from the European call option after 2 years is Max(0, Asset price$_{2Y}$ − $50). Asset price$_{2Y}$ is the price of the stock after 2 years as defined in Table 4.3.

As in the one-period binomial tree, we can hedge this exposure by creating a replicating portfolio whose value matches the payoff of the option. So far we have the option values, OV, at maturity but we need to calculate the option price at the trade date. In order to do this, we need the option values A and B after the first period. This is where the technique of *valuing back down the tree* is relevant (Figure 4.8).

Let us start by calculating the value of the call option at node A.

In order to calculate the value of an option, we need to determine the value of the replication portfolio, i.e., the amount of stock that we need to buy or sell and the amount of money that we need to borrow or lend.

In this example, we have assumed that the trader sells a call option. As before, the trader will have to buy a certain amount of stock and borrow money to replicate the payoff from the

Table 4.3   Two-period binomial tree for a call option

Stock price after 2 years ($)	$45.12	$52.25	$60.5
Payoff/value of the call at maturity	$0	$2.25	$10.5

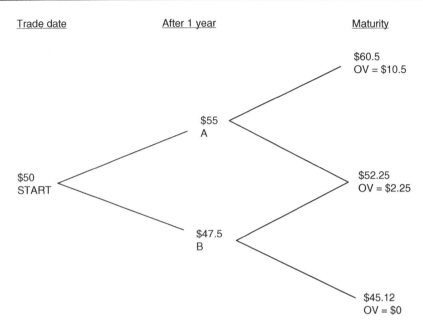

Trade date   After 1 year   Maturity

$60.5
OV = $10.5

$55
A

$50 $52.25
START   OV = $2.25

$47.5
B

$45.12
OV = $0

Figure 4.8   The option exposure

call. First, we need to calculate the amount of stock to be bought if we are at the node A. Using the formula introduced in section 4.1:

$$\frac{\text{Option value}_{up} - \text{Option value}_{down}}{\text{Asset price}_{up} - \text{Asset price}_{down}}$$

$$\frac{\$10.5 - \$2.25}{\$60.5 - \$52.25} = \frac{\$8.25}{\$8.25} = 1$$

We have an option that has a delta of +1. The value of the option moves by 100% of the movement in the underlying price, i.e., if the price of the stock rises by $1 then the price of the call option increases by $1 and vice versa. So, in order to replicate the payoff of the option position, the appropriate hedge is to buy one unit of stock, i.e., for every call option sold, the trader would need to hold one unit of the underlying asset at the node A.

The next question is how much will the trader need to lend or borrow at node A. We know that, from node A, there are two possible scenarios at maturity:

1. Number of shares held (1) × share price, $60.5 + cash position = the value of the option, $10.5
2. Number of shares held (1) × share price, $52.25 + cash position = the value of the option, $2.25

It is clear that the cash position is −$50 and the net present value of this cash position is −$50 × e^{(−0.06)} = −$47.09.

Following these calculations, we know now that the trader has to buy one unit of stock and borrow $47.09 at node A for every call option sold at trade date in order to replicate the payoff of the option.

The value of the call option at node A given by the value of the replicating portfolio is equal to $1 \times \$55 - \$47.09 = \$7.91$.

Following the same logic, we can calculate the amount of stock that needs to be bought and the cash position at node B.

$$\frac{\text{Option value}_{up} - \text{Option value}_{down}}{\text{Asset price}_{up} - \text{Asset price}_{down}}$$

$$\frac{\$2.25 - \$0}{\$52.25 - \$45.12} = \frac{\$2.25}{\$7.13} = 0.31$$

This calculation indicates that the value of the option moves by 31% of the movement in the underlying price, i.e., if the price of the stock rises by $1 then the price of the call option increases by $0.31. Therefore, to replicate the payoff on the option position the appropriate hedge is to buy 0.31 units of stock, i.e., for every call option sold the trader would need to buy and hold 0.31 unit of the underlying asset at node B.

To determine the cash position of the trader at node B, we know that there are two possible scenarios at maturity:

1. $0.31 \times \$52.25 + \text{cash position} = \$2.25$
2. $0.31 \times \$45.12 + \text{cash position} = \$0$

Therefore, the cash position is –$13.9, or in present value terms, $-\$13.9 \times e^{(-0.06)} = -\$13.09$.

So, the trader has to buy 0.31 unit of stock and borrow $13.09 at node B for every call option sold at trade date in order to replicate the payoff of the option.

The value of the call at node B is given by $0.31 \times \$47.5 - \$13.09 = \$1.63$. This is the value of the replicating portfolio.

Finally, we can calculate the value of the portfolio at the start date to determine the price of the call option. Again, we calculate the delta, in this case 0.84.

$$\frac{\$7.91 - \$1.63}{\$55 - \$47.5} = \frac{\$6.28}{\$7.5} = 0.84$$

If the price of the stock rises by $1, then the price of the call option will increase by $0.84. To replicate the payoff of the option position, the appropriate hedge is to buy 0.84 units of stock, i.e., for every call option sold, the trader needs to buy 0.84 units of the underlying asset.

To determine the cash position at inception, we know that:

1. $0.84 \times \$55 + \text{cash position} = \$7.91$
2. $0.84 \times \$47.5 + \text{cash position} = \$1.63$

The cash position is equal to –$38.3 or, in present value terms, $-\$38.3 \times e^{(-0.06)} = -\$36.07$.

The trader has to buy 0.84 units of stock and borrow $36.07 at the inception of the trade for every call option sold in order to replicate the payoff of the option. Hence, the call price is equal to **$0.84 \times \$50 - \$36.07 = \$5.93$.**

We now have all the values needed to reconstruct the two-period binomial tree (Figure 4.9).

Although we used the example of a European call option in the previous example, the technique of valuing back down the tree is clearly applicable to put options too.

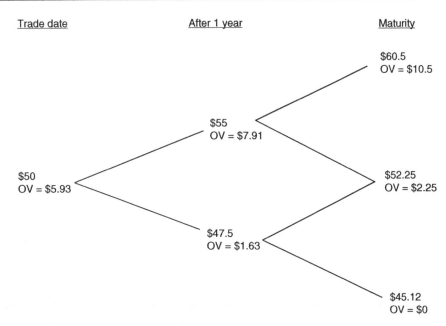

Figure 4.9   The option exposure completed

4.4   THE BINOMIAL TREE: A GENERALIZATION

In the simple binomial models that we have described in some detail in the section 4.1 and 4.3, the underlying asset price moves either up or down. The value of an associated option depends on the extent to which the asset price can move and not on the likelihood of the asset price moving up or down. This is key. The price of the option is a function of the portfolio that is used to hedge it and the value of that portfolio is the same if the underlying asset goes up in price or down in price from one time step to another. That is the point of the hedged portfolio.

If we think about the price moves in terms of state prices then the asset price will move by a certain amount from one node to another. If the asset price starts at a value S at a particular node, then it can be either uS or dS after the next time step. By extension, after the next time step, the asset price can take the values u^2S, if there are two consecutive up moves, d^2S, if there are two consecutive down moves, or udS if there is an up move followed by a down move or vice versa. Of course, if we assume that $u = 1/d$, then the binomial tree is able to recombine, i.e., udS is equal to S. In other words, if the asset price rises and then falls, it gets back to its original value. This is not an unrealistic assumption if we assume very short time steps.

The time steps can clearly be extended further and, pictorially, this will appear as a *binomial tree* (Figure 4.10).

In the tree, it should be clear that the nodes at the very top far right (i.e., at expiry) and very bottom far right can only be reached by one path, whereas the others can be reached by various means. These others are more likely to be reached given that there are more possible paths to reach them. The binomial tree therefore implies a probability density function for the possible outcomes for the asset price. If we think of u and d as state prices, i.e., rates of return, then the distribution of asset prices (assuming a large number of time steps) will be approximately log-normal.

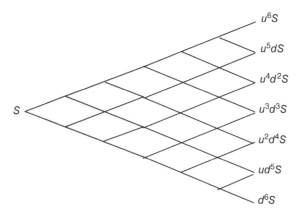

Figure 4.10   A binomial tree

In the example where we explicitly solved for the price of a European call option with a two-step binomial model, we used a technique called valuing back down the tree. This approach can be extended to the binomial tree just described. Let us assume that we have generated a binomial tree of asset prices out to the final maturity date of the option using a large number of time steps. At maturity, we know the distribution of the asset prices and so we know the distribution of the values of the option. Since we know the values of the option at each possible node at expiry, however, we can determine their values one node back. How can we do this? Well, we know that, in a risk-free world, the value of an option can be thought of as the expected value using risk-neutral probabilities and the appropriate discount rate, in this case, the risk-free rate. Then, of course, if we have the values for the option one time step back, we can calculate the values of the option one more time step back. In this way, we can get back to the spot price of the option value.

It is possible to do this on a spreadsheet, although, in practice, the binomial model will be programmed.

4.5   EARLY EXERCISE AND AMERICAN OPTIONS

American options are easily handled in the binomial model. The technique is essentially the same as for European options except in one respect. There must be no arbitrage opportunities at any of the nodes. Arbitrage is possible if our theoretical value for the option drops below the payoff from early exercise. If so, then it is clearly preferential to exercise early. Consequently, at each node on the binomial tree, it will also be necessary to test for this condition. If the value of the option is less than the payoff, then the value of the option is replaced by the value of the payoff. Otherwise, the derived value for the option is as before.

4.6   VOLATILITY CALIBRATION

By now, it should be obvious that while the probabilities of up and down moves in the price of the underlying asset are irrelevant in pricing options, the extent of the price moves is very relevant. When setting up a binomial (or trinomial) tree, one needs to set state prices u and d that are consistent with the desired level of implied volatility. In other words, if the trader believes that the underlying asset price will show average volatility of, say, 10% over the life of the option, then how does this translate into estimates of u and d?

Assuming that the total number of time steps is sufficiently large, then the option price calculated using the binomial tree will converge to the analytical solution for the option price that comes from the Black–Scholes formula (which we will introduce in Chapter 5) assuming that the level of implied volatility is equal in both cases.

In what follows, we will show how to calibrate the parameters u and d to match the desired level of implied volatility. Recall that u is equal to the ratio of the underlying price in the "up" scenario to the underlying price at inception and d is equal to the ratio of the underlying price in the "down" scenario to the underlying price at inception. Basically u and d can be thought of as the rate of return in the up and down world respectively.

In the binomial model, at each node, there are two possible moves. There is an up move and a down move. Using u and d as previously defined and p as the probability of an up move in the risk-free world, then the variance of the rate of return can be calculated as:[3]

$$\text{Variance} = pu^2 + (1 - p)d^2 - [pu + (1 - p)d]^2$$

If we assume that asset prices tend to show returns that are close to being normally distributed we will set $u = 1/d$.

Now, if σ is our assumed level of *annualized* implied volatility, then we can say that the variance given in the equation above has to be equal to $\sigma^2 \Delta t$, where Δt is the length of each time step in the binomial tree and is measured as fractions of a year. We can multiply through by Δt since variances are additive. Also, we are assuming that the implied volatility, σ, is constant across the tenor of the option. So, for example, if we have two time steps per year and the annualized volatility is σ, then the variance for each 6-month time step would be $\sigma^2/2$. Likewise, if we have four time steps per year and the annualized volatility is σ, then the variance for each 3-month time step would be $\sigma^2/4$. If we have 250 time steps (approximately the number of business days in a year), then the variance for each business day step would be $\sigma^2/250$.

So, to calibrate the parameters u and d such that the level of annualized implied volatility, σ, is consistent, we need the following to hold:

$$pu^2 + (1 - p)d^2 - [pu + (1 - p)d]^2 = \sigma^2 \Delta t$$

Recall, however, that the probability of the up move in the risk-free world is given by:

$$p = \frac{e^{rT} - d}{u - d}$$

and that $d = 1/u$, we find the following values for u and d:

$$u = e^{\sigma \sqrt{\Delta t}}$$

and

$$d = \frac{1}{u} = e^{-\sigma \sqrt{\Delta t}}$$

---

[3] Variance $(X) = E(X^2) - E(X)^2$ where $E(X^2)$ is the expected value of X^2, $E(X)^2$ is the expected value of X square and X can take the values u or d, with probabilities p and $(1 - p)$ respectively. Therefore $E(X^2) = pu^2 + (1 - p)d^2$ and $E(X^2) = (pu + (1 - p)d)^2$.

Hence, when setting up a binomial model, choose a time step that allows for a sufficiently large number of nodes and u and d that are consistent with the implied volatility that is relevant for the particular option that is being priced.

SUMMARY

In this chapter, we discussed the basics of the binomial model. The binominal model is perfect for understanding the ideas of delta hedging and of risk-neutral pricing and, as such, should be part of any introductory book on option pricing. In practice, however, there are much better numerical methods available to price options and to determine their Greeks. Consequently, although we will occasionally refer to the binomial model in later chapters, we will not be returning to it in any great detail. Just remember that delta hedging is used to reduce risk and, having delta hedged, we no longer need to worry about the probability of the underlying asset price rising or falling when calculating the price on the option. We just need to worry about the volatility. This is key.

5

The Fundamentals of Option Pricing

In this chapter, we discuss the basics of option pricing. There is some mathematics but we have kept it to a minimum. We will discuss the basic terminology in options and options pricing and we will explain why volatility of asset prices is important but the direction of movement is not. We will look at the nature of the time value of options, i.e., the price of optionality. We will discuss the Black–Scholes framework for pricing options and begin looking at the idea of the delta of an option and how it is relevant to the construction of portfolios that have no directional exposure. Finally, we will move on to option replication and risk-neutral valuation.

5.1 INTRINSIC VALUE AND TIME VALUE OF AN OPTION

5.1.1 Introduction and definitions

The essential feature to consider when building a framework for option pricing is related to the idea of intrinsic value and the time value of an option. We will use IVO_t to denote the intrinsic value of the option at time t and TVO_t to denote the time value of the option at time t.

For a call option, the intrinsic value at time t *is the difference, if positive, between the actual price of the underlying at time* t *(S_t) and the strike price (K); if this difference is negative, the intrinsic value is equal to zero since the option has no intrinsic value.*

For a call option: $IVO_t = \max(S_t - K, 0)$

For a put option, the intrinsic value at time t *is the difference, if positive, between the strike price (K) and the actual price of the underlying at time* t *(S_t); if this difference is negative, the intrinsic value is equal to zero since the option has no intrinsic value.*

For a put option: $IVO_t = \max(K - S_t, 0)$

The intrinsic value of an option is a purely deterministic number and, at any given time, equals the payoff of the option if it were to expire at that time.

From the lower boundary conditions introduced previously, we have respectively:

$$C_t \geq \max(0,\ S_t - K\,DF(t,\ T))$$

and

$$P_t \geq \max(0,\ K\,DF(t,\ T) - S_t)$$

where C_t and P_t are respectively the price of a call option and a put option at time t and $DF(t,\ T)$ is the discount factor applicable to a cash flow payable at T and valued at t.

What these boundary conditions are telling us is that the price of a call or a put option on a non-dividend paying stock cannot be lower than the respective intrinsic value (provided that the strike price is discounted using the appropriate discount factor). In other words, if the price of an option on a non-dividend paying asset were to be less than the intrinsic value, then it would be easy to take advantage of an arbitrage opportunity.

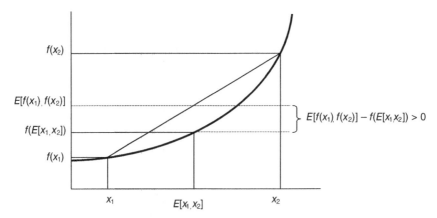

Figure 5.1   Jensen's inequality

Ignoring the impact of interest rates for the time being (i.e., assuming that the discount factor is equal to 1), *the price of an option has to be higher than its intrinsic value*. The difference between the two is generally referred to as the *time value of the option*. It will always be a non-negative quantity.

Calculating the intrinsic value of an option is mathematically trivial and so the core objective of option pricing techniques is to assess the time value of the option. The most common way to interpret the time value is to think about it as the value of the optionality left in the option, i.e., how much more than the intrinsic value the option buyer is willing to pay (or symmetrically the option seller requires to receive) in order to buy (sell) the right to trade the underlying asset at the strike price.

5.1.2   Jensen's inequality

The very nature of the time value of options lies in a well-known mathematical inequality, generally known as *Jensen's inequality*. Let us go through this concept in more detail.

Jensen's inequality states that the expected value of a convex function (such as the payoff of a call or a put option) is greater than or equal to the function of the expected value or, in other words, that if X is a random variable and f is a convex[1] function, then:

$$f(E[X]) \leq E[f(X)]$$

where E denotes the expected value.

Graphically, Figure 5.1 shows Jensen's inequality for a generic convex function.

How is Jensen's inequality applicable to our framework for option pricing? First, let us note that the payoff of a European option is indeed a convex function of the underlying price.

Once happy with that, assume that we want to calculate the price of a call option on a non-dividend paying stock, with the option expiring in 1 year. Let us start with a very simple example. If the expected value of the underlying asset at the expiry of the option is equal to

---

[1] A function defined on an interval is called convex if the graph of the function lies below the line segment joining any two points of the graph.

100 and if the strike price of this call option is also 100, then we can apply the option payoff function to the expected value of the underlying:

$$\max(E(S_T) - 100, \, 0) = \max(100 - 100, \, 0) = 0$$

However, the purpose of option pricing is to calculate the expected value of the option payoff, i.e., $E[\max(S_T - 100, \, 0)]$.

Since $\max(x - K, \, 0)$ is a convex function, Jensen's inequality guarantees that:

$$E[\max(S_T - 100, \, 0)] - \max(E(S_T) - 100, \, 0) \geq 0$$

In other words, the option price has to be, at least, higher than its intrinsic value.

Jensen's inequality suggests that the time value of an option has to be positive or, in other words, the option price has to be higher than its intrinsic value. Once we understand *why* it has to be higher, it is time to move to the next fundamental question: *how much higher?* Once we are able to answer this, we will know the value of the option. Before going through this crucial question, however, we offer a few remarks about *what makes it higher*.

5.1.3   Time value of an option

It is the uncertainty about the price of the underlying asset at the option expiry date that makes the value of an option higher than its intrinsic value or ensures that the time value of the option is a positive quantity.

To understand this fundamental concept, let us go back to our initial example and consider that we know that the final price of the underlying is going to be a known quantity that we will call F (this is obviously a very unrealistic assumption but it is very useful to develop some fundamental intuition about these fundamental concepts).

If we already know the price of the underlying at expiry, we will also know the payoff of our call option written on it (the strike price was assumed to be equal to 100). Ignoring for now the impact of the discount factor, we can conclude that the option price is going to be zero whenever $F < K$ and is going to be equal to $F - K$ whenever $F > K$.

In a world with no uncertainty about the future realization of asset prices, the value of the call option is equal to its intrinsic value (adjusted by the appropriate discount factor as we will see). As far as basic theory on option pricing is concerned, we will use the concept of asset price volatility as a main source of uncertainty.

5.2   WHAT IS VOLATILITY AND WHY DOES IT MATTER?

Volatility is a statistical measure of the variability of asset price returns over time. Typically, volatility is calculated as the annualized standard deviation of the returns of an asset over a certain period of time. At this point it may be worth recalling that the standard deviation σ of a random variable X is defined as:

$$\sigma = \sqrt{E[(X - \mu)^2]}$$

where $\mu = E[X]$.

In finance, the random variable X represents asset price returns. In practice, when calculating historical volatility based on a particular time series, it is often assumed that $\mu = 0$ (since, in most practical cases, it tends not to be statistically different from zero).

To understand fully the importance of volatility in the context of option prices, we are going to present various examples of asset price dynamics in a world of "very low volatility", i.e., a world with very little uncertainty about the future structure of asset prices. This is in stark contrast to a world of "very high volatility", where uncertainty about the future path of asset prices is very high. Of course, the concepts of "low volatility" and "high volatility" defined in this way are clearly vague. They can be understood on a comparative basis, i.e., a "low volatility" environment compared against a "high volatility" environment.

For instance, let us label "low volatility" as an environment where the price of the underlying asset at option expiry is most likely going to be within a range of 98 to 102. On the other hand, let us label "high volatility" as an environment where the range is much wider, say 80 to 120. It is very simple to observe that in the "low volatility" environment, the maximum payoff for a call option with strike equal to 100 is $\max(102 - 100, 0) = 2$ and in the "high volatility" environment the maximum payoff for the same call option is $\max(120 - 100, 0) = 20$:

Maximum call option payoff under "low volatility": $\max(102 - 100, 0) = 2$
Maximum call option payoff under "high volatility": $\max(120 - 100, 0) = 20$

Clearly the maximum payoff in the high volatility world is significantly higher than in the low volatility world.

This is not enough to prove formally that the option price when volatility is high has to be higher than the price of the same option when volatility is low, but the example is a useful starting point to develop the intuition in that direction. The fundamental idea is that since the buyer of the option *has the right* to decide whether to exercise the option or not, and he will obviously do it only when it is convenient for him, *he should attach more value to an option written on an underlying asset that is likely to show higher volatility, i.e., higher dispersion of the outcomes*. This is because owning an option carries *limited downside risks* and all the non-profitable outcomes are discarded simply by not exercising the option.

What about the case of the put option? In the "low volatility" environment, the maximum payoff for a put option with strike = 100 is $\max(100 - 98, 0) = 2$ and in the "high volatility" environment the maximum payoff for the same put option is $\max(100 - 80, 0) = 20$:

Maximum put option payoff under "low volatility": $\max(100 - 98, 0) = 2$
Maximum put option payoff under "high volatility": $\max(100 - 80, 0) = 20$

Again, the maximum payoff from the put option in the high volatility framework is significantly higher than in the low volatility framework. Figures 5.2 and 5.3 summarize these fundamental concepts for a "high volatility" environment and for a "low volatility" environment respectively.

The previous examples, however simple, should provide some comfort that *option prices* (both for calls and puts) *are positive functions of the future volatility of the price of the underlying asset*. We will revisit this in more detail in section 6.5, when we discuss option vega. For the time being, however, do keep in mind the positive dependency of the price of the option on the future volatility of the price of the underlying asset, i.e., all else the same; for an underlying asset with high volatility, option prices should be higher than for an underlying asset with low volatility. Ultimately, this is embedded in the nature of the option since it is the *right* to buy or to sell that determines the convexity in the payoff function.

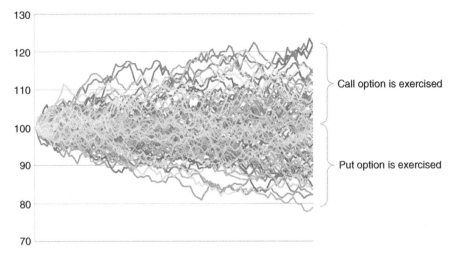

Figure 5.2   An example of high volatility environment

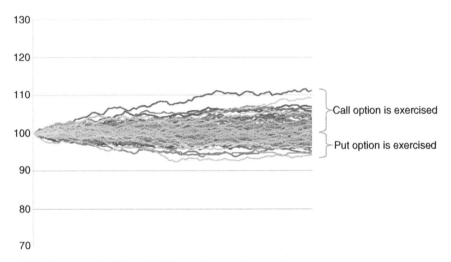

Figure 5.3   An example of low volatility environment

5.3   MEASUREMENT OF REALIZED VOLATILITY AND CORRELATION

As discussed in section 5.2, the volatility of an asset is the annualized standard deviation of its log-returns. In Chapter 6 we will introduce the so-called *implied volatility*, i.e., the volatility that can be derived or inferred from live, traded options markets. In this section we aim to describe how to calculate the *historical volatility* of an asset, i.e., the realized volatility based on the observation of its prices. The starting point is the time series of the asset price observed with a certain frequency (say daily, weekly or monthly):

$$S_0, \, S_1, \, S_2, \dots, \, S_n$$

where $n + 1$ is the number of observations. We can now calculate the time series on the n log-returns (which we indicate with r_i with $i = 1, 2, \ldots, n$):

$$r_i = \ln \frac{S_{i+1}}{S_i}$$

and the average:

$$\bar{r} = \frac{1}{n} \sum_{i=1}^{n} r_i$$

The standard deviation of the log-returns is going to be equal to:

$$\sigma_{\text{freq}} = \sqrt{\frac{1}{n-1} \sum_{i=1}^{n} (\bar{r} - r_i)^2}$$

However, as $\bar{r}$ generally tends to be close to zero (especially when we are looking at daily returns), it is very often omitted in the formula above which therefore becomes:

$$\sigma_{\text{freq}} = \sqrt{\frac{1}{n-1} \sum_{i=1}^{n} r_i^2}$$

This is the volatility of the asset, assuming a certain frequency: if we start from daily observation we will have daily volatility; weekly observation will give us weekly volatility and so on. In general, however, market participants refer to annualized volatility. To annualize the volatility we have to multiply σ_{freq} by an "annualization" factor that will be equal to the square root of the number of observations with the chosen frequency in 1 year: for instance, if we started from daily observations on business days, we can calculate the annualization factor and square root of the number of business days in 1 year (generally around $250 \sim 260$), i.e., something around 16; starting from weekly observation we can annualize the volatility multiplying the standard deviation calculated above by $\sqrt{52}$ and for monthly observation the annualization factor is going to be equal to $\sqrt{12}$.

Sometimes it is also useful, as we will see, to calculate the historic correlation of two assets (say S and P); in this case the starting point will be the observations of the two time series taken at the same observation time:

$$S_0, S_1, S_2, \ldots, S_n$$
$$P_0, P_1, P_2, \ldots, P_n$$

where, as before, $n + 1$ is the number of observations. We can now calculate the time series on the n log-returns (which we indicate with s_i and p_i with $i = 1, 2, \ldots, n$):

$$s_i = \ln \frac{S_{i+1}}{S_i}$$
$$p_i = \ln \frac{S_{i+1}}{S_i}$$

the averages:

$$\bar{s} = \frac{1}{n} \sum_{i=1}^{n} s_i$$

$$\bar{p} = \frac{1}{n} \sum_{i=1}^{n} p_i$$

the covariances:

$$\sigma_{S,P} = \frac{1}{n-1} \sum_{i=1}^{n} (s_i - \bar{s})(p_i - \bar{p})$$

and the standard deviations:

$$\sigma_S = \sqrt{\frac{1}{n-1} \sum_{i=1}^{n} (\bar{s} - s_i)^2}$$

$$\sigma_P = \sqrt{\frac{1}{n-1} \sum_{i=1}^{n} (\bar{p} - p_i)^2}$$

The historical correlation $\rho_{S,P}$ can be now calculated as:

$$\rho_{S,P} = \frac{\sigma_{S,P}}{\sigma_S \sigma_P}$$

As discussed the average values $\bar{s}$ and $\bar{p}$ are often assumed to be equal to zero, simplifying the formulae above.

5.4 OPTION PRICING IN THE BLACK–SCHOLES FRAMEWORK

In their seminal work in 1973 ("The Pricing of Options and Corporate Liabilities", published in the *Journal of Political Economy*), Fischer Black and Myron Scholes developed a framework for pricing vanilla options that constitutes the fundamental building block for the modern theory of option pricing. In this section, we will describe the basic assumptions and conditions underlying this framework and present the relevant formulae for pricing call and put options.

The key assumptions underlying the framework are:

1. The prices of the underlying asset are log-normally distributed with constant (and known) drift and volatility;
2. The possibility of short selling of the underlying asset without incurring significant non-interest costs;
3. Frictionless markets, i.e., transactions are not subject to any trading costs or taxes;
4. Unlimited liquidity, perfect divisibility and continuous trading of the underlying asset, for both purchases and sales;
5. No dividend or other sort of cash flows associated with ownership of the underlying asset;
6. The absence of arbitrage opportunities;
7. A constant risk-free interest rate, r, for all maturities.

When these assumptions hold, the price of a call option and of a put option calculated in t are respectively:

$$C = S\,\mathrm{N}(d_1) - K\,\exp[-r(T-t)]\,\mathrm{N}(d_2)$$
$$P = K\,\exp[-r(T-t)]\,\mathrm{N}(-d_2) - S\,\mathrm{N}(-d_1)$$

where:

$$d_1 = \frac{\ln(S/K) + \left(r + \sigma^2/2\right)(T-t)}{\sigma\sqrt{T-t}}$$

$$d_2 = \frac{\ln(S/K) + \left(r - \sigma^2/2\right)(T-t)}{\sigma\sqrt{T-t}} = d_1 - \sigma\sqrt{T-t}$$

$\mathrm{N}(x)$ is the cumulative probability distribution function for a standardized normal variable (the probability that a standardized normal variable will be less than x), S denotes the spot price of the underlying asset, K the strike price, r the level of the interest rate (assuming continuous compounding), σ is the annualized volatility (we will discuss volatility extensively) and $T-t$ is the time to expiry (measured in years).

A mathematical proof of these equations is outside the scope of this book but we do wish to dig deeper into an intuitive understanding of what is going on here.

One of the reasons why the Black–Scholes framework gained so much success within the financial industry was because it allowed traders to price options more precisely and analytically. In addition, it had the somewhat non-intuitive result (at the time) that one could price options without having to make an assumption on the future directionality of the underlying asset, just on the future volatility.

How is this possible? At a first glance, it would seem obvious that pricing a call option or a put option requires an assumption on the directionality of the underlying. Surely, one can assume that, if an underlying asset is expected to increase in price terms, then that should positively affect the price of a call option (it becomes more likely for the call option to be in-the-money at expiry) and negatively affect the price of a put option (it becomes less likely for the put option to be in-the-money at expiry). If we double check the formulae for the call and put option presented above, however, we do not see any sign of directional expectation embedded in these formulae. So, how has it been possible to build a framework for option pricing without embedding any directional view on the underlying asset? Answering this question means understanding the essence of Black–Scholes pricing and the concept of risk-neutral valuation.

5.5   THE OPTION DELTA AND THE REPLICATION OF THE OPTION PAYOFF

Buying or selling a call or a put option involves a certain degree of directional exposure to the underlying asset. For example, if we buy a call option and do nothing else, we clearly would like the price of the underlying to go up, to increase the chance of positive payoff when the option expires. Vice versa, if we buy a put option and do nothing else, we would like the price of the underlying to go down, to increase the chance of a positive payoff when the option expires. Therefore, the price of the underlying has to be related somewhat with the price of the option (either the call or put) since it is the price of the underlying that ultimately drives the option payoff.

As we pointed out in section 5.4, however, the option price presented in the Black–Scholes framework does not seem to show any dependency on the expected future direction of the price of the underlying. In this section we will try to explain this apparent paradox. How is it possible that the price of an option (which is clearly affected by the future evolution of the asset price) does not seem to be impacted by the expected future direction of the underlying asset?

To get to the heart of this apparent paradox, we will introduce the concept of the *delta* of an option, which we can define as the first derivative of the option price with respect to the price of the underlying asset. In other words, by how much will the option price change when the price of the underlying changes. If C is again the price of a call option, P the price of a put option and S the price of the underlying asset, then the delta of the call option and of the put option are dC/dS and dP/dS respectively.[2]

In essence, the delta of an option is an implied (or synthetic) indicator of the degree of directionality of the option with respect to the underlying asset price. It is hopefully easy to see that, on the final expiration day, provided that the price of the underlying is well above the strike (for a call option) or well below the strike (for a put option), i.e., if the option is in-the-money, the delta of the call option will be equal to 1 and the delta of the put option will be equal to –1. This is due to the fact the options that we just described have virtually 100% probability of expiring in-the-money and, as a consequence, 100% chance of being exercised. Therefore, in this example, owning a call option is virtually the same as owning the underlying asset itself (i.e., the call option price C will behave like the price of the underlying asset S, hence $dC/dS = 1$) whereas owning a put option is virtually the same as being short the underlying asset (i.e., the put option price P will behave in the opposite way to the underlying asset S, hence $dP/dS = -1$).[3]

Symmetrically, if the price of the underlying is well below the strike for a call option or well above the strike for a put option, i.e., if the option is out-of-the-money, the delta of the option will be equal to 0 provided that the option expiry is close enough. This is because the option will most likely expire out-of-the-money and therefore will not exhibit any price movement.

From these initial remarks it should be clear that, during the life of a vanilla option, the delta will vary within a range from 0 to 1 (for call options) or from –1 to 0 (for put options) reflecting the higher or lower directional dependency as appropriate.

As we will discuss in more detail in the following chapter, delta is one of the most common "Greeks".[4] For now, however, it is important to emphasize that the delta of the option expresses a degree of directionality of the option price with respect to the price of the underlying asset (dC/dS and dP/dS respectively).

A key consequence of knowing the delta of an option is that it becomes possible to offset the directional exposure of the option by trading the underlying asset itself. A simple example will clarify this.

---

[2] If we were being mathematically accurate, we would use partial derivatives here, $\partial C/\partial S$ and $\partial P/\partial S$, but our focus is on the intuition, not the mathematics. We are hoping to explain the intuition rather than to provide rigorous proofs. In fact, a rigorous proof of the Black–Scholes pricing equation can extend to many pages of text while providing no new understanding of options.

[3] We note here that the delta of the underlying is always 1, since $dP/dP = 1$. This may sound trivial and/or obvious but we note it just in case it is neither.

[4] We will discuss the option Greeks thoroughly in Chapter 6 where we will also present the relevant analytical formulae and highlight their key features.

Let us assume that we can buy a call option on 1,000 shares of XYZ Plc with strike 1.1 when the spot price of XYZ is 1. If the delta of a single option is 0.4, also described as 40 delta (we will show in Chapter 6 how to calculate the delta[5]), this is like saying that buying an option on 1,000 shares has the same directional exposure currently as buying 400 shares of XYZ. This latter figure will increase or decrease as the price of XYZ moves up (increasing the likelihood of the option expiring in-the-money and therefore the option delta) or down (decreasing the likelihood of the option expiring in-the-money and therefore the option delta).

Consequently, if we own a call option on 1,000 XYZ, we can reduce the directional exposure of this position by selling 400 shares of XYZ in the market, bringing the total net directionality of the portfolio to zero. In other words, if the price of XYZ falls slightly, then the loss in the value of the portfolio from being long the call option on the 1,000 XYZ shares will be (as a first order approximation) offset by the gain from being short 400 shares (they could be bought back at the now lower price for a net gain). The net delta of the portfolio is equal to the sum of the delta from the options position and the delta from the position in the underlying asset. The call option in this example has a delta of 0.4 and so a call option on 1,000 shares has a delta of 400. The underlying share has a delta of 1 (as we noted earlier) and so a short position in 400 shares has a delta of –400. Hence the combined position of a call option on 1,000 shares plus a short position in 400 shares has a net delta of 0.

From this example it emerges how important it is to know the delta of an option since it allows us to offset at any time (i.e., to hedge) the directional exposure implied by the option.

As we shall see in Chapter 6, delta neutrality is, in fact, a "localized" characteristic. Every time the underlying price changes, the delta of the option will change. So, if you have an existing delta-neutral portfolio (perhaps you are long some put options and long some of the underlying asset) and the price of the underlying changes, the portfolio will no longer be delta-neutral. The portfolio will consequently start showing some degree of directional exposure with respect to the underlying asset price.

The obvious question arising at this point is (most likely) going to be, what would be the point of buying an option and then continuously trading the underlying asset to remove the directional exposure? The answer to this question will become clearer in sections 6.4 and 6.8 dedicated to gamma and to option trading. For now, however, let us just accept that some market participants are involved in such activity (for instance, option market makers, who provide other market participants with liquidity in options but, once traded, want to reduce as much as possible the directional exposure of their option positions while they still remain live).

5.6 OPTION REPLICATION

In this section, we will analyse the fundamental concept of option replication in a Black–Scholes framework. We will construct a practical example and describe it step by step.

As we will continually point out through this book, the price of an option can be seen as the cost of replicating its payoff by trading the underlying security. The basic assumption here is that the underlying security is a tradable instrument. We will conduct our analysis from the point of view of the option seller; obviously the option buyer will have the identical and opposite point of view.

---

[5] The analytical formula for calculating the delta of a call option is $N(d_1)$, where the function N is the cumulative probability distribution function for a standardized normal variable that we introduced in section 5.4. We will discuss this in much more detail in Chapter 6.

In order to construct our example we will define a cash account, denominated in the same currency as the option and the underlying security. The basic assumption in this case is that, at the very beginning, we will start from a zero cash balance. The cash account is credited with the option premium that is received when we sell an option (recall that we are taking the option seller's point of view) and will be debited with the amount of money required to build the replicating portfolio. We will assume that, every day, there will be interest accruing on any outstanding cash balance and that this accrued interest itself will become part of the cash balance from the following day. The accrued interest will be positive in the case of a positive cash balance and negative in case of a negative cash balance.

To recap the assumptions underlying our example:

- The underlying security is tradable.
- We start from a zero cash account.
- Interest is accrued on a daily basis and becomes part of the cash account on the following day.

Now imagine that we had just sold a call option on one share of a non-dividend paying stock with a spot price of 100 and volatility of 20%. We will also assume a strike price of 110, an interest rate of 5% and an option time to expiry of 1 year.

We can verify, using the analytical formulae presented earlier, that the Black–Scholes price of this option is 6.04 and that the delta of the option is around 45%. What does this mean? Because we are selling the option, we are receiving a premium of 6.04 and we have to buy 0.45 units of the underlying security at an outlay of 45 (spot price of 100 per unit) to make our position delta-neutral. Note that selling a call option gives us a short delta position that we have to offset by buying the underlying asset in order to neutralize the delta. Our position is:

- We are long 0.45 shares of the underlying security.
- We are short the call option.
- We have a negative cash balance of $6.04 - 45 = -38.96$ in our cash account (the difference between the price of the option that we received and the amount we had to spend to purchase the underlying asset to neutralize the overall delta of the portfolio). This negative cash balance can be seen as an overdraft where the applicable interest rate is equal to 5%.

At this point we will have to consider the frequency of our delta re-hedging. As time passes and the price of the underlying moves, the delta of our option will change (at least during the times when the market for the underlying stock is open). However, it is just not possible in practice to continuously trade the underlying stock in order to re-hedge our option position – hence, the need for an assumption as to the frequency of the delta rebalancing. For the purpose of this exercise, it is assumed to be daily. The important caveat here is that this will not necessarily be the case in practice.

During 1 day, we assume the underlying price moves by 3% to 103. What is the profit and loss of our first day of option replication?

To calculate it we will have to re-price the option assuming the new level of underlying price (103) and 1 day less to the expiry. This price turns out to be roughly 7.45, implying a loss on the short option position equal to $6.04 - 7.45 = -1.41$. How has our delta hedge performed? Owning 0.45 shares of the underlying asset implies a profit of $0.45 (103 - 100) = 1.35$. It is also important to include in our calculation the interest charge on our negative cash account, equal to 0.005. The total P/L of our positions for the first day is therefore $1.35 - 1.41 - 0.005 = -0.065$. Why did we lose money?

We ask you to be patient regarding this very important issue. The reason will become clearer in the next few chapters. For the time being, let us check the status of the portfolio delta (after the underlying price moved up by 3%) and the cash account after the first day of trading. As a consequence of the higher price of the underlying, the option delta increased from 45% to roughly 51%. In any case, what is important to note at this stage is that the increased option delta will require an additional purchase of 0.06 units of the underlying asset in order to keep the delta-neutrality, with a financial outlay of $0.06 \times 103 = 6.18$. At the end of the trading day, the balance in the cash account will be equal to the balance as of the previous day (–38.96) minus the interest charged on that negative balance for the first day (0.005) minus the 6.18 outlay for the purchase of the additional 0.06 units of underlying. The total cash account at the end of the second trading day will therefore be $-38.96 - 0.005 - 6.18 = -45.145$. On top of this, we will have the long position on 0.51 units of underlying security (0.45 purchased initially and 0.06 purchased on the following day) worth $0.51 \times 103 = 52.53$ and a short position in the call option, now priced at 7.45.

Right now, it should be becoming clear that this is an iterative process such that (daily in our example) the price of the underlying asset is known and, as a consequence, the appropriate delta rebalancing takes place. The process is repeated iteratively until the call option expires, when two scenarios are possible:

1. The price of the underlying asset is at or below the strike price. In this scenario, we can realistically assume that the delta has been approaching zero, which implies that we have been selling back the underlying asset during the life of the option. Furthermore, as the option expires out-of-the-money, we are left with some residual amount in the cash account that reflects the option premium that we originally received and the result of the trading activity in the underlying asset, plus the net accrued interest paid or received.
2. The price of the underlying asset is above the strike price. In this scenario, we can assume that the delta has been approaching 1, which implies that we have been buying more and more units of the underlying asset during the life of the option and we now own one whole unit. Furthermore, since the option expires in-the-money, it is going to be exercised by the buyer. Consequently, we will have to sell the unit of the underlying asset that we own; this transaction will take place at the strike price and we will therefore receive the corresponding amount of 110. Afterwards, we will be left with zero units of the underlying asset and with some residual amount in the cash account that, as observed in scenario 1, reflects the option premium that we originally received and the result of the trading activity in the underlying asset, plus the net accrued interest paid or received.

As the analysis shows, whether the option expires in- or out-of-the-money, the equity position and options position will cancel each other out, and we will be typically left with a residual amount in the cash account that constitutes the total profit or loss (hopefully profit!) registered during the entire life of the trade.

5.7 OPTION REPLICATION, RISK-NEUTRAL VALUATION AND DELTA HEDGING REVISITED

Now that we have analysed the concept of option replication via delta hedging and risk-neutral option pricing, let us link all these concepts together.

The basic idea of delta hedging is to remove the directional risk arising from an option position. In this context, what we call directional risk is the risk with respect to movements in the price of the underlying security. In other words, we are trying to neutralize the impact on the net worth of a portfolio due to changes in the price of the underlying security. Since we are only trading the underlying security to offset the delta of the option, we are not removing all the inherent risks. Why is that so important? What are the other risks? Let us clarify this with an example.

Consider two traders: Mrs Bull and Mr Bear. Mrs Bull (not surprisingly) has a very bullish view on a stock, whereas Mr Bear is extremely bearish. Assume now that both Mrs Bull and Mr Bear agree on the expected volatility of the stock for the coming months.[6] If Mrs Bull and Mr Bear need to price a call option on that stock independently, they will come up with the same price. This is because the option pricing framework that they are going to use will allow them to remove the directionality risk from their net option position. This does not mean that both Mrs Bull and Mr Bear will follow the delta-hedging replication exactly in the same way; but, if they want to, they can. This is the crucial concept at the heart of risk-neutral pricing. Both traders are in a position to remove the directional risk from their implied options positions by trading the underlying security. The fact that each option trader will likely choose to hedge their positions in a completely different way is a separate issue. The option traders *are in a position to do it whenever they believe it is appropriate.*

In other words, what we are stressing here is not just the formulaic option pricing, itself a mere application of a formula based on a model. What the framework has produced is *not only a price but also a trading strategy* (i.e., option replication via delta hedging) that allows the option trader to replicate the payoff. To state it in a slightly different way, *the price is not a price unless it is accompanied by a unique trading strategy that ensures full replication of the option.*

Thus far in our tale, we have assumed that the two option traders Mrs Bull and Mr Bear have a view that happens to be the same about the future volatility of the stock. Now let us assume Mrs Bull and Mr Bear hold completely different views on the volatility of the underlying security. Mrs Bull, who is indeed very bullish, may think that the stock will follow a very nice upward path with relatively contained volatility. Mr Bear, who is very worried about a price collapse, thinks that the underlying stock price will drop quite sharply and that the sell-off will be associated with very high realized volatility. Now, if asked to quote the price of the same call option independently, their prices will be completely different.

Mrs Bull will assign a much lower fair value to the option compared to Mr Bear. But was not Mrs Bull much more bullish on the prospects for the stock? Why should Mr Bear be willing to pay more than her for something that, at least in theory, Mrs Bull believes is more valuable? The answer to this question is vital to understanding the risk-neutral framework. Mr Bear has to be willing to pay more because he will be in a position to remove the directional risk arising from the long position in a call option. So his directional view does not and should not matter as far as option pricing is concerned. On the other hand, even if Mrs Bull is very bullish on the stock, she might not be willing to pay Mr Bear's price because she believes Mr Bear's price assumes a volatility that is far too high compared with what she expects.

To sum up, the risk-neutral valuation framework allows the trader to remove the directional risk with respect to underlying movements. It does not, however, allow the trader to remove the directional risk with respect to the volatility. To some extent, we could state that the trader is *shifting from the directional view on the underlying to a directional view on volatility.*

---

[6] We will return to this assumption in section 6.8 but, for now, we will take it as given.

5.8 OPTIONS ON DIVIDEND PAYING ASSETS

In section 5.4 we presented the Black–Scholes framework for non-dividend paying assets. In this section we aim to extend that framework to underlying assets that pay dividends. As discussed in section 2.4.1, a dividend can be expressed continuously (continuous dividend yield q) or discretely, i.e., fixed cash amount to be paid out in certain dates in the futures (called *ex dates*).

It is easy to show that the case of continuous dividend yield can be easily expressed as a non-dividend paying asset, allowing us to apply the formulae presented in section 5.4. In particular, let's assume that a certain asset P with initial price equal to P_0 pays a continuous dividend yield of q and let's compare it with an asset S with initial price equal to S_0 that does not pay any dividend.

Recalling the formulae of the forward presented in section 2.4.1, we note that, to allow absence of arbitrage, the respective forward prices for delivery in T have to be equal to:

$$\text{Forward}(P) = P_0 \exp[(r - q)T]$$

whereas:

$$\text{Forward}(S) = S_0 \exp[rT]$$

From an option pricing point of view, assuming that the volatility of the two underlying assets is identical, it should be noted that the two securities will have the same probability distribution in T if $S_0 = P_0 \exp[-q\,T]$. This can be easily verified calculating the forward price of the asset S as:

$$\text{Forward}(S) = S_0 \exp[rT] = P_0 \exp[-q\,T] \exp[rT] = P_0 \exp[(r - q)T] = \text{Forward}(P)$$

What we just showed is that a non-dividend paying asset S with initial price S_0 has the same forward price as a dividend paying asset P with initial price P_0 if and only if $S_0 = P_0 \exp[-q\,T]$.

This is equivalent to saying that if we use $P_0 \exp[-q\,T]$ as initial price for the dividend paying asset P (instead of P_0), we can "transform" the dividend paying asset in a non-dividend paying asset that has the same terminal distribution. In this way we can therefore easily modify the formulae presented in section 5.4 for assets that pay a continuous dividend yield obtaining:

$$\text{Call} = P_0 \exp[-q(T - t)]\,N(d_1) - K \exp[-r(T - t)]\,N(d_2)$$
$$\text{Put} = K \exp[-r(T - t)]\,N(-d_2) - P_0 \exp[-q(T - t)]\,N(-d_1)$$

where q is the continuous dividend yield. In this case:

$$d_1 = \frac{\ln\left(P_0 e^{-q(T-t)}/K\right) + \left(r + \sigma^2/2\right)(T - t)}{\sigma\sqrt{T - t}}$$

$$= \frac{\ln\left(P_0/K\right) - q\,(T - t) + \left(r + \sigma^2/2\right)(T - t)}{\sigma\sqrt{T - t}}$$

$$= \frac{\ln\left(P_0/K\right) + \left(r - q + \sigma^2/2\right)(T - t)}{\sigma\sqrt{T - t}}$$

$$d_2 = d_1 - \sigma\sqrt{T - t}$$

In the case of discrete dividend payments, it is possible to apply the formulae presented in section 5.4 assuming an initial price equal to the spot price minus the present value of the discrete dividend payments.

5.9   OPTIONS ON FUTURES: THE BLACK MODEL

In this section, we aim to extend our option pricing framework to options on futures. This extension will allow us to introduce a very useful option pricing formula (the so-called "Black formula") where we can input the forward price directly; this will be incredibly useful for options on currencies and commodities as well. Let us proceed step by step. The first step is to get comfortable with the idea that the term structure of a futures contract is flat (and equal to the current price of the futures contract itself) or, in other words, that the forward price of a futures contract is equal to the futures price itself. We appreciate that this may not seem intuitive at first glance. Therefore, we present a simple example to try to shed some light on this.

If we look at the term structure of a commodity, for instance crude oil, we will see that it is possible to negotiate futures contracts expiring in different months. As discussed in Chapter 1 the term structure can assume different shapes depending on the levels of the futures prices for different expiries. Let us now focus on a specific expiry, say Dec 2015. Assume that the price of the Dec 15 contract on crude oil is equal to $90 per barrel. Let us now try to answer the following question: what is the forward price for delivery on Dec 14 of our futures contract expiring on Dec 15? In trying to answer this question, assume that today we are entering a forward contract expiring on Dec 14. It means that today we agree the price to pay (or to receive) on Dec 14 in order to enter a position in the Dec 15 futures contract. When analysing the pricing of a forward contract in Chapter 2, we calculated this price assuming absence of arbitrage and we showed that, in general, a forward price can be seen as the price of the underlying that allows replication of the exposure arising from the forward contract in the absence of arbitrage opportunities. In particular in section 2.4, we linked the forward price to the spot price and the cost of carrying the position until the forward contract expires. If we want to use the same framework to calculate the no-arbitrage price of a forward on a futures contract, we need to ask ourselves what is the cost of carrying the position in a futures contract (say the Dec 15 contract) until the expiry of the forward (Dec 14). The answer is that, at least as a first approximation, we can assume this cost to be sufficiently close to zero. This is due to the fact that trading a futures contract does not involve an initial cost[7] (if you buy a stock or a bond or an option, you will have to pay for it). Therefore, we can assume as a first approximation that the exposure in a futures contract is not funded, nor entitles you to receive any yield. This is the reason why the term structure of an individual future contract is in theory flat and equal to the current price of the futures itself.

In the Black–Scholes framework extended to dividend paying assets, there is an easy shortcut to force an underlying to have a flat forward term structure. This can be done (surprisingly simply) assuming that the dividend yield is equal to the interest rate. Recalling section 5.8, if we assume that $q = r$ the forward price of the futures F is going to be equal to:

$$\text{Forward}\,(F) = F_0 \exp[(r - q)\,T] = F_0 \exp[(r - r)\,T] = F_0 \exp[0] = F_0$$

---

[7] It does involve the payment of a margin, but this margin is returned when the position in closed.

Therefore with a little "trick" we forced the forward price of the futures asset F to be equal to its current price *for all delivery dates of the forward*. What this implies is that it becomes very easy to price options on futures. We can just use the formulae in section 5.8 and assume $q = r$. The results will be:

$$\text{Call} = \exp[-r(T - t)][F_0 \, N(d_1) - K \, N(d_2)]$$
$$\text{Put} = \exp[-r(T - t)][K \, N(-d_2) - F_0 \, N(-d_1)]$$

In this case:

$$d_1 = \frac{\ln\left(F_0/K\right) + \left(\sigma^2/2\right)(T - t)}{\sigma\sqrt{T - t}}$$
$$d_2 = d_1 - \sigma\sqrt{T - t}$$

This is normally known as the "Black formula". It can be compared with the traditional Black–Scholes formula but the Black formula is easier to use whenever the forward price is readily available in the market. This is the typical case for currency and for commodity options or, more generally, whenever the forward contract of an underlying asset is very liquid and easy to trade.

5.10   MONTE CARLO PRICING

5.10.1   Introduction to the Monte Carlo technique

So far we have analysed closed formulae option prices. This has been possible because under certain assumptions (as discussed) the price of vanilla options can be calculated using closed formulae. However, this is not always the case; even within the Black–Scholes framework, certain non-vanilla derivatives cannot be priced with a closed formula. In particular some of the derivatives that we will analyse in Chapters 9 and 10 require a different approach. Monte Carlo simulation is a very powerful tool that allows the pricing of a great variety of non-vanilla derivatives assuming the Black–Scholes pricing framework or even different frameworks.

The Monte Carlo pricing technique uses random numbers to generate simulated paths for asset prices in the future. Although the name was probably inspired by the small Mediterranean principality famous for its casinos, the Monte Carlo technique was actually pioneered by nuclear physicists in the early twentieth century rather than by Europe's professional gamblers. It is an extremely flexible mathematical tool and all derivatives can be priced with it, provided that a model for the dynamics of the underlying asset prices is available or, at a pinch, there is reliable historical data[8] that you expect to provide a reasonable framework for the asset's future price behaviour.

The technique consists of the following broad steps:

1. A series of prices for a particular underlying asset, called a path, is generated into the future. Although the process will use a random number generating technique, the price series is not random in the sense that the analyst will input a proposed model dictating the way in which prices for the asset are expected to behave. So, for equities, the underlying process may be a random walk with drift, while, in the case of interest rates, as discussed in Chapter 1,

---

[8] In Chapter 1, we discussed how most asset prices actually appear ostensibly to follow random walks (with drifts). With this in mind, it would seem reasonable to use random number generators to model simulations of future price paths for financial assets.

there may be mean reversion around an average rate with a lower bound to ensure that rates cannot go negative. Each relevant time step between the evaluation date[9] and the maturity date will have a price. Often, this means estimating the closing values for the underlying asset price for each day into the future until the maturity of the derivative.
2. Using this price series, all future cash flows from the derivative are determined. In other words, one treats the price series created in step 1 above as if it were real market price data.
3. The cash flows for the derivative are discounted (using an appropriate discount rate for each) and then summed to provide the net present value of the derivative (for the given price path).
4. Steps 1 and 2 are repeated a very large number of times[10] and the resulting net present values of the derivative for each path are averaged out. This average is the estimate of the spot price of the derivative.

The steps just outlined seem easy enough but, of course, there is always a catch; when something seems too easy, it generally is. The main difficulty in using Monte Carlo techniques comes from the need for an appropriate model to generate the price of the underlying asset. The random paths generated must be done so in a way that is consistent with the known empirical history of the underlying asset price and that the models chosen provide reasonable guides for that asset's future behaviours.

For any user of the Monte Carlo technique, there are a few things that need to be kept in mind:

1. The Monte Carlo price of a derivative is always going to be an "approximate" price, since the number of paths that could be used to compute the price of the derivative is finite. It is like trying to understand if a dice is honestly balanced by throwing it many times. After 60 throws, it is very unlikely that there will have been 10 throws each of 1, 2, 3, 4, 5 and 6. It is much more likely that a distribution something like 12, 13, 8, 6, 7 and 14 is achieved. This does not mean, *per se*, that the dice is unbalanced, however. It just means that the "true" characteristic of the dice can only be discovered by many more throws.
2. The Monte Carlo technique can also be used to provide an estimate for the Monte Carlo "error" that goes with the estimate of the price of the derivative. That is to say, a measure of the uncertainty surrounding the price. For instance, the price of a particular exotic option could be, say, 3.86% of the notional with an uncertainty of 0.12%. This uncertainty (or error) is usually expressed in terms of standard deviations and it is interpreted as there being a 66% probability that the "true" price of the option is between 3.74 and 3.98% of notional. Note that 3.86% − 0.12% equals 3.74% and 3.86% + 0.12% equals 3.98%.
3. Increasing the number of paths simulated in the Monte Carlo process will tend to reduce the Monte Carlo error but only in proportion to the square root of the number of paths. So, for example, doubling the number of paths only reduces the error by a factor of the square root of two (about 1.4), i.e., from 0.12 to 0.085%. The number of paths used in a typical Monte Carlo run will depend on the specific application but, as mentioned earlier, will generally be in the range of upwards of tens of thousands.

---

[9] The date on which the derivative is to be priced.
[10] Thousands of times in most cases.

4. The Greeks[11] computed by Monte Carlo techniques can be very "noisy", especially when the payoffs from the derivative being priced contain some sort of digital condition. It is possible to make a "correction" to the payoff on the derivative in order to obtain some smoothing of the resulting Greeks, for example by replacing a digital payoff condition with a large call spread. In this case, the resulting price for the derivative will likely be an overestimate of the "true" price, i.e., it will be an over-hedged price.

5. In most Monte Carlo techniques, the random number generators used to create the paths are not entirely random. Empirically, they will generate so-called pseudo-random numbers, i.e., a sequence of numbers which has most of the statistical properties of a series of truly random numbers but which has been generated in a deterministic way. Theoretically, this implies that a particular random series may be repeated at some point in the process, although one would need to be calculating a very large number of paths.

6. The most common pseudo-random number generator requires an initial seed number (an integer number) to start off the generation of the particular sequence of random numbers. Some commentators believe that there is such a thing as a "magic seed" but, unfortunately, this is not the case. For some of the pseudo-random number generators, in particular for the Mersenne-Twister, which is probably the most common, it is recommended to use a long number as the seed. Do not use 0 or 1 as the seed. This will be a very bad choice. Choose a seed with as many digits as available.

7. The time step used in a Monte Carlo simulation varies greatly depending on the derivative to be priced. In derivatives that involve daily observations (such as barriers), one will need daily time steps; for monthly observations, monthly time steps are needed and so on. For some fixed income derivatives, one may be able to use weekly or monthly time steps. For those underlying assets that have highly volatile price dynamics, it may be appropriate to have short time steps.

8. Monte Carlo pricing is very costly in terms of computational power. Even with modern computers, the time needed to calculate Greeks using a Monte Carlo technique can be noticeable. It is often very tempting to speed up the process by reducing the number of paths or the number of time steps but one then has to be certain that the results are accurate enough for the problem.

5.10.2 Generation of a Monte Carlo path

The basic idea behind the generation of a Monte Carlo path is relatively simple. Start from the present state of the market, i.e., the current price of an underlying asset, and compute the state after the next time step, i.e., the future price of that asset. Then, treat the new state as the new starting point and compute the state for the next time step. Repeat until the maturity date of the derivative.

The difficult piece of the process lies in computing the change in the asset value across a single time step. Let us think about the following simple example, taking the price of gold (denominated in USD).

Let $S(0)$ be the spot price of gold today. How does one compute $S(1)$, the price of gold tomorrow? Well, what do we know about the empirical behaviour of the gold price? In the first instance, we know that the gold price often trends so that we know that the price of gold

---

[11] We will get back to the concept of "Greeks" in Chapter 6; for the time being we can define the Greeks as the sensitivities to those market variables involved in determining the option price.

tomorrow can be expected to be higher (in the case of a bullish trend) or lower (in the case of a bearish trend) than today. What is the extent of this trend? We could look at the recent history to determine the trend or we could assume a trend change in line with interest rate. Whatever is decided, the price tomorrow may not be the same as the price today. This should be reflected in the Monte Carlo simulation. Second, we know that the gold price is volatile around the trend. This volatility also needs to be reflected in the simulation.

In its simplest version, the formula for a Monte Carlo step will look like this:[12]

$$S(1) = S(0) \times \exp \left[\text{yield} \times dt + \text{vol} \times W \times \text{sqrt}(dt) \right]$$

where dt is the length of the time step, $t(1) - t(0)$, W is a random number taken from a random-number generator,[13] and vol is the volatility of the asset price over the time step. If the yields and the volatilities are annualized, then dt will need to be expressed in years. So, if the time step is 1 business day, dt may be 1/250 (assuming there are 250 business days in a year).

In general, for the generic step number k:

$$S(k) = S(k - 1) \times \exp \left[\text{yield} \times dt + \text{vol} \times W \times \text{sqrt}(dt) \right]$$

To calculate $S(k)$ we will need an estimate of the yield and of the volatility. This is our pricing model. No matter how many times we run the Monte Carlo process, the appropriateness of the answer that we get will depend upon the validity of these initial assumptions. One way to get the initial estimate of the volatility may be to analyse the structure of implied volatilities in the options market for gold.[14] While this may not be the "correct" measure of future volatility, it has, at least, the feature that any vanilla options that are used to hedge the derivative being priced will have the same level of implied volatility. In this way, the Greeks from the Monte Carlo process and the Greeks on the vanilla options are, in a sense, comparable.

In the case that one is attempting to model the behaviour of forward prices rather than the future behaviour of spot prices, a couple of tweaks need to be made to the model just outlined:

1. Unlike the behaviour of spot prices over time, specific forward prices will tend not to have drift, i.e., the expected future level of a forward asset price is the same as the present level of the forward asset price. As a consequence, there is no drift term in the above equation for the Monte Carlo simulation of an asset price on a particular forward date.
2. Since different forward dates will have different associated volatilities, each forward will need to be simulated separately. In other words, for a trade, say, with a 1-year maturity, contingent on observations of the prompt forward contract, a Monte Carlo path will consist of 12 simulations, one for each of the observed forwards.

Pricing models with two or more factors are typically used in the case of pricing assets based on forward prices. Since each forward will be a source of randomness, this translates into having distinct random numbers in the computation of the Monte Carlo steps. The equation for a step in a two-factor forward model used to price a derivative might look like:

$$FT(k) = FT(k - 1) \times \exp \left[\text{vol1} \times W1 + \text{vol2} \times W2 \right] \times \text{sqrt}(dt)$$

---

[12] The yield term, in this case, is the "drift" measure that we have highlighted before. The equation for $S(t)$ is a classic random walk with drift.

[13] Most random-number generators will assume a standard Gaussian distribution for the random numbers.

[14] We will define implied volatility in Chapter 6; for the time being, think of implied volatility as the volatility that using the Black–Scholes formulae allows us to replicate option prices observable in the option markets.

In order to make things clearer, we invite the reader to look at the spreadsheet "Chapter 5 – Monte Carlo" in which we will show a simple example of a one-step Monte Carlo that we will use to price a vanilla option. Obviously there is no need for Monte Carlo to price a vanilla option as a closed formula is available. However, our aim is to show that Monte Carlo allows us to replicate the same price that we could get using the Black–Scholes closed formula once the same assumption underlying the Black–Scholes framework is embedded in the Monte Carlo paths.

The first tab does not describe a real Monte Carlo (as it can be understood from the weird name "Deterministic Monte Carlo"). The reason why we included it is because we find it extremely useful to understand these concepts. In this case we are not running random simulations but we take 999 values distributed uniformly in the range [0, 1] (as it can be seen in column F, basically from 0.001 to 0.999) and we invert the standard cumulative normal function to get our normal variables (column G). We associate to each normal variable the corresponding asset price return (column H) and asset price at expiry (column I) consistent with market data and option features in the left-hand side. From the asset price at expiry we calculate the payoff of the call option that we aim to price (column J), we average this price (cell C14) and discount the average value to obtain our Monte Carlo price (cell C15). For comparison we include also the Black–Scholes price (cell C20).

The second tab (called "Stochastic Monte Carlo") presents a real example. It is basically the same as the previous tab, but in this case the numbers sampled from the uniform distribution are really random; therefore every time you force Excel to recalculate (pressing Shift+F9 or Cmd+= on a Mac), a new set of random variables is generated generating a new Monte Carlo price. In this case in cell C16 we also included the standard error of the Monte Carlo price obtained. If the reader believes the standard error is too large, we suggest increasing the number of scenarios to improve the quality of the price and reduce the error.

5.11   OTHER PRICING TECHNIQUES

5.11.1   Partial differential equation

Another widely used technique to price exotic derivatives is the numerical solution of a partial differential equation, PDE. We do not plan to go into the mathematical details of PDE-pricing here although the fundamental idea consists of the following steps, where we focus on the example of a European call option of strike K and expiry T:

1. Select a time step dt and set up a grid with $t(0) = 0$, $t(1) = dt$, $t(2) = 2dt, \ldots, t(N) = T$. The corresponding asset prices will be $S(0), S(1), \ldots, S(N)$. The former goes from the evaluation date to the expiry date of the call option. Usually the grid will be a constant-step grid with the logarithm of the asset's price.
2. For the last step $t(N)$, assign the value the call option's payoff assumes if fixed at the corresponding asset level, i.e., assign the call option payoff formula $\max(S(N) - K, 0)$ to the point corresponding to $S(N)$.
3. The value of the derivative at each time point can be calculated using a partial differential equation. The value of the derivative at the time step $t(N - 1)$, conditional on a particular price level Sj, can be estimated knowing the value of the option on step tN, as well as the volatility surface and drift of the asset and the interest rate. Although this is true in theory only for infinitesimal time steps, it can be a very good approximation if the steps are short enough.
4. Repeat step 3 going backwards in time one step until initial time $t(0)$ is reached.

In practice, it will not make a great deal of sense to use a PDE to price a vanilla European call option since an exact[15] analytical solution actually exists. PDEs are used only for more exotic derivatives, American options and Barrier options being prime examples. PDE solutions can be as accurate as required; their accuracy can be increased by increasing the number of time steps and strike steps in the grid.

Regular users of PDE estimation techniques will tend to have their own tricks of the trade. Regardless of these, however, PDE techniques have many advantages over Monte Carlo pricing. PDE prices do not, for example, have a random component to their results, such as the Monte Carlo error. PDE methods are also faster than Monte Carlo techniques for pricing equivalent derivatives.

So, why do we not price everything using PDE methods? The reason is known as "the curse of dimensionality". When adding more assets to a Monte Carlo technique, the increase in computational cost is linear. A simulation with four assets, for example, costs four times the computer time as a simulation with just one asset. With PDE methods, however, the cost increases exponentially with the number of underlying assets. If one normally prices a derivative on, say, gold using a grid with 200 strike points then, in order to price a derivative based on four underlying assets with similar accuracy (i.e., some kind of structured product), the strike grid will need to contain 200^4 points, i.e., 1.6 billion points. This is completely unfeasible.

In practice, PDE methods are used with problems of one or two dimensions, i.e., derivatives with one or two underlying assets, e.g., a commodity with an FX rate. In some cases, three-asset PDEs can be made to work effectively but this is already borderline and a Monte Carlo technique might actually be faster (for a similar level of accuracy). Finally, note that very limited use of PDE methods can be applied when the underlying asset references specific forwards since each forward would have to be treated as a separate asset in the PDE. It is very rare, for example, for exotic derivative trades on commodities to reference just one or two forwards. Instead, PDEs are mostly used to price derivatives on commodities that reference spot prices (e.g., precious metals and indices).

5.11.2 Binomial/trinomial tree pricing

For completeness, we should mention that those types of trades that can be priced using a PDE method can also be priced using a binomial or, less commonly, a trinomial tree. These techniques are essentially a simplification of the PDE approach. While they are often discussed in the academic literature and we ourselves used a binomial tree approach to price simple options in an earlier chapter, they do tend to provide less accurate and less stable results than do PDE methods in the presence of a volatility smile. As a consequence, market participants are now tending towards other pricing techniques. Binomial and trinomial trees may still have a place in derivative pricing, however, since they are excellent educational tools.

5.12 PRICING TECHNIQUES SUMMARY

In Table 5.1, we summarize the pros and cons of the various pricing techniques that we have discussed thus far in this book.

---

[15] Assuming, of course, that the underlying assumptions of the Black–Scholes model apply.

Table 5.1   Comparison among different pricing techniques

Technique	Pros	Cons
Analytic – exact	Fast, accurate and stable	Very limited set of payoff profiles can be priced
Monte Carlo	All complex payoffs are supported	Very slow; Monte Carlo error; stability of Greeks is poor
PDE	All complex payoffs are supported	Slow; curse of dimensionality
Binomial/trinomial tree	All complex payoffs are supported	Less accurate than PDE methods

5.13   THE EXCEL SPREADSHEET "OPTION REPLICATION"

5.13.1   Introduction and description of the spreadsheet

In this section, we describe a practical example of option replication that can be found in the spreadsheet called "Chapter 5 – Option Replication". The spreadsheet is based on a random generation of a path for the underlying asset price; the random generation is such that the price of the underlying follows a log-normal distribution with given parameters. Each random generation can be seen as a sample of a Monte Carlo (so this spreadsheet can be also seen as a basic example of generation of Monte Carlo path). We suggest you set the calculation option of your Excel to "Manual" and to press Shift+F9 (or Cmd+= on a Mac) to generate a new random path. We will start from the first tab (called "Option replication") and we will analyse the second tab ("Replication with different vol") shortly.

On the left-hand side, it will be possible to change the market data (i.e., spot price at inception, level of interest rates and volatility – respectively cells C5, C6 and C7) and the option details (such us the strike price – cell C11). For simplicity we will assume expiry in 1 year's time, 100 time steps (ignoring weekends and holidays) and the absence of dividends. Interest rate calculations are based on continuous compounding.

The simulated random path for the spot price of the underlying asset is consistent with the Black–Scholes assumption on the dynamic of the underlying price itself (i.e., a log-normal distribution with drift equal to the interest rate and volatility specified as an input). Based on the defined inputs, the price and delta of a call option is calculated (the strike price can be defined as an input); furthermore the spreadsheet simulates an option replication throughout the life of the option itself allowing you to see in detail how the replication works. At the last time step, we will assume that the option expires and we will calculate the total Profit & Loss of the option replication. All the calculations are performed from the option seller's point of view and daily re-hedging. It goes without saying that option buyer will run exactly the opposite position. Each time step can be seen as an individual trading day.

The relevant columns (from column E) are:

1. *Generation of a random path of the underlying spot price*
   Time step: it identifies each of the 100 time steps.
   Time to expiry: defined in years. As noted earlier, we will price a 1-year option, and so, at the first time step, the time to expiry will be exactly equal to 1.

Discount factor to expiry: the discount factor applicable for each single time step; it will obviously converge to 1 as the expiry approaches.

Random generated number: a random number drawn from a standard normal distribution (i.e., normal distribution with mean equal to zero and variance equal to 1). The way we are generating the random numbers is to use the Excel random-number generator (Rand() function that generates a random number according to a uniform distribution[0, 1]) to which we apply the inverse of a cumulative standard normal distribution.

Time step return: the random return of the asset price for each time step, generated consistently with the random number drawn and assuming a log-normal distribution for the underlying stock (see section 5.10.1 for further details on how to generate a random price path).

Underlying spot price: the path of the price of the underlying security randomly generated according to each time step return.

2. **Calculation of option price and delta**

    d1 and d2: calculated at each step using the Black–Scholes formula applied to the market environment prevailing at each step (i.e., underlying spot price, time to expiry, etc. . . .).

    Call option price: the price of the call option calculated at each step using the Black–Scholes formula applied to the market environment prevailing at each step (i.e., underlying spot price, time to expiry, etc. . . .).

    Call option delta: the delta of the call option calculated at each time step.

3. **Calculation of cash balances from options and delta hedging and related interest**

    Cash balance at the start of the time step: it is assumed to be zero at inception (time step 0 in cell Q4) and for each of the following time steps is assumed to be equal to the cash balance outstanding at the end of the previous time step (which we will introduce shortly) plus the interest charged in each period on this outstanding cash balance (also the interest charge will be presented shortly).

    Change in cash balance from option premium/payoff: this column describes the cash amount received (hence the positive sign of the cell R4) when the call option is initially sold minus the cash amount that will have to be paid to the call option buyer if the option expires in-the-money (hence the negative sign of the cell R104 whenever the option expires in-the-money, i.e., we are assuming a cash-settled option). At all other time steps, it is equal to zero.

    Change in cash balance from option delta hedging: at the time step zero (i.e., as soon as the option is sold), cell S4 is equal to the amount that the call option seller will have to pay to buy a portion of the underlying price defined according to the delta (we are assuming perfect divisibility of the underlying asset); in the subsequent time steps, it represents the amount that will have to be paid or received to rebalance the delta hedging. At each time step, this amount will be negative if the delta compared to the previous time step is increasing and therefore an additional quantity of underlying asset will have to be bought; it will be positive if the delta compared to the previous time step is decreasing and therefore a certain quantity of underlying asset will have to be liquidated. In the last time step, cell S104, it is going to be equal to the proceeds of liquidating all holdings in the underlying asset (if any) as the option is expiring and no further delta hedging is required.

Cash balance at the end of the time step: simply equal to the cash balance at the beginning of each time step (i.e., of each trading day) adjusted by the changes in cash balances occurring in that day. It is worth noticing that this is the quantity on which the interest will be charged/paid (as it is assumed to be the amount of cash outstanding at the end of each trading day). It is also important to point out that the cash balance outstanding at the end of last time step (cell T104 in our example) will be equal to the amount left over to the option seller once the underlying asset held as delta hedging has been fully liquidated and the option payoff has been settled. In other words, this final quantity can be seen as the total Profit & Loss that the option and the associated shares transactions to delta hedge the option have generated over time.

Interest on outstanding cash balance: the interest rate charged or received at each time step on the cash balance outstanding at the end of it. It is added to the cash balance at the start of the following time step.

The calculation so far could be enough to identify the total Profit & Loss of the option position and the delta-hedging activity performed accordingly. However, in the columns described shortly we will be showing different ways to express the same result. We invite the reader to analyse this carefully as it is very important to understand option replication and the risk-neutral framework described in this chapter.

4. ***Calculation of Profit & Loss (P&L)***

Option P&L (seller's point of view): the Profit & Loss of the option trader (from the perspective of the option seller) arising from the short position in the option; it can be seen simply as the difference between the option price calculated in the previous time step and the option price calculated in the current time step. Therefore, it is going to be a negative quantity when the option price increases (remember, we are analysing the seller's point of view) and a positive quantity when the option price decreases.

Delta-hedging P&L: the Profit & Loss of the option trader arising from the ownership of the underlying asset according to the option delta; for each time step, it can be seen as the option delta observed in the previous time step times the difference in the price of the underlying asset.

Total P&L: it is simply the cumulative sum of Option P&L, Delta-hedging P&L and Interest on outstanding cash balance. The total P&L observed in the last time step (cell Y104) has to be the same as the cash balance outstanding at the end of the last time step (cell T104).

To complete the analysis, we also added a column that shows the call option replication over time (column AA). At the first time step (cell AA4), it is simply assumed to be equal to the option premium received by the option seller; in any subsequent time step it is equal to the value as of the previous time step plus the Delta-hedging P&L plus the Interest on outstanding cash balance. The value of the call option replication in the final step (cell AA104) minus the actual call option payoff can be seen as the total P&L of the trader (obviously equal to the total P&L calculated previously).

To sum up, the spreadsheet described above should give you a practical representation of the day-by-day activity assuming daily re-hedging to be delta neutral. On the chart on the right-hand side (at the right of column AC), we plot the dynamic of the option price prevailing at each time step and also the replication performed by the option seller assuming daily re-hedging.

The table "Output" located in the range B14–C23 summarizes the key output of each scenario. You can see that the total Profit and Loss is calculated in three ways that are basically identical: it is calculated as option replication minus option payoff (cell C19), as residual cash balance outstanding after the option expiry (cell C20) and cumulative P&L from the option position and the implemented delta-hedging activity (cell C21). The table "Output" also includes a calculation of the realized volatility observed during the life of the option for each simulated scenario.

If you keep generating new random paths and observe the chart described, you will notice that sometimes the replicating path and the call option path are perfectly overlapping. However, sometimes the replication will be higher at expiry: this means that the trader will make an overall profit during the life of the option. In the case when the replicating path is lower than option price, this will mean that the replicating strategy was not profitable enough and the trader will incur a loss.

5.13.2   Why the replication is not perfect

What if the volatility used to calculate the option price and replicate the payoff is materially different from the actual volatility of the underlying?

We now move one step further and we will show what can happen within the framework we have just described when a wrong "choice" of expected volatility over the life of the option is made. In order to do so we move to the following tab of the spreadsheet (called "Replication with different vol"). This sheet has only one change compared with the one we have been working on so far. In this sheet, we can assume a volatility to calculate the option price and delta (cell C7, Volatility used to price/hedge) but we can simulate the underlying price dynamic based on a different volatility (cell C8, Volatility used to simulate the path). The other parts of the sheet are basically identical to what we have already seen; however, in this case we can clearly analyse what happens when the volatility used to simulate the path of the underlying asset is materially different from the volatility used to price and hedge the option. For instance, if we assume that these two values are very different (for instance, 30% and 15% respectively), you can easily observe that the option replication will almost surely fail (and the trader will incur losses that for certain scenarios can be substantial). The example clearly suggests that selling volatility at a level that is materially lower that the realized volatility will almost certainly result in a loss. By contrast, selling it at a materially higher level will almost certainly result in a profit (i.e., in many scenarios, the proceeds resulting from the option replication strategy at expiry will exceed the option payoff).

SUMMARY

Let us try to sum up the concepts discussed so far regarding option pricing. What have we discussed so far?

- The basic terminology of options and options pricing
- The nature of time value, i.e., price of the optionality and how it related to Jensen's inequality
- Asset return volatility and why it is relevant for pricing options

- The Black–Scholes framework
- The delta of an option and why it is relevant when constructing portfolios that have no directional exposure (at least locally, i.e., for small variation of the price of the underlying asset)
- Option replication and risk-neutral valuation

To repeat, *pricing an option is not merely a probabilistic exercise.*[16] An option price cannot be considered as such if it is not accompanied by a hedging strategy that allows a payoff replication under some condition. It cannot be taken for granted that, in practice, such a hedging strategy is going to be followed religiously, but anyone who trades options has to be in a position to be able to follow the replication strategy if he or she wishes to do so.

The replication strategy is based on the replication of the option payoff by trading the delta of the option. It is designed to remove, as much as possible, the directional exposure arising from the option position. It should not be seen as a way to offset all the risks coming from the option position but only the risks that can be expressed as pure directional exposure (often referred to as delta risk, i.e., the first derivative of the option price with respect to the price of the underlying as we have pointed out several times).

Expressing a price as a weighted average of the option payoffs according to a certain probability distribution has little to do with no-arbitrage pricing, as it would condition the option price on a certain opinion on the distribution of the relevant states of the world. If this were the case, it should be obvious that different market participants would have (and will have) different probability distributions in their minds and greatly varying discount rates at which they would discount risky future cash flows. Therefore, we would have many different possible prices for a single option (we would probably end up having a different option price for each market participant). However, they could not be considered risk neutral. *Risk neutrality requires that the price of the options is independent of the individual views of each market participant.* The way this is achieved is by the no-arbitrage condition. In other words, the risk-neutral price is independent of the view of the individual market participant because any price different from the risk-neutral price would imply an arbitrage opportunity. Consequently, in the Black–Scholes framework, risk neutrality is guaranteed by the absence of arbitrage, i.e., the risk-neutral price is the only price that prevents arbitrage from taking place.

From a probability point of view, the distribution that is consistent with the risk-neutral price (also called the risk-neutral probability distribution) *is the only distribution such that the risk-neutral price can be expressed as the expected value of the payoff at expiry.* This probability distribution turns out to be completely independent of each market participant's opinion and it is only driven by the risk-neutral condition. The risk-neutral probability distribution should not be seen as a probability distribution assigned by the market. It is nothing more than the probability distribution that, *if used to calculate the expected value of the payoff at expiry,* would exactly result in the risk-neutral price.[17]

---

[16] When we say that pricing an option is not a probabilistic exercise, we mean that the option price is not a weighted average of the option payoffs under various states of the world. Option prices arise instead from arbitrage-free conditions. This will become more obvious when we discuss the binomial tree approach to option pricing.

[17] Perhaps think of it as a probability distribution that can be used to price options if we want to express those option prices as expected values.

To sum up, in the Black–Scholes framework the price of an option is the cost of replicating that option payoff at expiry via trades in the underlying asset. It has to be seen as coupled with a trading strategy (replication via delta hedging) that allows that replication to be implemented. There is a unique probability distribution such that the price of the option can be expressed as the expected value of the payoff at expiry. Even if it does not seem obvious at first glance, there is a two-way correspondence between the price of the option considered as the cost of replicating the payoff and the price of the option considered as the expected value of that payoff under the risk-neutral probability distribution.

6

Implied Volatility and the Greeks

In this chapter, we continue the discussion of the option Greeks that we began in Chapter 5, where we looked at delta. Although it is possible to consider each of the Greeks quantitatively, it is also important to understand intuitively how they operate; to do so we need to describe first the concept of implied volatility.

6.1 IMPLIED VOLATILITY

Volatility has a central role to play in options pricing. In the Black–Scholes framework, volatility is the only input that is not directly observable (as opposed to the price of the underlying asset or the level of the interest rate) but its role is crucial since an over- or underestimation of the actual volatility relative to the implied volatility during the life of the option may have serious consequences in terms of the profit and loss of the options replication via the delta-hedging process or trading in the underlying to replicate the option. So far we have not been very clear on how an option trader will arrive at the volatility input. In some cases, it will be estimated from historical data. In other cases, it may simply be an exogenous input.[1]

In this chapter, we will shed some light on volatility and its significance in the options markets. At the end of this chapter we will show an example of the behaviour of the implied volatility of the EUR/USD FX rate and the S&P 500 Index based on real data.

Before proceeding, let us start from a very simple (and unrealistic but useful) example. Assume, if you will, that we live in a world that has yet to discover the concept of financial options. Assume also that 100 relatively educated financial market participants are in a room being presented with the new concept of a "plain vanilla call option" on a tradable underlying security with which they are familiar, gold for the sake of argument. Now assume that the spot price of gold is $1,600/oz and that, having presented the idea of the call option, we ask those 100 people to start estimating a fair price for an at-the-money call with a 1-year expiry. Each person shows the price that he or she would be willing to pay (bid price) to buy this option, or the price that he or she would require to receive (ask–offer price) to sell it, or both prices at the same time. What we are trying to build here is an example of a very primitive options market. In such a market, we would expect each individual person to show, at least initially, prices based mainly on where they expect gold to be trading when the option expires. In other words, those people who have a very bullish view on gold may be tempted to show an aggressive (i.e., relatively high) bid price for the call option (and a very conservative, low offer price or no offer price at all), whereas those people who believe gold has little chance of increasing in price before the option expires may be willing to offer this option at a low price. This directional stance may be also coupled with some broader risk aversion arguments: given that buying a call option offers downside limited to the premium paid and potentially unlimited

---

[1] There are many ways to forecast future volatility. Most rely in some way on extrapolating past volatility data. The most popular technique is probably the GARCH model and its many extensions. Discussion of the details of GARCH is outside the scope of this book, although the mathematics is relatively straightforward and interested readers should hold little fear in investigating further.

upside, whereas the opposite is true in the case of sale, some may be tempted to show an aggressive bid and/or a more conservative offer just to address these risk aversion concerns. Irrespective of the individual opinions, if we expect this price discovery process to be relatively orderly (i.e., people not offering below somebody else's bid or bidding above somebody else's offer) such that there are no straightforward arbitrage opportunities (i.e., opportunities to earn riskless profit simply crossing inconsistent bid–offer prices), we should come up with a set of bid prices and a set of offer prices such that *the highest bid is lower than the lowest offer* (this will ensure the impossibility of crossing inconsistent bid–offer prices).

At the end of this price discovery process, suppose the highest bid (best bid) for our 1,600 strike call (at-the-money) with 1-year expiry is $120/oz and the lowest offer (best offer) is $130/oz. We have a market price. In other words, we have a price that somebody is willing to pay to buy the option and a price that somebody is asking to receive in order to be willing to sell it.

What may sound like a trivial game can actually lead to very profound insights into option pricing: when getting to our 120–130 bid–offer price for the call option, we did not make any assumption about the process governing the price of the underlying asset nor did we make any assumption about the price of the option itself. What is more, without even involving the concept of volatility of the underlying asset, but simply relying on the directional expectation of the people in the room, we have been able to get to an option price. The obvious question is, given how primitive this option pricing process was, did we converge to *the right option price*? This is where it gets more interesting, as there is no such concept as a "right price" or a "wrong price". Once the inconsistent bids and offers (leading to straightforward arbitrage opportunities) are discarded, all prices are in a certain sense "good prices". The key point to note here is that we have been able to determine a *market price*; a very primitive one, but still a market price. Once this market finds its equilibrium between demand and supply, leading to the 120–130 bid–offer prices, it becomes impossible to identify obvious arbitrage opportunities. The only available choices left to the market participants are to buy the option at the best offer ($130), to sell it at the best bid ($120) or to do absolutely nothing and just wait for the market price to change. Therefore, even in this very primitive market, with just one option and its underlying, we have a market price for this option that excludes any *a priori* arbitrage opportunity.

One may feel very puzzled at this point. Why put in all this effort trying to learn about options and related pricing and hedging, if everything can be solved by a bunch of random relatively well-educated people gathered in a room?

In reality, we need option pricing models, because the financial world is much more complicated. It may be easy to come to some agreement on the market price of an individual option but it would be impossible for "the 100 people in the room" to come up with consistent prices across all securities without the help of more sophisticated models. Also, how would we know how to hedge the risks involved in trading options? In other words, even in our primitive case of the 120–130 bid–offer on the 1-year at-the-money option on gold, it would be very difficult to assess what the level of directional risk is (basically the option delta) arising from trading this option. To derive the delta, we will have to define a model for the dynamic of the underlying asset as well as for the dynamic of the option price. The Black–Scholes framework is exactly that, i.e., it makes assumptions on both the underlying asset and the option price dynamics to evaluate the price of the option consistently.

To sum up, while our "primitive" option price is a legitimate market price, more sophisticated models are required to move forward (i.e., to price a multitude of options in a consistent way and also to evaluate risk appropriately). So, has our primitive option price anything to do with the option price we could calculate within the Black–Scholes framework? Of course, it does. Since both the price of the underlying and the level of the interest rate (in this case we assumed it to be equal to 0) are both directly observable and the strike price and option tenor are assigned, *the only "free" (i.e., not yet assigned) input is the volatility*. We invite you to verify that using the Black–Scholes formula for the price of the call option (assuming a zero interest rate and no convenience yield for gold), the "primitive bid price" of $120 would be obtained assuming a volatility of around 18.8%, whereas the "primitive offer price" of $130 would be obtained assuming a level of volatility of around 20.4%.

As it should be increasingly clear at this stage, we are using the Black–Scholes formula *the other way around*, i.e., we are using it to identify the level of volatility such that the option price retrieved using the formula matches the option price observed in the market. As you can see in the example above, the bid–offer expressed *in price terms* 120–130 has now been translated into a bid–offer expressed *in volatility terms* (18.8–20.4%). From now on, we will refer to the volatility calculated in this way as the *implied volatility, i.e., the level of volatility that is backed out of the Black–Scholes formula using actual options prices trading in the market.*

The trouble is, we cannot invert the Black–Scholes formula analytically, i.e., it is impossible to come up with a closed formula that expresses the volatility as a function of all the other variables (including, obviously, the option price). Therefore, the implied volatility is generally identified via an iterative process of trial and error that allows us to calculate the implied volatility with the desired level of accuracy. A very simple example of this is shown in the spreadsheet "Chapter 6 – Implied Volatility".

What is crucially important about the idea of implied volatility is that it allows us to add an additional dimension when thinking about the price of a derivative, opening the door to the concept of *volatility trading*. So, from now on, we should think about any option not only as a way to obtain a certain payoff depending on the price of the underlying asset but also as way to take a position on the implied volatility derived by an option price itself, or as a way to take a position on the potential divergence between implied volatility and likely future realized volatility (at this stage it is useful to recall the example described in section 5.13.2 where we showed the potentially big replication error that can occur when the volatility used to price and delta hedge an option is materially different from the volatility of the future path of the underlying asset). These fundamental concepts will be clarified in more detail in section 6.8, once the basic ideas about sensitivities of options prices have been discussed. At this stage, we close the section with a very common aphorism about implied volatility that almost every option trader would have heard. "The implied volatility is the wrong number that, used in the wrong formula, gives the right price for the option."

6.2 THE GREEKS

Generally speaking, the Greeks are the sensitivities of the option price with respect to each of the variables used to calculate the price itself. In the following sections we will describe the most common Greeks and the dynamics that they should be expected to follow.

6.3 DELTA AND ITS DYNAMICS

6.3.1 Definition and calculation

In Chapter 5, we discussed the option replication strategy. At the centre of this is the concept of option delta. Delta is the first derivative in calculus of the price of an option with respect to the price of the underlying security.

Before going into further detail, we should recap some of our previous observations on delta presented in section 5.5.

- The delta of the underlying itself is 1. This is essentially a trivial consequence of the definition of delta, since the first derivative of a variable with respect to itself is clearly equal to 1.
- The delta of a long plain vanilla call is within a range of 0 to 1.
- The delta of a long plain vanilla put is within a range of −1 to 0.

It is now time to introduce some jargon. An option position is said to be *long delta* if it generates a profit in the case of an upward movement in the price of the underlying security and a loss in the case of a downward movement. By contrast, an option position is said to be *short delta* if it is set to generate a loss in the case of an upward movement in the price of the underlying and a profit in the case of downward movement.

Analytically it can be shown that the delta of a plain vanilla call is equal to $N(d_1)$ and the delta of a plain vanilla put is $N(d_1) - 1$, where the function N is, as noted in section 5.4, the cumulative probability distribution function for a standardized normal variable and where:

$$d_1 = \frac{\ln{(S/K)} + (r + \sigma^2/2)(T - t)}{\sigma\sqrt{T - t}}$$

In the formula above, S is the spot price of the underlying asset, K is the strike price of the option, r is the interest rate (assuming continuous compounding), σ is the volatility and $T - t$ is the residual life of the option (expressed in years).

In Figure 6.1, we plot the delta of a generic call option as a function of the price of the underlying security. We have assumed a plain vanilla call option with a strike price equal to \$100, a 6-month expiry, written on a generic non-dividend paying stock. Interest rates are assumed to be 0 and implied volatility is set equal to 20%. As the chart clearly shows, the delta is a monotonically increasing function of the price of the underlying; for a plain vanilla call option, its values are within a range of 0 (for out-of-the-money options) to +1 (for in-the-money options).

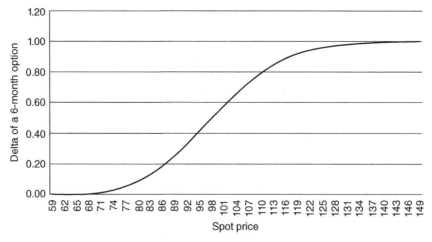

Figure 6.1   Call option delta as a function of the underlying price

6.3.2   The dynamics of delta

In this section, we will present, both intuitively and qualitatively, some key conclusions regarding the sensitivity of delta to changes in the main pricing parameters. The sensitivity of delta relative to the price of the underlying (briefly introduced in the section 6.3.1) will be analysed thoroughly in the section 6.4 on gamma (dDelta /dSpot) but, first, let us consider how delta changes over time.

1. The change in delta with respect to the time to expiry

In general, all else being equal, the delta of a plain vanilla option that is in-the-money will tend towards 1 (for a call option) or towards −1 (for a put option) as the expiration date approaches. On the other hand, all else being equal, the delta of a plain vanilla option that is out-of-the-money (either a call or put) will converge to 0 as the expiration date approaches. This result can be easily tested empirically but it will be useful to appreciate the dynamics intuitively.

Let us think about it this way. We know that, during the life of the option, the delta will be within a range of 0 to 1 (in the case of a call option) and −1 to 0 (in the case of a put option). We also know that, at expiry, the delta of a call option tends to 1 if the option is in-the-money (i.e., if the option is likely to be exercised). At this point, the holder of the option buys the underlying asset at the strike price. Therefore, owning the option is equivalent to owning the underlying. On the other hand, the delta will tend towards 0 if the option is out-of-the-money. In this case, the option will not be exercised and, consequently, there will be no dependency of the option price on the price of the underlying security. If we think about the evolution of delta over time in these terms, it is not difficult to see the convergence to 1 in the case of in-the-money call options and convergence to 0 in the case of out-of-the-money call options. The same analysis applies to a put option, although, in that case, the delta tends to −1 in the case of in-the-money options.

Figure 6.2 represents delta as a function of the spot price of the underlying for different expiries (volatility is assumed constant and equal to 20%). On the right-hand side of the chart,

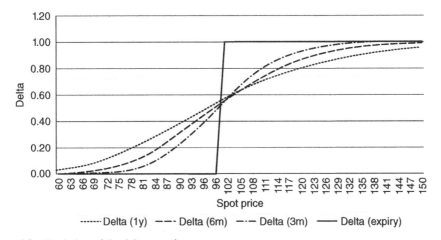

Figure 6.2   Evolution of the delta over time

we observe the behaviour of the delta for *in-the-money* options (i.e., where the spot price is higher than the strike price), while the left-hand side of the chart shows how the delta changes in the case of *out-of-the-money* options (i.e., spot price lower than the strike price). Note that, on the expiration date (or very close to it), the delta tends to assume a discontinuity (as the solid line shows). This is due to the fact that, at the expiry date or sufficiently close to it, even small variations in the price of the underlying asset around the strike price can cause the option to change from in-the-money to out-of-the-money or from out-of-the-money to in-the-money. Consequently, it is possible to observe sharp swings in the delta as the "moneyness" of the option changes from in-the-money to out-of-the-money and vice versa.

2. The change in delta with respect to implied volatility

The analysis of the sensitivity of the delta of an option with respect to the implied volatility used to price the option is a little more complicated than the analysis of the sensitivity with respect to time, but not unduly so.

Let us begin with an example of an *out-of-the-money* option with a *low volatility* underlying. Due to the low volatility, the probability that the underlying price will cross the strike before the expiry is relatively low. Intuitively, at least locally, we should therefore not expect to see a strong dependency of the option price to the price of the underlying. In other words, we should expect a relatively low delta. If the volatility then starts to increase, however, we would expect a higher probability of the option expiring in-the-money. This increases the dependency of the option price to the price of the underlying, i.e., it increases the delta of the option.

What about the case of an in-the-money option? In this case, we can see that the opposite is true. For an in-the-money option, low volatility increases the chance of the underlying price staying above the strike. In other words, it increases the probability that the option will be exercised, thereby increasing the delta of the option, other things being equal. Of course, as is probably obvious by now, if the volatility then increases, there will be a higher chance of the underlying dropping below the strike price prior to expiration, and therefore reducing the delta of the option.

Figure 6.3 summarizes this first for out-of-the-money (OTM) options (top) and second for in-the-money (ITM) options (bottom).

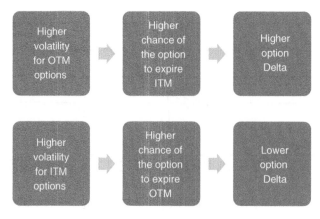

Figure 6.3   Change in delta with respect to implied volatility

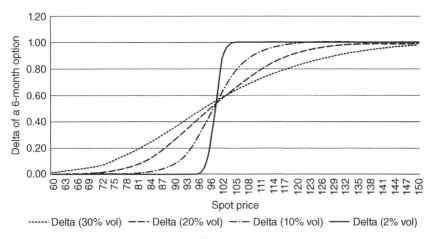

Figure 6.4   Option delta as a function of volatility

We can, of course, display graphically the sensitivity of the delta to volatility for both in-the-money and out-of-the-money options. Figure 6.4 shows the delta of a 6-month call option with strike price of 100 for different levels of volatility. As before, the right-hand side of the chart shows the behaviour of the delta for in-the-money options (i.e., spot price higher than the strike price), whereas the left-hand side shows how the delta changes with respect to volatility in the case of out-of-the-money options (i.e., spot price lower than the strike price).

Figure 6.4 is actually very similar to that showing the sensitivity of the delta to the time to expiration of the option. For example, we can see that higher volatility produces the same effect as increasing the time to the expiry. In both cases, the chances of an out-of-the-money option ending in-the-money will increase and delta will therefore rise.

6.4   GAMMA AND ITS DYNAMICS

Delta is clearly an important feature of an option since it expresses the link between the option's price changes and movements in the option's underlying. However, delta is far from constant and changes readily as the price of the underlying changes. As a consequence, option traders are typically also interested in the relationship between the delta and the underlying price, i.e., the second derivative of the option price with respect to the price of the underlying. This is generally referred to as the gamma of the option.

In general, gamma can be seen either as the first derivative of the delta with respect to the price of the underlying (dDelta/dSpot) or as the second derivative of the price of the option with respect to the price of the underlying (d²Option/dSpot²).

In a sense, gamma is therefore a measure of convexity, since it measures how the first-order sensitivity, the delta, changes with respect to the price of the underlying asset itself or the speed of the changes in delta as the underlying moves.

Although the proof is outside the scope of this book, we would note that, analytically, it can be shown that the formula for the gamma of a plain vanilla call or put option is equal to:

$$\frac{N'(d_1)}{S\sigma\sqrt{T-t}}$$

where:

$$d_1 = \frac{\ln(S/K) + (r + \sigma^2/2)(T - t)}{\sigma\sqrt{T - t}}$$

$$N'(x) = \frac{1}{\sqrt{2\pi}}e^{-x^2/2}$$

and the variables are defined in section 6.3.1.

Before describing in detail how gamma evolves over time and with respect to changes in the spot price or in volatility, it is probably useful to spend some time explaining intuitively what being long or short gamma actually means in practice.

First, let us think about a long gamma position. We begin with an option trader who is long a call option and short the underlying asset, such that the overall directional exposure, i.e., the delta, is 0 (or as close to 0 as is possible). The trader is long the call and he is also long gamma. This is probably not obvious but bear with us. As the price of the underlying moves up or down, the delta of the option will change according to the gamma. Since we are looking at a call option, the option's delta will increase as the underlying price rises. At the same time, however, the delta of the short position in the underlying asset stays the same.[2]

The net result of a rise in the price of the underlying is an increase in the overall net delta of the trader's position. The delta exposure of the option increases but the delta exposure coming from the short position in the underlying remains the same. Therefore, as the price of underlying goes up, the overall delta exposure of the trader's position increases. In order to get back to a delta-neutral position, the trader must sell more of the underlying. This can be done *at the higher price.*

What would have happened if the price of the underlying had gone down instead of up? As the price goes down, the delta of the option decreases. Again, however, the delta of the short position in the underlying stays the same. The net result of a drop in the price of the underlying is a reduction in the net delta of the overall position. To get back to a delta-neutral position, the trader must buy more of the underlying asset, but, obviously, *at a lower price.*

What is hopefully clear from this example is that an option trader who is long a call option (and delta hedged with a short position in the underlying) seems always to be "on the right side" whenever the market moves. If the price of the underlying goes up, the trader will have to *sell* the underlying asset (at the *higher* price) and if the price of the underlying goes down, the trader will have to *buy* the underlying asset (at the *lower* price). The option trader is "buying low and selling high" (generally a desirable position to have) thanks to the long gamma exposure that arises from being long a call option (and short the underlying asset).

Obviously there must be a drawback in what seems otherwise to be a win–win situation for the trader. We will come back to this in detail in section 6.6.2 but, for now, we note that it has something to do with the decline in the time value of the option experienced by the trader as he or she holds the long position in the option towards expiry and/or the fact that he or she paid premium in order to be long the option in the first place.

Figure 6.5 summarizes the examples that we just described above. Recall that the trader is *long gamma* in both cases.

---

[2] The delta on a long position in the underlying asset is always 1 and so the gamma implied by a long position in the underlying is 0 by definition. The delta on a short position in the underlying asset is clearly always −1. Hence, the gamma implied by a short position in the underlying asset is also 0.

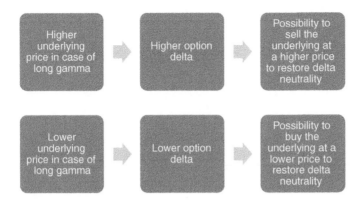

Figure 6.5   Long gamma exposure

What if, instead of being long a call option, the trader was long a put? In this case, the trader needs to be long the underlying asset in order to delta hedge his exposure. We leave it to you to consider the exposure inherent in the case of a long put option (and a consequent long position in the underlying asset to hedge the overall delta exposure) and then to verify that the trader will still be in a "buy low and sell high" position.

In fact, it should be possible to demonstrate that, in order to be in the advantageous position of being able to "buy low and sell high", it is not the particular type of option (call or put) that is important but whether the option trader is long or short an option.

Now, let us assume that the trader is short an option. The trader, who is short a call (or put), will try to maintain the overall delta position relatively close to 0 but, in this case, he or she will always be "on the wrong side" of the market. Whenever the price of the underlying goes up, the trader will have to *buy* the underlying asset (at a *higher* price) and when the price of the underlying goes down, the trader will have to *sell* (at a *lower* price). The option trader ends up having to "buy high and sell low" thanks to the short gamma exposure, which arises from being short the option (call or put), and the desire to hedge the delta. In this case, the trader appears to be in a less advantageous position than before but he or she is compensated by the fact that the short option position is losing time value with the passage of time (or that the trader earned premium at the outset from selling the option). We will return to this in section 6.6.2.

Figure 6.6 summarizes the example that we just described. Recall that the trader is now *short gamma* since he or she has sold the option.

1. The sensitivity of gamma with respect to the price of the underlying

Gamma is sensitive to the price of the underlying. You might want to think of this sensitivity as, basically, a third derivative of the option price with respect to the price of the underlying. Gamma tends towards 0 as the underlying price diverges from the strike. Gamma is maximized when the price of the underlying (or more accurately, the forward price of the underlying) is close to the strike price.

Consider why this might be the case. As the underlying price rises, in the case of the call, or falls, in the case of the put, the option becomes more and more "in-the-money". Consequently, its delta will tend towards $+1$ in the case of the call or -1 in the case of the put.

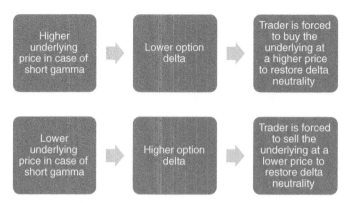

Figure 6.6   Short gamma exposure

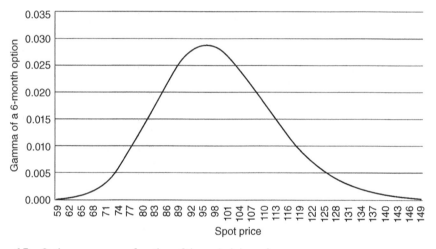

Spot price

Figure 6.7   Option gamma as a function of the underlying price

If the option is heavily in-the-money, the delta will not change much irrespective of the change in the price of the underlying. The delta has to stay close to +1 or −1 depending on whether it is a put or a call. But if the delta is not changing much, then its rate of change must be close to 0. In other words, gamma is close to 0. The same argument can be applied for deeply out-of-the-money options. In this case, irrespective of whether we are looking at a call or a put, the delta will stabilize close to 0. Changes in delta will be strictly limited and so gamma must be close to 0.

The gamma of a vanilla call or put cannot assume negative values and, since it converges to 0 as the price of the underlying increases or decreases, it is easy to think about a sort of bell-shaped function (Figure 6.7).[3]

---

[3] That the gamma function is bell shaped can also be determined by observing that gamma is the first derivative of delta and that the functional form of delta is represented by a *cumulative distribution of a normally distributed random variable*. Since the derivative of the cumulative distribution of a function is the function itself, then the shape of the gamma function has to be the normal distribution.

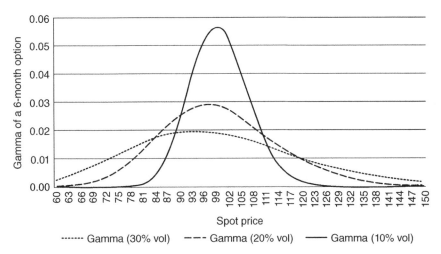

Figure 6.8   Option gamma as a function of volatility

2. The sensitivity of gamma with respect to volatility

What about the sensitivity of the option gamma with respect to the level of implied volatility that has been used to price the option? Consider the example of an out-of-the-money option with an underlying asset price that is exhibiting low volatility. In this case, due to the low volatility, the probability that the price of the underlying will cross the strike price before the expiry date is relatively low. Consequently, we should not expect to see a strong sensitivity of the delta of the option to changes in the price of the underlying asset. In other words, we should expect a relatively low gamma. As the volatility starts to increase, however, we should expect a higher probability that the option will expire in-the-money, thereby increasing the sensitivity of the option delta to the price of the underlying asset. In other words, gamma should increase. As volatility changes, gamma is expected to change and gamma rebalancing may be required at different levels of volatility (Figure 6.8). The opposite is true for at-the-money or close to at-the-money options, as Figure 6.8 shows. In this case, the lower the volatility, the lower is the probability that the option will flip from in-the-money to out-of-the-money or vice versa; therefore, in a low volatility regime, the gamma will be higher because any change of the price of the underlying will trigger bigger change of the delta.

3. The sensitivity of gamma with respect to time to expiration

Given the discussions on delta in section 6.3.2 and how it changes with the passage of time, it should be relatively easy to derive, at least intuitively, how gamma evolves as the expiry date approaches. In general, we can say that, all else being equal, the gamma of a plain vanilla option will always tend to 0 (both for a call and put option). If the option at expiry is in-the-money, its exposure will be the same as a (long or short) position in the underlying asset. This carries no gamma exposure since the delta is "sticky" at 1. On the other hand, if the option at expiry is out-of-the-money, its delta will be "sticky" around 0 and so there is no gamma exposure. So, in the case of in-the-money or out-of-the-money options, the option gamma will tend to disappear as expiry approaches. A more delicate situation occurs if the option happens to be

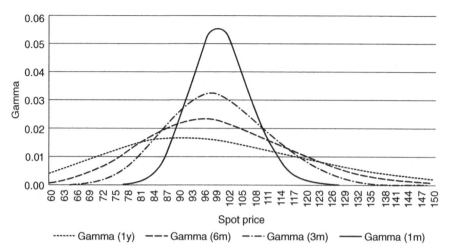

Figure 6.9   Evolution of the gamma over time

right at-the-money very near to the expiry date. In this case, a very unstable gamma is likely to be observed. For small increases or decreases in the price of the underlying, the option delta will quickly converge to 1 or 0 (in the case of the call) or to −1 to 0 (in the case of the put). At this point, when gamma is highly unstable, traders should be careful not to overstate the importance of the gamma figures as they can rise to high values but are subject to very sharp changes in a relatively short timeframe.

Figure 6.9 depicts the evolution of the gamma over time for both in-the-money and out-of-the-money options.

6.5   VEGA AND ITS DYNAMICS

Vega is the first derivative of the option price with respect to the volatility of the underlying asset.[4]

Before we discuss the key analytical results, let us consider some of the main features that we observe:

- Vega of the underlying asset price itself is always 0. Volatility is a measure of the dispersion of the asset price. Volatility is "caused" by changes in the asset price. The asset price is not "caused" by the level of volatility.
- The vega of a plain vanilla call option is always positive and so is the vega of a plain vanilla put.
- The vega of a deeply in-the-money-option (where its delta will be 1 or very close to 1) or a deeply out-of-the-money option (where its delta will be 0 or very close to 0) will be 0 or very close to 0.

As we have already done for the other Greeks, let us introduce the relevant jargon. A position is said to be *long vega* if it generates a profit in the case of a rise in the volatility

---

[4] It is worth pointing out at this stage that the concept of vega is somewhat in conflict with the assumption underlying the Black–Scholes model that, as discussed, assumes constant volatility. However, as we will see, vega is a crucial concept.

of the underlying asset and a loss in the case of a decline in the volatility of the underlying. Conversely, a position is said to be *short vega* if it generates a loss in the case of a rise in the volatility of the underlying and a profit in case of a decline.

Analytically, it can be shown that the vega of a plain vanilla call or put is equal to:

$$S\sqrt{T-t}N'(d_1)$$

where:

$$d_1 = \frac{\ln(S/K) + (r + \sigma^2/2)(T-t)}{\sigma\sqrt{T-t}}$$

$$N'(x) = \frac{1}{\sqrt{2\pi}}e^{-x^2/2}$$

and the variables are defined (as usual) as in section 6.3.1.

The vega calculated from these equations measures the change in the price of the option for a 100 percentage points change in the volatility (say from 25 to 125%). It is much more common to express vega as the sensitivity of the option price to a 1 percentage point change in the level of volatility (say from 25 to 26%), which requires one to divide the vega obtained from the formula above by 100. In any case, one should use care when calculating vega to avoid any confusion about the scale.

1. The sensitivity of vega with respect to the price of the underlying

As we pointed out, the vega of a deeply in-the-money option (where its delta will be 1 or very close to 1) or a deeply out-of-the-money option (where its delta will be 0 or very close to 0) will be 0 or very close to it. The logic is similar to that already described for gamma. As the price of the underlying asset increases (decreases) and a call (put) option becomes more and more in-the-money, the price of the option will increase and get closer and closer to its intrinsic value. If the option is sufficiently in-the-money, its vega will stabilize at levels converging on 0 since the behaviour of the option price converges on the behaviour of the underlying asset itself. As we noted before, however, the underlying asset has no vega exposure. Consequently, as the option gets more and more in-the-money, it will lose its sensitivity to volatility (hence the convergence of vega to 0). The same logic applies to deeply out-of-the-money options. If the option is sufficiently out-of-the-money, its vega will again stabilize at levels converging on 0 (both for call and put options) as the time value of the option will disappear and the option will get more and more worthless. In this case, the option loses its sensitivity to all the various pricing inputs, including volatility. Figure 6.10 summarizes this discussion. As we can observe, similarly to gamma, vega also has the bell-shaped characteristic of the normal distribution.

2. The sensitivity of vega with respect to the time to expiry

In general, we can say that, all else being equal, the vega of a plain vanilla option will tend to 0 (for both call and put options) as expiry approaches. If the option at expiry is in-the-money, its exposure will be the same as a (long or short) position in the underlying asset which, as we know, carries no vega exposure. On the other hand, if the option at expiry is out-of-the-money, its value is going to disappear (and so will its vega). So, in the case of in-the-money options and out-of-the-money options, the option vega will tend to 0 as expiry approaches.

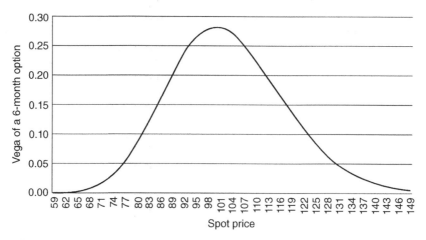

Figure 6.10   Option vega as a function of the underlying price

The general evolution of vega over time can be seen in Figure 6.11 (where we have the same 100 strike price, a volatility of 25% and zero interest rates). When the option expiry is still far away (say 1 year), the vega shows "fat tails". As the expiry approaches, however, the tails of the vega function get thinner and the dynamic that we observed (i.e., the vega converging on 0 for deep in-the-money or out-of-the-money options) becomes increasingly stronger. In other words, the effect of the reduction in the time to expiration on vega is to reduce progressively the range of prices within which changes in volatility have meaningful effects. For long-dated options, not only will vega tend to be bigger but its effects are observable even for large deviations of the price of the underlying asset from the strike price. As expiry approaches, however, vega starts to shrink considerably and its effects are meaningful only to the extent that the price of the underlying asset stays relatively close to the strike price.

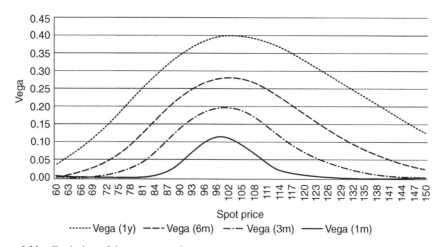

Figure 6.11   Evolution of the vega over time

3. *The sensitivity of vega with respect to volatility of the underlying*

The sensitivity of the option vega with respect to the volatility that has been used to price the option is a little more complicated to explain although it is clearly not impossible.

Start with the example of an out-of-the-money option on an asset whose price is exhibiting low volatility. Due to the low volatility, if the option is sufficiently out-of-the-money, the probability that the underlying price will cross the strike price before expiry is relatively low, causing the option price to be very low too. Therefore, at least locally, we should not expect to see a strong sensitivity of the option price to changes in the volatility of the underlying (i.e., we should expect a relatively low vega). If the volatility starts to increase, however, we should expect a higher probability of the option expiring in-the-money, thereby increasing the sensitivity of the option price to the underlying volatility itself, i.e., increasing the vega of the option.

What about the case of an in-the-money option with low volatility? Similar to the out-of-the-money case that we just described due to the low volatility, the probability of the underlying price crossing the strike price before expiry is relatively low. The delta of the option, in this case, will tend to be relatively close to 1 and, therefore, at least locally, we should not expect to see a strong sensitivity of the option price with respect to the volatility of the underlying (i.e., we should again expect a relatively low vega) since the option price is expected to behave very similarly to the price of the underlying. If the volatility starts to increase, however, we should expect a higher probability of the underlying crossing the strike price, thereby increasing the chances of the option expiring out-of-the-money. This dynamic will tend to increase the sensitivity of the option price to the underlying volatility itself, i.e., to increase the vega of the option.

To understand what happens in the case of at-the-money or close to at-the-money options, it may be useful to take a look at the first derivative of vega with respect to the volatility term σ. From the functional form of vega presented above, it can be seen that:

$$\frac{d\text{Vega}}{d\sigma} = S\sqrt{T-t}N'(d_1)\frac{d_1 d_2}{\sigma} = \text{Vega}\frac{d_1 d_2}{\sigma}$$

where the variables are defined (as usual) as in section 6.3.1.

As vega is always a positive quantity, it can be seen that the only way for dVega/dVol to assume 0 values is if either d_1 or d_2 are equal to 0. Recalling the expressions for d_1 and d_2, we can show that to get d_1 equal to 0 we need:

$$\ln(S/K) = -(r + \sigma^2/2)(T-t)$$

and to get d_2 equal to 0 we need:

$$\ln(S/K) = (r + \sigma^2/2)(T-t)$$

Assuming an option that is priced with 20% volatility and 6 months to expiry, ignoring for the time being the impact of interest rates, we get d_1 equal to 0 when:

$$\ln(S/K) = -0.01$$

and we get d_2 equal to 0 when:

$$\ln(S/K) = 0.01$$

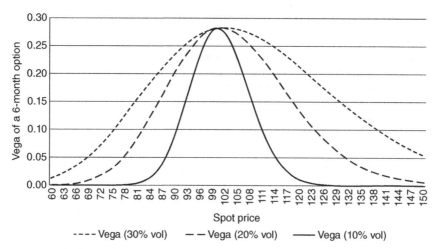

Figure 6.12   Option vega as a function of volatility

Consequently, for typical values of volatility and when the option is not too far from expiry, dVega/dVol is 0 when the spot price of the underlying is not too far from the strike (1% away in logarithmic terms in our example), i.e., when the option is close to at-the-money.

To sum up, we can complete our analysis by saying that out-of-the-money vanilla options (both calls and puts) show a positive sensitivity for vega with respect to volatility (i.e., positive dVega/dVol, known as positive volatility convexity), whereas for at-the-money options this sensitivity is very close to 0 (i.e., neutral dVega/dVol or neutral volatility convexity).

Figure 6.12 summarizes these findings. When the option is not too far from being at-the-money, the magnitude of vega is not particularly affected by the level of volatility. For in-the-money or out-of-the-money options, the vega profile for different levels of volatility will diverge sharply (only to converge again when the options become really deeply in-the-money or out-of-the-money).

Option traders should not underestimate the importance of the dynamics that we just described, since it relates to the second derivative of the option price with respect to volatility. Being a second derivative, it is basically a measure of convexity and will show how much vega is expected to change when volatility itself moves. This is a really crucial variable for a trader intending to keep a specific overall vega exposure. As volatility moves, the overall vega will change and a vega rebalancing will likely be required at different levels of volatility.

The Black–Scholes framework, assuming constant volatility, might not be adequate to capture this second-order effect that, from time to time, has proven to be potentially very disruptive to hedging activity. We will go back to this when discussing more sophisticated pricing models that attempt to take this into account.

6.6   THETA AND ITS DYNAMICS

6.6.1   Definition and calculation

The theta of an option is the first derivative of its price with respect to the time to expiry, i.e., how the price of the option changes just for the passage of time.

Before we discuss the key properties of theta, let us highlight some of the main features that we observe:

- The theta of the underlying asset is always 0. Its price clearly shows no dependency with respect to time.
- The theta of a plain vanilla call is negative and so is the theta of a plain vanilla put. If you are long a simple call or a put, the value of that option position will fall from one day to the next if everything else remains the same.
- The theta of a deeply in-the-money option (where its delta will be 1 or very close to 1) or a deeply out-of-the-money option (where its delta will be 0 or very close to 0) will be 0 or very close to it.

Again, some typical jargon. A position is said to be long theta if it generates a profit as time elapses, i.e., if nothing changes, then some profit will be registered day after day simply as a result of the passage of time. Conversely, a position is said to be short theta if it generates a loss as the time elapses, i.e., if nothing changes, some loss will be incurred with the passage of time.

Analytically, it can be shown that the theta of a plain vanilla call is equal to:

$$-\frac{SN'(d_1)\sigma}{2\sqrt{T-t}} - rKe^{-r(T-t)}N(d_2)$$

where, as usual:

$$d_1 = \frac{\ln(S/K) + (r + \sigma^2/2)(T-t)}{\sigma\sqrt{T-t}}$$

$$d_2 = \frac{\ln(S/K) + (r - \sigma^2/2)(T-t)}{\sigma\sqrt{T-t}}$$

$$N'(x) = \frac{1}{\sqrt{2\pi}}e^{-x^2/2}$$

and the variables are defined (as usual) as in section 6.3.1.

The theta of a plain vanilla put is equal to:

$$-\frac{SN'(d_1)\sigma}{2\sqrt{T-t}} + rKe^{-r(T-t)}N(-d_2)$$

where d_1, d_2, the function N' and the variables are defined as above.

From these equations, it should be possible to verify that the theta of a call option is always negative (as it is calculated as the sum of two negative numbers) and the theta of a put is likely to be negative, unless $rKe^{-r(T-t)}N(-d_2)$ is greater than $(SN'(d_1)\sigma)/(2\sqrt{(T-t)})$ (which is unlikely especially if the level of interest rates is low).

In the formulae above, the calculated theta will be an annual number. The most common way to represent theta is with respect to the passage of one calendar day (in which case the number obtained by the formula will have to be divided by 365) or one business day (in which case it will have to be divided by the number of business days in a year, typically assumed to be between 250 and 260).

Before we discuss the sensitivity of theta with respect to the various option pricing factors (i.e., the price of the underlying, volatility and time to expiration), it is worth recalling the section 6.4 on gamma and the "buy low, sell high" feature that is typical of long gamma positions and the "buy high, sell low" in the case of short gamma positions. At that time, we described the long gamma position as a potentially desirable one but noted that there has to be a price to pay in order to enter a long gamma position. As we anticipated, that "price" is the theta. At the same time, we also pointed out that the theta can be also seen as the price required by whoever takes a short gamma exposure to offset the not so desirable "buy high sell low" feature of that exposure.

6.6.2   Gamma versus theta: An equilibrium at the heart of option pricing

In this section, we will use a Taylor's series expansion to investigate the sensitivities of the price of a portfolio P (which we will shortly specify) with respect to the price of the underlying asset (S) and with respect to time elapsing (t).[5] The portfolio P is formed by a combination of a call option (C) and some quantity of the underlying asset itself. For the time being, we will assume constant volatility σ. The Taylor's series expansion gives us the following result for the portfolio P:

$$\Delta P = \frac{\partial P}{\partial S}\Delta S + \frac{\partial P}{\partial t}\Delta t + \frac{1}{2}\frac{\partial^2 P}{\partial S^2}\Delta S^2 + \frac{1}{2}\frac{\partial^2 P}{\partial t^2}\Delta t^2 + \frac{\partial^2 P}{\partial S \partial t}\Delta S \Delta t + \cdots$$

The expansion above allows us to express the change in the value of the portfolio, ΔP, as a function of the Greeks (delta $\partial C/\partial S$, theta $\partial C/\partial t$ and gamma $(\partial^2 C)/(\partial S^2)$) assuming small variation in the price of the underlying, ΔS, over a small time interval, Δt. Ignoring the terms Δt^2 and $\Delta t\,\Delta S$ (which are generally very small), we are left with:

$$\Delta P \cong \frac{\partial P}{\partial S}\Delta S + \frac{\partial P}{\partial t}\Delta t + \frac{1}{2}\frac{\partial^2 P}{\partial S^2}\Delta S^2$$

Assuming that we keep the portfolio delta hedged by owning the appropriate quantity of the underlying asset (i.e., making the term $\partial P/\partial S$ equal to 0 for the whole portfolio), we have:

$$\Delta P \cong \frac{\partial P}{\partial t}\Delta t + \frac{1}{2}\frac{\partial^2 P}{\partial S^2}\Delta S^2$$

So, we have a delta-hedged portfolio and we ask ourselves what is the condition on ΔS such that the value of the portfolio does not change over one unit of time (say, one business day)? We can rewrite the previous expression assuming that $\Delta P = 0$:

$$\frac{\partial P}{\partial t}\Delta t + \frac{1}{2}\frac{\partial^2 P}{\partial S^2}\Delta S^2 \cong 0$$

This can be written as:

$$\text{Theta } \Delta t + \frac{1}{2}\text{ Gamma } \Delta S^2 \cong 0$$

We arrived at this equation by making a couple of crucial assumptions. First, that the portfolio was delta hedged. Second, we assumed that the value of the portfolio did not change

---

[5] Hopefully, you will remember Taylor's expansion from your high school mathematics. If not, there are plenty of online resources devoted to it, especially on YouTube. For example, http://www.youtube.com/watch?v=jjltTORF2Jg.

with the passage of one business day. For this to be true, the condition above needs to hold. Now, this will be a special case but this simplified equation does suggest that theta and gamma somehow work in opposite directions.

Let us now replace theta and gamma with their respective analytical Black–Scholes expressions; we will assume a zero interest rate for simplicity. We can solve for the value of ΔS that keeps the value of the (delta-hedged) portfolio unchanged after one business day (we will assume 252 business days in 1 year). Replacing theta and gamma, we have:

$$-\frac{SN'(d_1)\sigma}{2\sqrt{T-t}}\frac{1}{252} + \frac{1}{2}\frac{N'(d_1)}{S\sigma\sqrt{T-t}}\Delta S^2 \cong 0$$

From which we obtain:

$$\Delta S^2 \cong \frac{\dfrac{SN'(d_1)\sigma}{2\sqrt{T-t}}\dfrac{1}{252}}{\dfrac{1}{2}\dfrac{N'(d_1)}{S\sigma\sqrt{T-t}}}$$

This can be simplified to:

$$\Delta S^2 \cong \frac{S^2\sigma^2}{252}$$

or, taking the square root of both sides:

$$\frac{\Delta S}{S} \cong \frac{\sigma}{\sqrt{252}}$$

The term $\Delta S/S$ can be seen as the relative change of the price of the underlying asset (basically the percentage change in the price of the underlying asset). This last expression provides us with a very important insight related to the relative change in the underlying price that is required for the gamma effect (the "buy high, sell low" effect in the case of short gamma or the "buy low, sell high" effect in the case of long gamma) to be balanced by the effect of theta over one business day.

As a first approximation we can say that if the annualized volatility, σ, is roughly equal to 16%, then the percentage change in the price of the underlying asset prices that balances theta and gamma over one business day is around 1%.

What does this mean in practice? First, it suggests that, from a long gamma perspective (say we are long an option priced using 16% volatility), we need *at least* a 1% change in the price of the underlying over one business day for the gamma effect ("buy low, sell high" in this case) to offset the negative theta that we will incur over that business day. Conversely, from the short gamma perspective (say we are short the option priced using 16% volatility), we need *no more than* a 1% change in the price of the underlying over each business day for the positive theta contribution to be offset by the negative impact of the gamma effect ("buy high, sell low" in this case).

For any given business day, the quantity $\Delta S/S\sqrt{252}$ can be thought of as the "annualized realized volatility" for that particular business day. The quantity, σ, can obviously be seen as the level of volatility implied for that particular option. The condition $\Delta S/S \cong \sigma/\sqrt{252}$ is therefore equivalent to saying that, for the theta and the gamma effects to be balanced over a given business day, the realized volatility registered that day has to be approximately equal to the implied volatility used when pricing the option. If the realized volatility is higher than the implied volatility, the trader with a long gamma exposure will gain. Conversely, a lower level of realized volatility compared with the implied volatility will be beneficial to the trader with a short gamma exposure. Of course, in making such generic statements, we need to remember the assumptions that both the long and the short gamma traders are keeping their respective portfolios delta neutral continuously.

At this point we invite the reader to revisit the spreadsheet introduced in Chapter 5 (Chapter 5 – Option replication) which shows the effect of having a realized volatility materially different from the implied volatility used to price and to revalue the option.

6.6.3   Dynamics of theta

1. The sensitivity of theta with respect to the price of the underlying

Similar to the situation with gamma and vega, the effect of theta will tend to 0 as the underlying price diverges from the strike price and will be maximized when the price of the underlying (or, more accurately, the forward price of the underlying) is at the strike price. Again, from an intuitive point of view and ignoring the impact of the interest rates, it is not all that difficult to see why this should be the case. As the underlying price increases (or decreases) and a call (or put) option becomes more and more in-the-money, the price of the options will increase and get closer and closer to the intrinsic price, reducing the time value left in the option. Thus, if the call (put) option is sufficiently in-the-money, its theta will stabilize at levels around 0 as the option price will lose its sensitivity to the time to expiry.

The same logic applies to deep out-of-the-money options. If the call (put) option is sufficiently out-of-the-money, its theta will again stabilize at levels at or close to 0 (for both call and put options) as the time value of the option will disappear and the option price itself will lose its sensitivity to the time to expiry.

Similarly to what we observed in the case of the gamma, since theta cannot assume positive values (the time value of an option cannot be negative) and it converges to 0 as the price of the underlying either increases or decreases, it is natural to expect a sort of bell-shaped function, as shown in Figure 6.13. Note that, in Figures 6.13–6.15, the theta is measured with respect to one business day, assuming 252 business days per year.

2. The sensitivity of theta with respect to the volatility of the underlying

What about the sensitivity of theta with respect to the volatility that has been used to price the option? Not surprisingly, this will be very similar to the analysis we did for gamma. We will start with an example of an out-of-the-money option on an underlying asset exhibiting low volatility. Due to the low volatility, the probability of the underlying price crossing the strike price before expiry is relatively low. We should expect to see a very low time value for the option and, hence, a very low option price, since the intrinsic value of the out-of-the-money option is equal to 0. Therefore, we would expect a low sensitivity of the option price with respect to the time to expiry (i.e., we should expect a relatively low theta). If the volatility starts to increase, however, we should expect a higher probability of the option expiring in-the-money, thereby increasing the time value of the option and the sensitivity of its price relative to the time to expiry, i.e., increasing the theta of the option. As the volatility moves, the overall theta is expected to change and re-hedging may become necessary.

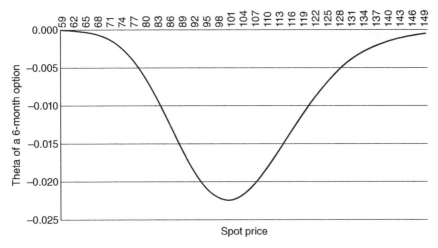

Figure 6.13   Option theta as a function of the underlying price

The same logic applies to in-the-money options. When the volatility is low, the probability of the underlying price crossing the strike before the expiry date (causing the option to expire out-of-the-money) is relatively low. Hence, at least locally, we should expect to see a very low time value for the option (as the option price will be approximately equal to its intrinsic value) and therefore a low dependency of the option price with respect to the time to expiry (i.e., a relatively low theta). If the volatility starts to increase, however, we should expect a higher probability of the option expiring out-of-the-money, increasing the time value of the option and therefore the sensitivity of its price to the time to expiry, i.e., increasing the theta of the option. Finally, for in-the-money options, as the volatility moves the overall theta is expected to change with the possible consequent need for a potential re-hedging. Figure 6.14 summarizes these conclusions (as usual for both in-the-money and out-of-the-money options).

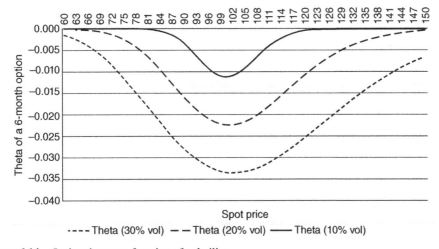

Figure 6.14   Option theta as a function of volatility

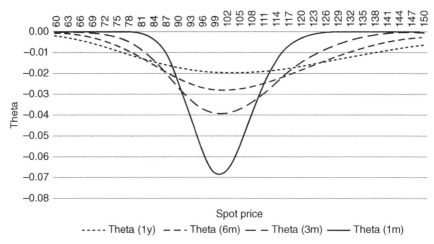

Figure 6.15   Evolution of the theta over time

3. The sensitivity of theta with respect to the time to expiry

If you understood the evolution of gamma over time, it should be relatively easy to understand, at least intuitively, the evolution of theta as expiry approaches. In general, we can say that, all else being equal, the theta of a plain vanilla option will always tend to 0 (both call and put option). It is probably not difficult to see why. If the option at expiry is in-the-money, its exposure will be the same as a (long or short) position in the underlying asset (which, by definition, carries no theta exposure). Likewise, if the option at expiry is out-of-the-money, its exposure is going to disappear (and so will its theta). Thus in the case of both in-the-money and out-of-the-money options, theta will have to disappear as expiry approaches.

A more delicate situation occurs when the option happens to be right at-the-money very close to the expiry date. In this case, the theta carried by an option can be quite significant (in particular for highly volatile underlying assets) since the uncertainty about whether the option is in-the-money or out-of-the-money will cause a relatively high time value to remain in the option and, therefore, a relatively high theta.

The evolution of theta over time can be seen in Figure 6.15 (both for in-the-money and out-of-the-money options).

6.7   RHO

The rho of an option is the first derivative of its price with respect to the interest rate. For options on non-dividend paying stocks, the sensitivity of interest rates arises from two sources. On the one hand, the interest rate modifies the value of the forward price of the underlying asset. On the other hand, it affects the discount factor used in the pricing process. Let us think about these two components separately.

From the point of view of the forward price of the underlying, it should be noted that a higher interest rate corresponds to a higher forward price and therefore will affect positively the price of a call option and negatively the price of a put option. From the point of view of the discount factor, higher interest rates correspond with lower discount factors and hence to lower prices for both call and put options. The opposite conclusions obviously hold in the case of lower interest rates.

Therefore, the impact on the call price of higher interest rate is mixed (positive because of the effect on the forward and negative because of the discounting effect). That said, it can be shown analytically that the effect on the forward price tends to outweigh the other effect (the rho of a vanilla call option is a positive quantity in the Black–Scholes world). On the other hand, the impact of higher interest rate on a put option is definitely negative since both effects tend to be negative.

Analytically it can be shown that, in the case of European call option on a non-dividend-paying stock, the rho is equal to:

$$\text{Rho} = K\,(T - t)\,e^{-r(T-t)}N(d_2)$$

and the variables are defined (as usual) as in section 6.3.1.

Whereas, for a European put option on a non-dividend-paying stock, the rho is equal to:

$$\text{Rho} = K\,(T - t)\,e^{-r(T-t)}N(-d_2)$$

where, as usual:

$$d_2 = \frac{\ln(S/K) + (r - \sigma^2/2)(T - t)}{\sigma\sqrt{T - t}}$$

6.8 OPTION TRADING

6.8.1 Taking a position on implied volatility or on implied versus realized volatility

Now that we have covered the main Greeks in some considerable detail, it is worth spending some time to discuss two different perspectives of volatility trading using options. As it should be clear at this stage, to a certain extent, the implied volatility can be seen *per se* as a tradable quantity with its own demand and supply dynamics. What this means, in practice, is that an option trader can in principle decide to take a long or a short vega exposure on a certain underlying asset by buying or selling the required quantity of options to achieve the desired vega exposure. When doing so, the trader will also typically decide the option expiry (or range of expiries) and the option strike (or range of strikes) that suits his or her views.

If the view is correct, the trader will be in a position to undertake a series of trades in the underlying based on delta hedging over the life of the option, or in subsequent options trades to obtain a profit at a later stage. For instance, assume that a trader buys vega on a certain underlying asset (buying vanilla calls or puts on that underlying) and that the implied volatility subsequently rises. All else being the same, the trader can now sell back the options at a higher price. Conversely, we can think about the example of a trader who is selling vega on a certain underlying asset (selling vanilla calls or puts on that underlying) and that the implied volatility subsequently falls. All else being the same, the trader can now buy back the options at a lower price.

If the trader's view is incorrect, however, and the implied volatility moves in the opposite direction compared with what was expected, the trader will obviously incur a loss, all else being equal.

It is worth reminding ourselves that, in the cases just described (i.e., whenever a bet on the implied volatility is the main purpose of the trade), the trader will typically keep the overall delta of the portfolio relatively neutral: this will allow the trader to focus and isolate the portfolio (as much as possible) from profits or losses due to the simple fluctuations in the price of the underlying asset (i.e., to focus mainly on the desired long or short vega exposure).

It is also important to note that, in general, the vega exposure itself can vary (and will typically vary) during the life of the trade as a consequence of changes in the price of the underlying asset, in the level of the implied volatility itself and also simply because of the passage of time. It is worth keeping in mind that the vega profile can change (even significantly) during the life of those trades that are meant to give the trader a desired vega profile. This clearly adds a certain level of complication since, in general, the trader will have to attempt to forecast not only the future evolution of the implied volatility that he or she intends to take a position on but also the expected vega exposure that results as a consequence of the evolution of the price of the underlying and of the implied volatility itself, as well as the passage of time that, in any case, tends to reduce the vega exposure of any portfolio.

Taking a position on the implied volatility, however, is not necessarily the main reason why a volatility trader may decide to buy or sell options. Another typical reason is the trader's own belief that the realized volatility that the underlying asset will exhibit in the future will be significantly different from the implied volatility tradable in the options market. If the trader's view is correct, it will be possible to "extract" a certain profit simply taking the option position (and continuously delta hedging it) and wait a certain amount of time to monetize as much as practicable the discrepancy between implied and realized volatility. For instance, a trader who believes that a certain stock is likely to have a sudden spike in realized volatility that is not reflected in the corresponding options market can buy a certain quantity of call or put options on that stock (keeping the overall position relatively delta neutral), in an attempt to crystallize profits from this view. If the stock subsequently experiences very volatile movements, the trader can take advantage of the "buy low, sell high" effect of the long gamma exposure that will allow him or her to more than offset the negative theta arising from the long option position. In this case, the trader does not necessarily need the *implied* volatility to go higher in order to obtain a profit (even though a higher implied volatility would be beneficial, since it is a long option exposure). All that is needed by the trader is a high realized volatility (higher than the implied purchased at the outset). In cases like this, since the main source of potential profit is the "buy low, sell high" effect arising from the option gamma, it might be worthwhile taking exposure via options that embed high gamma. Typically, this can be achieved by trading relatively short-dated options (say 1 month or even shorter). It should be noted that, as short-dated options tend to expire (obviously) in a short period of time, the options trader will face the risk that the timing of their options purchase is inaccurate, and the depreciation of the option portfolio due to theta is too great and can significantly reduce their potential gains.

6.8.2 Taking a position on the terminal payoff or re-hedging with a certain frequency

Aside from volatility trading, a market participant can trade options to take a particular view on the price of the underlying that will prevail when the option expires. In other words, to take a position on the terminal payoff of the option. In principle, if the aim of an option position is related to its terminal payoff, the trader is likely not to be too worried about the evolution of the implied volatility or the spread between implied and realized volatility (except for mark-to-market purposes) and therefore he or she is not likely to have very frequent re-hedging of the option portfolio (in principle the trader can also decide to run a naked option position, i.e., with no delta hedging at all). In section 6.8.1 we discussed the situation where a trader decides to take exposure on implied volatility or implied against realized volatility. In this case, it is very unlikely that the trader with a view on volatility will run naked option positions since they may well carry too strong a directional exposure. In this section, we will compare the two approaches to ensure that we fully understand the implications of both.

For the sake of simplicity, let us assume an options market where two types of option traders are operating: the directional option trader and the delta-hedged/volatility option trader. The directional option trader is only buying options, betting on the price of the underlying moving to a certain level or not moving beyond a certain level. The non-directional trader, on the other hand, always keeps his option book as much as possible delta neutral and only takes positions on implied volatility or on the difference between implied volatility and what he believes the future realized volatility will be.

We will now present some possible market regimes for the underlying asset (in terms of direction and realized volatility) and discuss what is the most likely course of action for the two traders on a case-by-case basis:

1. The underlying asset price is expected to be little changed or maybe having a mild upward trend. In this case, the directional trader may decide to sell at-the-money or slightly out-of-the-money put options to collect the option premium. He would probably decide not to buy call options since he is not sure that the potential upward movement will justify spending the premium. He might also decide to sell out-of-the-money call options, believing that the price of the underlying will not rise too much. The non-directional trader, on the other hand, is likely to sell options (either calls or puts or both) unless he believes the implied volatility is too low compared to the expected realized volatility.

2. The underlying asset price is expected to have a sharp upward trend. In this case, the directional trader is most likely to buy call options; he may consider out-of-the-money call options in order to increase the leverage of his exposure. He may also consider financing these call options by selling at-the-money or slightly out-of-the-money put options to reduce the total premium cost. The non-directional trader is likely to buy options (either calls or puts or both) unless he believes the implied volatility he will have to pay is too high compared with the expected realized volatility.

3. The underlying asset price is expected to have relatively trendless but highly volatile behaviour. In this case, the directional trader may decide to sell slightly out-of-the-money calls and/or puts to collect the option premium. Even if focused only on the terminal payoff, however, the trader will have to be aware of the risk of a volatile profile on his profit and loss due to the potential volatility of the underlying and the potential spikes in the implied volatility; for these reasons he may also consider buying deeply out-of-the-money options to contain excessive mark-to-market volatility of his portfolio. The non-directional trader is likely to buy options (either calls or puts or both) unless he believes the implied volatility he will have to pay is too high compared to the expected realized. He may want to buy relatively at-the-money options to benefit from the high gamma or also out-of-the-money options to benefit from the high volatility convexity.

4. The underlying asset price is expected to show a trendless profile with very low volatility. In this case, the directional trader will probably decide to sell at-the-money and out-of-the-money calls and/or puts to collect as much premium as possible. When doing so, however, he takes the risk that, if the view is wrong, he can face significant losses due to the potentially high leverage of the options sold. The non-directional trader is also likely to sell options (either calls or puts or both) unless he believes that the implied volatility being sold is too low compared with the future expected volatility. The price risks are similar to the directional trader.
5. The underlying asset price is expected to be flat or having a mild downward trend. The opposite of scenario 1 above.
6. The underlying asset price is expected to have a sharp downward trend. The opposite of scenario 2 above.

Obviously these are relatively simple example scenarios but they do highlight the wide range of choices that an option trader will have according to his view of the future. Other factors may affect the risk–return of these exposures, of course. In particular, volatility for at-the-money options can be different than volatility for out-of-the-money options while the implied volatility used to price call options can be different to the implied volatility used to price put options. We will look at this in more detail when discussing the *volatility smile*. Finally, liquidity for out-of-the-money options can be significantly lower than for at-the-money options, affecting the potential risk–return profile of the chosen option portfolio.

6.9   SOME ADDITIONAL REMARKS (IN Q&A FORMAT)

1. **Are options payoffs zero sum games (i.e., if the option buyer makes money, does the seller have to lose and vice versa)?**
   This is certainly true if one looks strictly at the payoff or the profit and loss of the option position taken in isolation. If the activity of trading the underlying asset is included, however, in the case of delta hedging, the profit and loss from this source needs to be included. For example, assume that the option buyer keeps the option position naked (i.e., he does not delta hedge it) but the option seller does delta hedge it. If the price of the underlying asset goes up and, at expiry, the option ends up being in-the-money, the option buyer will have a positive payoff but the negative payoff of the option seller will be (at least partially) offset by the delta-hedging activity.
2. **When an option is purchased, is it impossible to lose more than the premium paid for it?**
   This is certainly true for a naked option position, i.e., if an option is bought and nothing else is done. However, if a trader buys, say, a call option and starts delta hedging it by selling the underlying asset, he may end up losing more on the delta than what is made from the option payoff. This can happen if the underlying asset price increases slowly towards the strike but does not cross it. In this case, the trader is likely to lose the option premium paid when the option was bought but has a zero payoff at expiry since the call option expires out-of-the-money. In this case, the trader will suffer some loss on the underlying asset that was sold as the delta hedge, since its price went up, but not enough to bring the option into the money to offset the share position loss.

3. **When an option is purchased, does the realized volatility of the underlying need be high in order to make a profit?**

In principle this is correct but it is important to clarify that, as discussed in some detail, in order to take advantage of a potentially high realized volatility (higher than the implied one), frequent delta-hedging activity is generally required. When delta re-hedging is performed, the option portfolio may accumulate a directional position that can easily overshadow any gain arising from a realized volatility higher than implied. Delta hedging in practice (since in real life it is not done continuously as the Black–Scholes model postulates) is a highly path-dependent process, and timing decisions on delta hedging can, in practice, result in highly variant returns for different traders, even those who began with identical positions.

6.10 AN EXAMPLE OF THE BEHAVIOUR OF IMPLIED VOLATILITY: EUR/USD RATE AND S&P 500 IN 2010–2012

We conclude this chapter by presenting the evolution over time of the 1-month implied volatility of the EUR/USD FX rate and the S&P 500 Index.[6] Figures 6.16 and 6.17 should be useful for shedding some light on how volatility in certain asset classes has been changing over the years 2010–2012. Although outside the scope of this book to discuss in detail the events highlighted below, we trust the charts will be helpful to get familiar with the behaviour observed and the orders of magnitude involved.

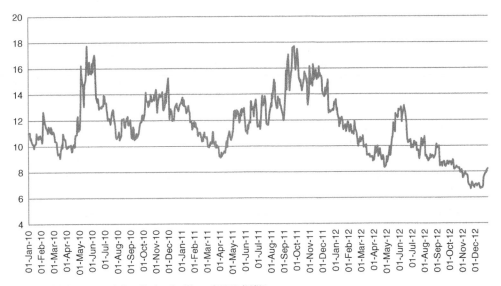

Figure 6.16   1-month implied volatility of EUR/USD rate

---

[6] For the volatility of the EUR/USD FX rate we are using the 1-month implied volatility for delta neutral straddles. As a proxy of the 1-month implied volatility of the S&P 500 Index we are using the VIX Index (for a more detailed description of the methodology of calculation of this index, please refer to www.cboe.com/VIX).

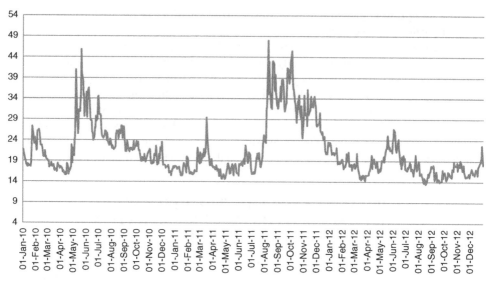

Figure 6.17   VIX Index

SUMMARY

In this chapter, we continued the discussion of the option Greeks that we began in Chapter 5. In Chapter 5, we concentrated on delta. In this chapter, we looked at delta in more detail but we also added gamma, vega, theta and rho. Although it is clearly possible to look at each of the Greeks quantitatively, our overriding aim was to describe and explain each of the Greeks intuitively. If we can understand each of the Greeks intuitively, we are in a position to understand and assess the Greeks of a portfolio of vanilla options as well as the Greeks of more exotic options such as barrier options (which we will meet in Chapter 8).

Delta is the first derivative of the price of an option with respect to the price of the underlying security. The delta of a long plain vanilla call is within a range of 0 to 1, while the delta of a long plain vanilla put is within a range of −1 to 0. All else being equal, the delta of a plain vanilla option that is in-the-money will tend towards 1 (for a call option) or towards −1 (for a put option) as the expiration date approaches. On the other hand, the delta of a plain vanilla option that is out-of-the-money (either a call or a put) will converge to 0 as the expiration date approaches.

Gamma is the first derivative of the delta with respect to the price of the underlying. Gamma is therefore a measure of convexity, since it measures how the first-order sensitivity, the delta, changes with respect to the price of the underlying asset itself. Gamma tends towards 0 as the underlying price moves away from the strike. Gamma is maximized when the price of the underlying (or, more accurately, the forward price of the underlying) is at/close to the strike price. Gamma of vanilla calls and puts cannot assume negative values. Given the comment on delta we can say that, all else being equal, the gamma of a plain vanilla option will always tend to 0 (both for a call and a put option). If the option at expiry is in-the-money, its exposure will be the same as a (long or short) position in the underlying asset. This carries no gamma exposure since the delta is "sticky" at 1. On the other hand, if the option at expiry is out-of-the-money, its delta will be "sticky" around 0 and so there is no gamma exposure. So, in the case of in-the-money or out-of-the-money options, the option gamma will tend to disappear as expiry approaches. A more complicated situation occurs if the option happens to be right at-the-money very near to the expiry date. In this case, a very unstable gamma is likely to be observed. For small increases or decreases in the price of the underlying, the option delta will quickly converge to 1 or 0 (in the case of the call) or to -1 or 0 (in the case of the put).

Vega is the first derivative of the option price with respect to the volatility of the underlying asset. The vega of a plain vanilla call option is always positive and so is the vega of a plain vanilla put. The vega of a deeply in-the-money option (where its delta will be 1 or very close to 1) or a deeply out-of-the-money option (where its delta will be 0 or very close to 0) will be 0 or very close to 0. In general, we can say that, all else being equal, the vega of a plain vanilla option will tend to 0 (for both call and put options) as expiry approaches.

The theta of an option is the first derivative of its price with respect to the time to expiry, i.e., how the price of the option changes just for the passage of time. The theta of a plain vanilla put or call is negative. The theta of a deeply in-the-money option (where its delta will be 1 or very close to 1) or a deeply out-of-the-money option (where its delta will be 0 or very close to 0) will be 0 or very close to it. Similar to the situation with gamma and vega, the effect of theta will tend to 0 as the underlying price moves away from the strike price and will be maximized when the price of the underlying (or, more accurately, the forward price of the underlying) is at the strike price. In general, the theta of a plain vanilla option will always tend to 0 (both call and put option). If the option at expiry is in-the-money, its exposure will be the same as a (long or short) position in the underlying asset (which, by definition, carries no theta exposure). Likewise, if the option at expiry is out-of-the-money, its exposure is going to disappear (and so will its theta). Thus in the case of both in-the-money and out-of-the-money options, theta will have to disappear as expiry approaches. A more complicated situation occurs when the option happens to be right at-the-money very close to the expiry date. In this case, the theta carried by an option can be quite significant (in particular for highly volatile underlying assets) since the uncertainty about whether the option is in-the-money or out-of-the-money will cause a relatively high time value to remain in the option and, therefore, a relatively high theta.

The rho of an option is the first derivative of its price with respect to the interest rate. For options on non-dividend paying stocks, the sensitivity of interest rates arises from two sources. On the one hand, the interest rate modifies the value of the forward price of the underlying asset. On the other hand, it affects the discount factor used in the pricing process. From the point of view of the forward price of the underlying, higher interest rates correspond to higher forward prices and therefore will affect positively the price of a call option and negatively the price of a put option. From the point of view of the discount factor, higher interest rates correspond to lower discount factors and hence to lower the price for both call and put options. The opposite conclusions obviously hold in the case of lower interest rates. Consequently, the impact on the call price of higher interest rate is mixed (positive because of the effect on the forward and negative because of the discounting effect). That said, the effect on the forward price tends to outweigh the other effect (the rho of a vanilla call option is a positive quantity in the Black–Scholes world). On the other hand, the impact of higher interest rate on a put option is definitely negative since both effects tend to be negative.

7

Volatility Smile and the Greeks
of Option Strategies

As we already mentioned in Chapter 6, "Implied Volatility", the Black–Scholes formula is very often used "the other way around", i.e., to derive (or back out) the level of volatility that, when used in the formula as an input, allows one to obtain the market price of the option. As we have seen extensively, this procedure allows market participants to retrieve what is commonly known as *implied volatility*. In this chapter, we want to move one step forward, calculating implied volatility, not just on a specific strike and expiry, but across different strikes and across different option maturities. This is extremely important, as there is no guarantee that the level of implied volatility is going to be the same across different strikes and/or different maturities.

7.1 THE VOLATILITY SMILE – WHY IS THE IMPLIED VOLATILITY NOT FLAT ACROSS DIFFERENT STRIKES?

Let us start from the analysis of volatility across different strikes. This will lead us to an observation of the so-called volatility smile.

In the following section, we plot the volatility smile (or skew) for some unspecified underlying asset and discuss the typical shapes that are generally observed. Figures 7.1 and 7.2 are based on an at-the-money level of 100; typically these charts are based on volatility for at-the-money or out-of-the-money options, for a given expiry: therefore, on the right-hand side it is possible to see the volatility of out-of-the-money call options whereas on the left-hand side the volatility of out-of-the-money put options can be observed.

A common theme is to have volatility at (or close to) the at-the-money strike lower than the volatility levels prevailing on the out-of-the-money strikes (both call and put options). This is what is often referred to as the volatility smile; the choice of name should be quite obvious from the graph in Figure 7.1.

Another typical theme (quite frequent in equity options) is to have volatilities corresponding to out-of-the-money put options (left-hand side) generally higher than at-the-money volatilities (in the centre of the chart) that are, themselves, higher than the volatilities corresponding to out-of-the-money call options (right-hand side). We show this in Figure 7.2 and it is often referred to as volatility skew. In this example, the implied volatilities clearly refer to call options.

The obvious questions at this stage are: (1) why can volatility exhibit meaningful differences across different strikes, and (2) what is driving these differences?

1. Volatility tends to be higher for strikes that can be reached or crossed if some sort of "crash event" or "extreme event" occurs. A common example of this phenomenon can be observed in equity derivatives markets where, generally, lower strikes tend to have higher levels of implied volatility compared with higher strikes. This can be thought of as the additional risk

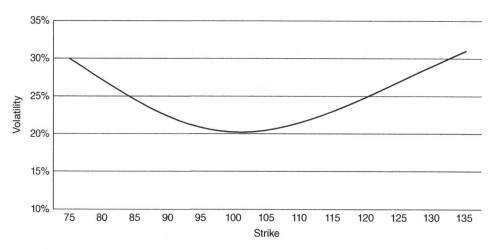

Figure 7.1   Example of volatility smile

premium that the buyer of the puts is willing to pay in order to buy protection from a drop in the price of the underlying (or, symmetrically, the additional risk premium that the seller of puts requires in order to be willing to sell that protection). This reflects the typical market belief that a falling stock market is likely to be more volatile than a rising stock market. The same is not always true for other asset classes, however. In commodities, for instance, it is not unusual to observe that the additional risk premium is charged on the upside (i.e., call options) rather than the downside (i.e., put options). This may be because the market perceives a risk of sharp and volatile increases in commodity prices due to supply shocks (e.g., in the case of the crude oil market, to periods of rising geopolitical tensions in the Middle East) or due to overall risk aversion (e.g., in the case of gold).

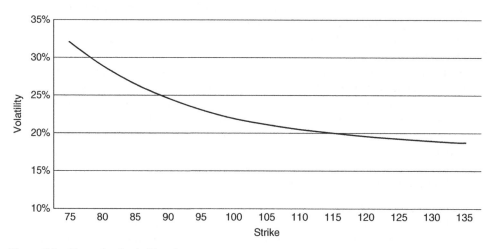

Figure 7.2   Example of volatility skew

2. Out-of-the-money options sometimes have higher levels of implied volatility in order to compensate the option seller for the negative volatility convexity that he or she will face as a consequence of selling out-of-the-money options.[1] To clarify this very important point, let us consider a very simple example of an option trader who has been asked to price a deeply out-of-the-money option (whether it is a call or put does not really matter in this example) in the knowledge that he or she will, realistically, only be able to cover the vega risk only for strikes close to the at-the-money. The question faced is, what level of volatility is needed in order for the trader to be willing to sell the deeply out-of-the-money option? Should it be the same as the at-the-money volatility or will some additional risk premium have to be taken into account? As we discussed in section 6.5, the seller of a deeply out-of-the-money option is facing a negative volatility convexity position, i.e., for increased levels of volatility, the trader's negative vega position will rise, forcing him or her to buy volatility at higher levels.[2] Conversely, for decreased levels of volatility, the trader's negative vega position will decrease forcing him or her to sell volatility at a lower level (assuming, again, an overall vega-neutral position). If the market for options with out-of-the-money strikes is not particularly liquid and the option seller can only realistically hedge a short vega position by buying options with at-the-money or close to at-the-money strikes, then it is quite possible that the option seller (the trader, in this case) will require additional risk premium, reflected in a higher option price (which manifests itself in an increased level of implied volatility), in order to sell options with out-of-the-money strikes. In this way, the higher option price will compensate for the risk associated with the hedging mismatch that arises from the negative volatility convexity of the combined position (i.e., short options with out-of-the-money strikes and long options with at-the-money strikes). This truth in fact holds for any derivative: if a dealer or seller of a derivative will incur additional costs due to illiquidity or difficulty in matching cash flows in order to adequately hedge themselves, the price of the derivative should rise accordingly.

Referring back to the discussions of risk reversals and butterflies in Chapter 3, note that the steepness of the volatility skew is relevant in the calculation of risk reversal prices while the convexity of implied volatility is important in the prices of butterflies.

7.2 THE "STICKY DELTA" AND "STICKY STRIKE" APPROACHES TO DESCRIBING VOLATILITY SMILE

There are two approaches generally used to describe volatility smile in numerical terms; the *sticky delta approach* and the *sticky strike approach*.

In the *sticky delta* approach, the implied volatility for each expiry is expressed in terms of the delta of the option. This approach is typically adopted in FX and commodity options. For example, for each expiry, the volatility of the 50 delta and 25 delta options (calls and puts) are quoted. Often, the 10 delta options are also quoted (again, for both calls and puts) which means five strikes for each expiry. The example in Table 7.1 is based on a hypothetical 3-month option on a foreign exchange rate (say the EUR/USD rate).

---

[1] In particular, this is true for deeply out-of-the-money options where the gap risk (i.e., the risk of the price of the underlying asset having a sudden and unexpected jump) that the option seller is taking is much higher than what he or she would take for at-the-money or slightly out-of-the-money options.

[2] Assuming the trader wants to keep the overall position vega neutral.

Table 7.1 Volatility quoted as a function of the delta

Delta	Volatility
10 delta put	11.5%
25 delta put	10.5%
50 delta (call or put)	9.0%
25 delta call	8.5%
10 delta call	8.25%

Table 7.2 Volatility quoted as a function of the strike

Strike	Volatility
1,400	16.5%
1,450	15.5%
1,500	15.0%
1,550	14.0%
1,600	13.5%

Note that, with the sticky delta approach, the implied volatility at each option strike price is essentially a function of the option delta and, by extension, of the change in the price of the underlying asset.[3] So, if the implied volatility of the asset "exhibits" sticky delta behaviour then it also means that, if the implied volatility of the 25 delta call, say, is equal to 8.5% then, as the spot price moves higher, the new 25 delta call will be priced implying the same implied volatility of 8.5%. Clearly, the actual strike price will have risen along with the increased level of spot price.

Conversely, in the *sticky strike* approach, the implied volatility for each expiry is expressed in terms of the option strike itself. This may be expressed in absolute price terms (such as a 1,500 call on the S&P 500 Index). This approach is typically adopted in the case of equity options (single stocks or indices); Table 7.2 below shows a hypothetical example of volatility quoted in terms of absolute strike level.

With the sticky strike approach, each strike has a certain implied volatility associated with it and this implied volatility will be a function neither of the future price dynamic of the underlying asset nor of the passage of time. So, if the implied volatility of the asset "exhibits" sticky strike behaviour then, for example, if the implied volatility of the 1,500 strike on the S&P 500 Index is equal to 15%, the 1,500 strike will retain the same volatility of 15% regardless of whether the underlying spot price moves higher or lower.

The dynamic behaviour of the volatility skew over time will be much more complex than our discussion of the sticky delta and sticky strike approaches would suggest. In a sense, they are static representations of how traders might attempt to quote implied volatilities as spot prices change. They are not meant to be theories of how implied volatility will evolve in practice over time. As such, both these approaches should be considered as simplified representations of how traders may quote implied volatilities across different strikes as spot prices change by small amounts.

---

[3] As well as of the passage of time.

Over time, and irrespective of the way in which traders quote implied volatility across different strikes, the dynamics of volatility skew can approximately be seen as the combination of three different kinds of movement as described in Figure 7.3:

1. Parallel shifts in the volatility skew

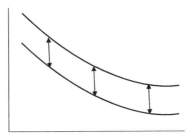

2. Changes in the slope of the volatility skew

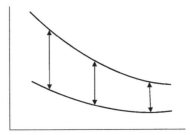

3. Changes in the convexity of the volatility skew

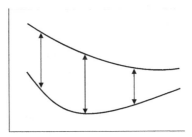

Figure 7.3 Dynamics of volatility skew

We will revisit this later in section 7.5.

7.3 THE VOLATILITY TERM STRUCTURE – WHY IS THE IMPLIED VOLATILITY NOT FLAT ACROSS DIFFERENT EXPIRIES?

In the previous section, we discussed some of the reasons for the non-flat implied volatility structure that we generally see across different options strikes for the same basic option structure on a specific underlying asset. In a similar fashion, we will now discuss why implied

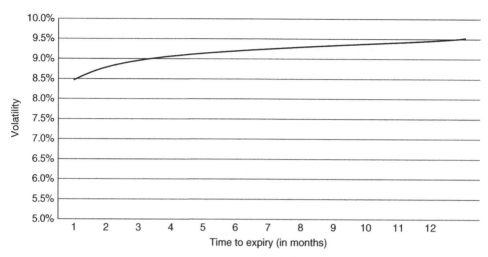

Figure 7.4   Example of upward sloping volatility term structure

volatility tends not to be constant across different expiry dates. This will allow us to introduce the concept of volatility term structure, i.e., to express the dependency of implied volatility on option tenor.

In general, for many underlying assets, the volatility term structure tends to be upward sloping, i.e., longer expiries tend to have a higher implied volatility than shorter expiries. This is essentially a reflection of additional risk and liquidity premia that are embedded at the back end of the volatility term structure. This is the case, at least in general, for equities, foreign exchange rates and certain commodities (such as gold) as highlighted in Figure 7.4 (showing, for example, the volatility term structure for at-the-money options of an underlying such as the EUR/USD foreign exchange rate).

However, under certain market conditions, it is possible to observe a different shape for the volatility term structure. In particular, during times of distressed marked conditions or on the days immediately preceding a big event, it is often possible to observe a downward-sloping volatility term structure in some assets, at least at the very front of the curve. This is probably due to the heightened chances of sharp moves in asset prices in the immediate future as a consequence of factors that are otherwise perceived to be temporary (Figure 7.5).

On the other hand, there are underlying assets with an implied volatility term structure that is structurally downward sloping. This is the case for certain commodities, such as oil and natural gas, and it is often due to the fact that the prices of the short-term futures contracts on these assets may tend to be more volatile than the prices of the long-date futures contracts.

7.4   THE VOLATILITY SURFACE – COMBINING SMILE AND TERM STRUCTURE

Having discussed volatility skew and the volatility term structure, it is natural to combine the two. This is the *volatility surface* (Figure 7.6).

Implied volatility is itself a market with its own demand and supply dynamics across different strikes and different parts of the term structure. It is not necessarily possible to interpret the

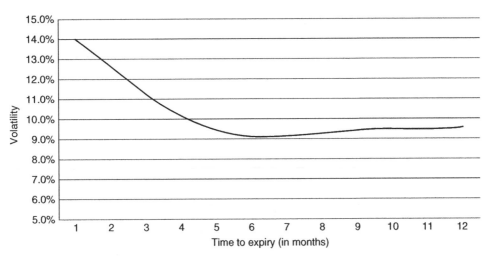

Figure 7.5   Example of inverted volatility term structure

different shapes to the volatility surface in terms of market expectations of future volatility at certain points in the future and for certain strikes. In practice, the volatility surface can be very hard to interpret since it is the result of the multitude of interactions between many different sets of market participants (i.e., banks, corporates, fund managers, insurance companies, etc.) acting for very many different reasons and sometimes restricting their focus only to specific parts of the volatility surface. Under certain market conditions and where different market participants act on different parts of the volatility surface, strong pressure can be exerted on certain parts of the surface itself, causing strong observable anomalies. For instance, when there is strong demand for long-dated options, which is met only by supply in shorter-dated

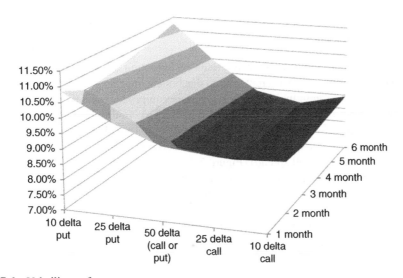

Figure 7.6   Volatility surface

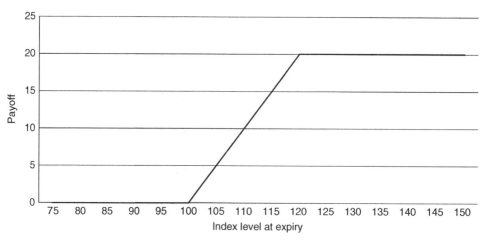

Figure 7.7   Payoff profile of a 100–120 call spread

options. In this case, it may be that we observe a significant steepening of the volatility term structure that, depending on the strength of the various flows involved, may take a long time to be absorbed by the market.

7.5   ANALYSING THE GREEKS OF COMMON OPTION STRATEGIES

Having analysed, in some detail, the common Greeks of vanilla options, it is time to extend the analysis to the most common option strategies, such as call and put spreads, strangles, straddles and butterflies. Since these strategies can be derived from combinations of vanilla options, the Greeks of each strategy will also be combinations of the Greeks of the individual options that compose the strategies themselves. What follows is a detailed discussion of these.

7.5.1   Vertical call or put spreads

Vertical call or put spreads, as previously discussed in section 3.6, are a combination of two vanilla call or put options with different strikes, one bought and one sold. For instance, a trader could own a long position in the 100 call on a certain equity index and be short a 120 call on the same index, both options having, say, a 6-month expiry. In this case, the trader is said to be long the call spread.[4] The maximum payoff that this call spread can offer to its buyer is 20 index points, earned if, at expiry, the price of the underlying index is greater than or equal to 120 (the high strike of the call spread) (Figure 7.7).

Since the call spread can be seen as the combination of two individual call options, it is natural to expect that the total delta of the call spread is going to be the sum of the delta of the two individual calls. The trader in this case would be long delta on the option bought (the 100 strike call) and short delta on the option sold (the 120 strike call). To assess whether the combined delta exposure is long or short, it is useful to notice that the call with the low strike

---

[4] The "long" position is derived from the long position in the call options with the low strike.

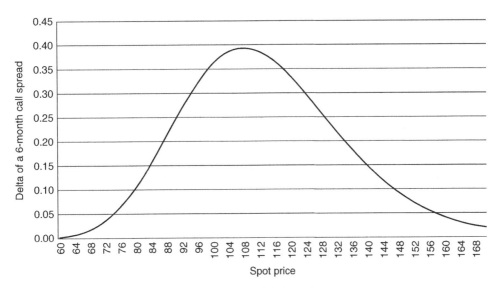

Figure 7.8   Call spread delta as a function of the underlying price

(100 in this case) is always going to have a delta that is equal to or higher than the delta of the option with the high strike (120 in this case). So, since the option that the trader is long has higher delta than the option that the trader is short, the trader's overall delta is going to be positive. However, as the price of the underlying asset moves away from the price range within the two strikes, it is natural to expect the delta to converge to zero. This is due to the fact that any further movement of the price of the underlying asset above the high strike or below the low strike will not have (at expiry) any meaningful effect on the payoff.

Figure 7.8 highlights the delta profile of the call spread above, expressed as a function of the price of the underlying index. It is worth noting that the delta is maximized when the underlying index is trading between the two strikes.

Conversely, it can be shown that, if the trader is long a put spread (i.e., long a put high strike and short a put with lower strike), the overall position is going to have negative delta (or, in the common jargon, is "short delta").

The analysis of the net gamma profile for long call spreads is slightly more complicated. As we have discussed in section 6.4 (when we analyzed the gamma profile of a vanilla option), when an option moves further and further out-of-the-money, its gamma will converge to zero. For the 100–120 call spread, as the price of the underlying index increases, the gamma of the 120 call will tend to be higher than the gamma of the 100 call. Since the trader is short that option, the overall gamma position will turn negative. On the other hand, as the price of the underlying index falls, the gamma of the 100 call will tend to be higher than the gamma of the 120 call and as the trader is long the 100 call option, the overall gamma position will turn positive.

So, as is hopefully clear from Figure 7.9, a trader who is long a call spread will see the gamma exposure switch from positive to negative when the underlying price is sufficiently close to the high strike and from negative to positive when the underlying price is sufficiently close to the low strike. The net gamma position will obviously tend towards zero when the

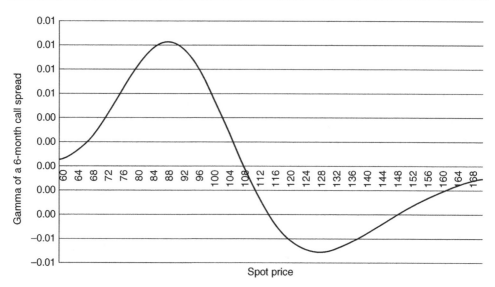

Figure 7.9   Call spread gamma as a function of the underlying price

price of the underlying is significantly higher than the high strike or significantly lower than the low strike since the delta converges on zero in these regions.

Geometrically, one can see this from the chart of the delta of the call spread (Figure 7.10) and recall that the gamma is the first derivative of the delta. This will be positive up to the level of highest delta, negative beyond that level, eventually converging again to zero.

Turning to a long put spread position: net gamma exposure switches from positive to negative when the underlying price is sufficiently close to the low strike (recall that the trader is short this option) and from negative to positive when the underlying price is sufficiently close to the high strike (the trader is long this option).

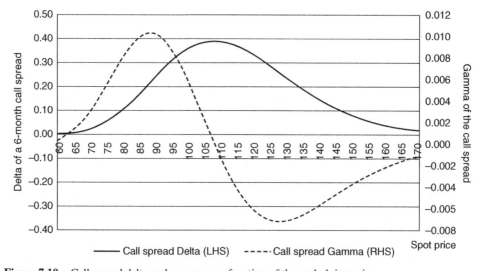

Figure 7.10   Call spread delta and gamma as a function of the underlying price

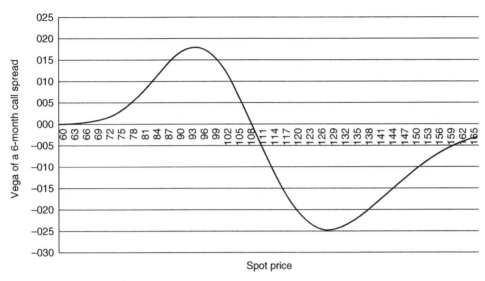

Figure 7.11   Call spread vega as a function of the underlying price

What about the other Greeks? For vanilla options, vega will tend to have the same sign as gamma and theta will tend to have the opposite sign. We can use this result. For a long call spread exposure, for example, vega will flip from positive to negative as the price of the underlying rises and from negative to positive as the price of the underlying falls (Figure 7.11).

The opposite is true for theta as Figure 7.12 shows. Note that both vega and theta will converge to zero as the underlying price moves sufficiently away from the strike prices.

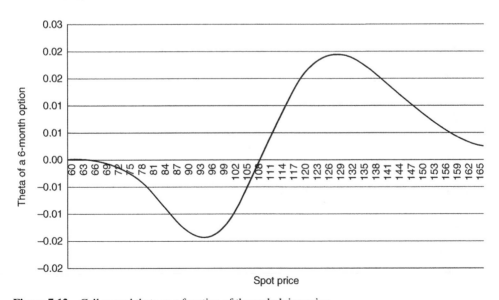

Figure 7.12   Call spread theta as a function of the underlying price

7.5.2 Straddles and strangles

The Greeks of straddles and strangles show many similarities since they both consist of a simultaneous purchase (a long straddle or strangle) or sale (a short straddle or strangle) of a call and a put with the same maturity. The difference is related to the strikes of the call and put that are bought or sold. The strikes are equal in the case of a straddle and different in the case of a strangle.

Looking first at the delta – this is slightly more complicated than in the case of the vertical spread since its sign can switch from positive to negative and vice versa but the analysis should still be relatively straightforward.

Let us start with an example of a trader who is long a 100 straddle on a generic equity index. To calculate the delta of the overall position, it is again useful to decompose the straddle in its two components, i.e., a 100 strike call option and a 100 strike put option, both long positions (in this case). The two options will give the trader two opposite delta exposures: a long delta exposure arising from the call option and a negative delta exposure arising from the put option (remember that the trader purchased both of them).

In this case, the sign of the overall delta exposure will be clearly equal to the sign of the delta exposure of the option that has the greater delta (since its delta will prevail over the other one). When the price of the underlying asset goes up, the long delta exposure of the 100 strike call option will increase and the short delta of the 100 strike put option will decrease. Together, we see an increase in the overall delta of the straddle. On the other hand, as the price of the underlying asset goes down, the long delta of the 100 strike call option will fall and the short delta of the 100 strike put option will increase. This time around, we see a decrease of the overall delta. Figure 7.13 summarizes this. It's worth noting that, for higher spot prices the delta will asymptotically converge to $+1$ whereas, for lower prices, the delta will asymptotically converge to -1.

The same approach can be applied to a long strangle position with the difference being that, if the price of the underlying ends up in the range between the two strikes, then the

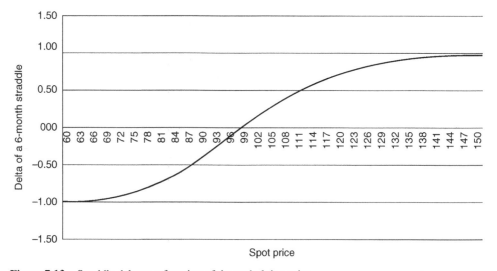

Figure 7.13   Straddle delta as a function of the underlying price

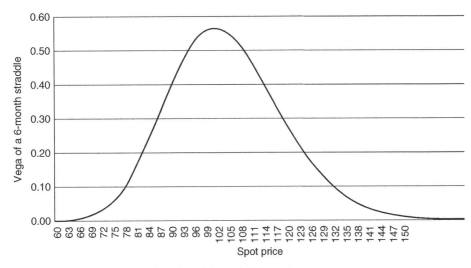

Figure 7.14   Straddle vega as a function of the underlying price

option delta will converge to zero as the expiry date approaches since both the call and put options will expire out-of-the-money (or, at least, the likelihood of expiring out-of-the-money will increase).

The signs on gamma, vega and theta are relatively straightforward since they only depend on whether the straddle or strangle has been bought or sold. For a long straddles or strangle position, gamma and vega will be positive and theta will be negative. Conversely, for a short straddles or strangle position, gamma and vega will be negative and theta will be positive. For simplicity, we only show the chart of the evolution of vega of a straddle with respect to the price of the underlying asset. Interested readers may wish to replicate similar charts for gamma and theta (but remember that the sign of theta is going to be opposite to the sign of vega and gamma) (Figure 7.14).

7.5.3   Risk reversals

Risk reversals are a combination of the purchase (sale) of a call option and the simultaneous sale (purchase) of a put option with a lower strike. As may be obvious by now, the Greeks of a risk reversal are going to be the sum of the Greeks of the two positions in the individual options. Clearly, when a call option is purchased and a put option is sold, the overall delta position is long.

The gamma, vega and theta positions of the risk reversal are slightly less obvious since they involve both a long and a short option position.

As should be clear from the analysis of the call and put spreads, the net gamma, vega and theta exposure depends on how close is the underlying asset price to the high strike (the call strike) or to the low strike (the put strike). Assuming a trader bought a 110 call option and sold a 90 put on a generic asset, the long position in the call option gives a long vega and gamma position and a short theta position, whereas the short position in the put option will give a short vega and gamma position and a long theta position. The vega, gamma and theta of each option will tend to assume their maximum values when the price of the underlying is close

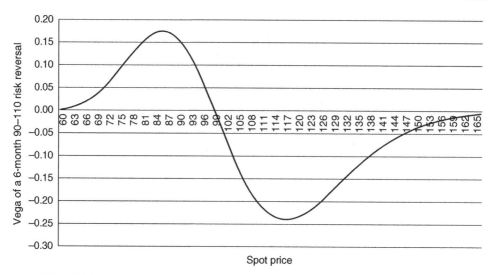

Figure 7.15   Risk reversal vega as a function of the underlying price

to the respective strike price. So, the closer is the price of the underlying to the strike price of the call option (110 in our example), the Greeks arising from the call option will prevail. As the underlying price approaches 110, the trader will tend to get longer vega and gamma and shorter theta. On the other hand, as the price of the underlying moves closer to the strike of the put option (90 in our example), the more that the put option Greeks will prevail, causing the trader to be shorter vega and gamma and longer theta.

In Figure 7.15, we present the dynamic of the vega for a risk reversal. Interested readers may wish to replicate similar charts for gamma (hint, the shape should be similar) and theta (hint, it should have a symmetrical shape).

What clearly emerges from the example above is that a key feature of risk reversals is that the profile of the price of the underlying asset will strongly affect the vega, gamma and theta. Not only the magnitude *but also the sign* of the Greeks, which flip from positive to negative or vice versa as the price of the underlying moves closer to one strike or to the other strike.

Risk reversals are often used as hedges (we will discuss this more fully in sections 7.6 and 7.7). This is because, risk reversals exhibit a meaningful exposure to what is often referred to as dVega/dSpot.[5]

The dVega/dSpot is the first derivative of vega with respect to the price of the underlying asset. It expresses how vega changes with relatively small changes in the price of the underlying. We will discuss this topic in more detail later but, at this stage, it is important to stress that the sensitivity of vega with respect to the price of the underlying asset is among the most important variables on which the derivatives hedger will need to focus. A derivatives position that shows a very high absolute level of dVega/dSpot may end up requiring frequent re-hedging of the vega exposure, with potentially very high associated costs.

So, returning to our risk reversal example. Risk reversal prices are highly sensitive to the volatility skew of the underlying asset. Since the risk reversal involves taking a long (or short)

---

[5] dVega/dSpot is sometimes called vanna.

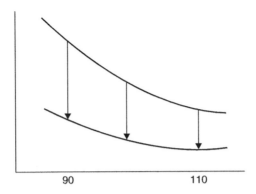

Figure 7.16   Flattening of the volatility skew

position in a given strike and a short (or long) position in a different strike, the risk reversal can be seen as an instrument that allows one to take a position on the skew directly.

To emphasize this very important concept, in buying a 110 call and selling a 90 put, all else being equal, the trader will benefit from any increase in the implied volatility of the 110 strike that occurs relative to the 90 strike. See Figure 7.16.

Conversely, the trader will incur a loss in the case of a fall in the implied volatility of the 110 strike (exposure is long vega on that strike) relative to the 90 strike (exposure is short vega on that strike) (Figure 7.17).

To sum up, the risk reversal is a way to trade and express a view on the steepness (or the flatness) of the volatility skew for a given expiry and it is also a common strategy to manage the dVega/dSpot of a derivatives portfolio.

7.5.4   Butterflies

A risk reversal is a way to trade the steepness or the flatness of the volatility skew for a given option expiry date, and a butterfly is a way to take a position in the convexity of the volatility skew.

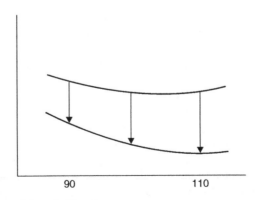

Figure 7.17   Steepening of the volatility skew

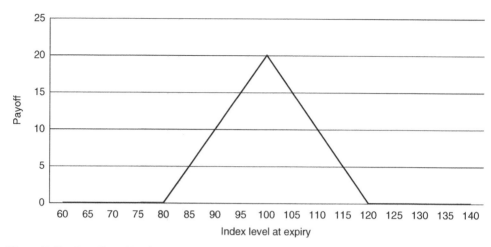

Figure 7.18 Payoff profile of a 80–100–120 butterfly

As we discussed earlier, there is some debate among the option purists on what exactly constitutes a butterfly. Technically, a butterfly spread involves only calls or only puts but we are happy to say that a short position in a straddle and a long position in a strangle also constitutes a butterfly. A very common example of this type of butterfly involves setting the centre strike exactly at the mid-point between the other two strikes. A payoff profile is represented in Figure 7.18; a 80–100–120 butterfly, where we assumed a long position in the wings, i.e., long a 120 strike call and a 80 strike put, and short position in the belly, i.e., short a 100 strike straddle.

The straddle is often referred to as the *belly* of the butterfly and the call and the put that are part of the strangle are often known as the *wings* of the butterfly. The symmetry of the butterflies we have just shown is derived from the fact that, as is commonly assumed, the strike of the straddle is exactly the average of the strikes of the strangle and the notional of each option bought and sold is identical.

However, as you may be able to verify, the butterfly that we have just described is not vega neutral, since the vega of the straddle tends to be higher than the vega of the strangle (due to volatility skew).

So, it is also very common to trade vega-neutral butterflies, where the vega neutrality can be easily achieved by reducing the amount of the straddle traded for the same amount of strangle (more on this shortly).

So, how to analyse the basic Greeks of a butterfly? We will assume a generic case of a trader who decides to go long the wings (strangles) and short the belly (straddle) of the butterfly, i.e., the strategy represented in Figure 7.18.

As the reader can easily observe from this chart, the trader's delta will tend to be relatively neutral if the price of the underlying is close to the strike of straddle and will turn slightly negative if the price of the underlying approaches the top strike of the strangle and slightly positive if it approaches the lower strike of the strangle. In both cases, if the notional of the straddle is equal to the notional of the strangle, the delta will converge to zero if the price of the underlying asset moves significantly higher than the top strike or significantly lower than the low strike of the strangle.

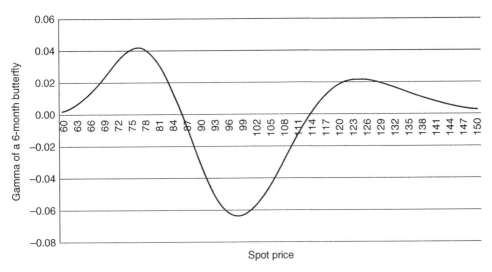

Figure 7.19   Butterfly gamma as a function of the underlying price

Given the behaviour of the delta, it is not difficult to determine the corresponding profile of the gamma. When the price of the underlying asset is close enough to the belly of the butterfly the gamma exposure is negative since the negative gamma position of the short straddle will tend to overwhelm the positive gamma of the long strangle. On the other hand, as the price of the underlying asset diverges sufficiently from the middle strike towards either the high or the low wing of the butterfly, the long gamma exposure arising from the top strike or the low strike of the strangle prevails and pushes the overall gamma exposure into positive territory (see Figure 7.19).

The full extent of the move into positive or negative territory is obviously a function of all the various parameters used to evaluate each option price (such as the volatility used to price each strike of the butterfly, the time to the expiry, etc.) as well as the notionals of the strangle and the straddle. As we said earlier, butterflies are not always symmetric, i.e., the relative notionals of the straddle and strangle can be different. For instance, the straddle can be "underweighted" to achieve vega neutrality for the butterfly as a whole. However, changing the notionals of each option that comprise the butterfly will also alter its gamma profile.

What about theta? The sign and the behaviour of theta are going to be the opposite of that just described for gamma. When the price of the underlying asset is close enough to the belly of the butterfly, the trader will have a positive theta exposure (since the positive theta of the short straddle will tend to overwhelm the negative theta of the long strangle). On the other hand, as the price of the underlying asset diverges sufficiently from the belly of the butterfly towards either the high or the low wing of the butterfly, the short theta exposure arising from the top strike or the low strike of the strangle will take over and push the overall theta exposure into negative territory. Again, the full extent of the move into positive or negative territory will be a function of the various parameters used for each option price as well as the relative notionals of the strangle with respect to the straddle.

Turning to vega. A butterfly can be constructed that is vega neutral at inception by setting the notional of the straddle such that the ratio of the notional of the straddle over the notional of the strangle is equal to the ratio of the vega of the straddle over the vega of the strangle. Mathematically, the condition for a butterfly to be vega neutral is:

$$\frac{\text{Straddle notional}}{\text{Strangle notional}} = \frac{\text{Straddle vega}}{\text{Strangle vega}}$$

Regardless of the actual net vega exposure at and around the belly of the butterfly, as the price of the underlying asset gets sufficiently close to either the top strike or to the low strike of the strangle, we should expect an increase in the vega exposure (recall that the trader sold the straddle and bought the strangle). This can arise from a reduction in an already-short vega position or an increase in an already-long vega exposure. Finally, there will be a tendency for convergence to zero for much higher or much lower spot prices. Therefore (and rather unsurprisingly), the behaviour of vega will be (at least qualitatively) very similar to that of the behaviour of gamma.

7.5.5   Butterflies and volatility convexity

The main reason that we chose to describe the butterfly as a combination of one straddle and one strangle is because, in our view, this is the easiest way to understand the volatility convexity (or dVega/dVol) embedded in the butterfly. In clarifying this crucially important concept, we strongly advise readers to use the example spreadsheet provided (Chapter 7 – Risk reversals & Butterflies) and, ideally, to build customized spreadsheets and pricing tools to familiarize themselves as much as possible with these concepts.

When discussing risk reversals, we mentioned the quantity dVega/dSpot, i.e., the derivative of the vega with respect to the spot price of the underlying asset, and we pointed out that the risk reversal is the typical instrument to hedge this quantity. When we began the discussion about vega, however, we also noted that there is another fundamental quantity related to the dynamic of vega, namely dVega/dVol (also known as volga). Volga is the first derivative of vega with respect to the underlying asset volatility or, as some prefer, the second derivative of the price of the option with respect to volatility.

dVega/dVol, or volga, is particularly important when considering exotic options, portfolio of derivatives and structured products. A detailed analysis of these topics, from a quantitative point of view, is clearly beyond the scope of an introductory book like this but we will try as much as we can to develop a simplified framework in order to highlight how dVega/dVol (and also dVega/dSpot) can affect the price of certain derivatives and how any misunderstanding of these derivatives can lead to serious mispricing and mis-hedging of individual derivatives positions or a derivatives portfolio as a whole. Our aim in this book is to inform readers about the existence of these risks and to suggest an indicative framework that allows one to detect when these second-order risks will arise in certain types of derivatives. At the end of this chapter we will also briefly discuss classes of models beyond Black–Scholes that try to address option pricing and hedging whenever the Black–Scholes framework is clearly not sufficient to provide a robust pricing and hedging solution.

At this stage, let us begin by showing that a butterfly is strongly affected by the dVega/dVol. As we discussed in section 6.5, when we analysed the vega behaviour for at-the-money or close to at-the-money options (we invite interested readers to verify numerically this behaviour using the pricing tools provided in the spreadsheet "Chapter 7 – Risk reversals & Butterflies"), the vega of a straddle tends to show little sensitivity to the level of volatility that is implied by the straddle itself. In other words, the dVega/dVol of the straddle tends to be relatively

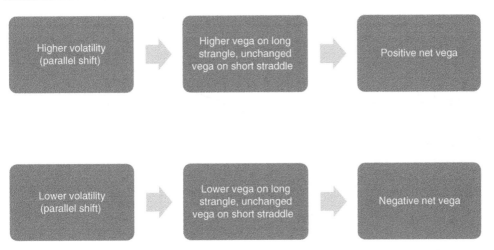

Figure 7.20   Positive volatility convexity

low (or even virtually zero). In the same section (6.5), however, we showed that the level of dVega/dVol tends to increase considerably for out-of-the-money options. As the strangle can be seen as a combination of two out-of-the-money options (one call and one put), it will embed a significant exposure to dVega/dVol.[6]

Going back to the butterfly example, we can see that it is comprised of an element that has a relatively insignificant dVega/dVol (the straddle) and an element that embeds a meaningful exposure to dVega/dVol (the strangle).

Recall now that we can always set the notional of the straddle in a way that makes the whole butterfly vega neutral. The final position will be a butterfly that is virtually vega neutral at inception but, at the same time, embeds either a positive dVega/dVol position (when the wings are bought and the belly is sold) or a negative dVega/dVol position (when the wings are sold and the belly is bought).

How about an example to reinforce this? Consider our previous example (introduced in 7.5.4) of a butterfly where the trader sells the straddle and buys the strangle setting the respective notionals such that the overall vega is zero for the current level of volatility. The trader is long the wings and we would expect this position to be long dVega/dVol. Is this the case? Starting from a position of vega neutrality, if volatility increases by the same amount for all three strikes then, all else being equal, there is going to be an increase in the vega position of the strangle and a substantially unchanged vega position of the straddle. In other words, the net vega position will become positive. On the other hand, if volatility sees a downward parallel shift, the vega of the strangle is going to decrease, with a substantially unchanged vega on the straddle, causing the net vega positions to become negative. In other words, the fly embeds, at inception, a neutral exposure to vega and a positive exposure to volga (dVega/dVol) (Figure 7.20).

In Figure 7.21, we plot the net vega of the butterfly (vertical axis) against the level of volatility (horizontal axis). The ratio of the notional of the straddle with respect to the notional of the strangle has been chosen such that the butterfly is vega neutral when volatility is at

---

[6] To be clear, it is important to recall that a long position in an out-of-the-money option, be it either a call or put, will always generate a positive dVega/dVol position. That is why the total dVega/dVol exposure of a strangle can be significant.

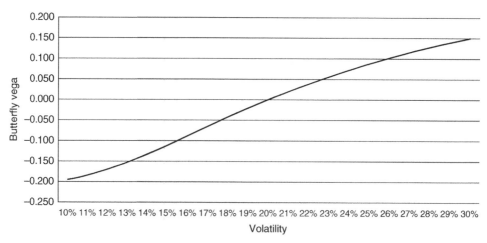

Figure 7.21   dVega / dVol profile of a 80–100–120 butterfly

20%; for simplicity, we have assumed that the volatility is constant for each strike (i.e., a flat volatility smile).

7.6 SOME ADDITIONAL REMARKS ON STRADDLES, RISK REVERSALS AND BUTTERFLIES

When we discussed the Black–Scholes framework, one of the key assumptions noted was related to the constant level of volatility assumed in pricing. We have observed, however, that volatility in the real world is not constant at all. More accurately, not only is volatility not constant over time but, as the existence of volatility skew shows, different strikes may have different levels of implied volatility while changes in the slope or in the convexity of the volatility skew are also possible, which is in direct contradiction to the Black–Scholes framework.

The plain vanilla options (or option strategies) that tend to be affected by these skew dynamics are:

1. Straddles. They tend to show a strong sensitivity to the absolute level of volatility (high vega) and very low sensitivity to dVega/dSpot and dVega/dVol. As such, they can be used to trade and to express views on the absolute level of volatility.
2. Risk reversals. The main feature is a high level of dVega/dSpot, minimal sensitivity to the absolute level of implied volatility (at least locally) and to the volatility convexity. Risk reversals are frequently used to take positions on the steepness of the volatility smile/skew.
3. Butterflies. The main feature is a high level of dVega/dVol with minimal sensitivity to the absolute level of implied volatility (at least locally) and to the slope of the volatility skew. They are typically traded to take position on volatility convexity.

The three strategies are so actively traded in some markets (typically FX and certain commodities) that the most common option quotes are precisely related to each of these. We will have volatility quotes for:

1. Fifty delta calls and puts (σ_{50}): they define a delta-neutral straddle.

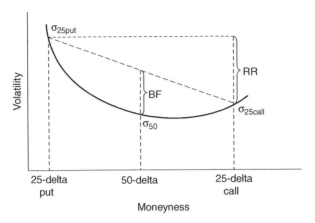

Figure 7.22   Risk reversal and butterfly

2. Risk reversals (*RR*): typically 25 delta risk reversals, i.e., the difference between the volatility of the 25 delta call (σ_{25call}) and the volatility of the 25 delta put (σ_{25put}), i.e., $\sigma_{25call} - \sigma_{25put}$. 10 delta risk reversals are often quoted too.
3. Butterflies (*BF*): typically 25 delta butterfly, i.e., the difference between the average volatility of the 25 delta call and 25 delta put and the 50 delta volatility; in formula: $(\sigma_{25call} + \sigma_{25put})/2 - \sigma_{50}$. 10 delta risk reversals are often quoted too.

From the formulae above, it is easy to infer the levels of σ_{25call} and σ_{25put} once the σ_{50}, *RR* and *BF* are specified:

$$\sigma_{25call} = \sigma_{50} + BF + {}^{1}\!/_{2}RR$$

and

$$\sigma_{25put} = \sigma_{50} + BF - {}^{1}\!/_{2}RR$$

It is often useful and to aid understanding to think of the quantities *RR* and *BF* in graphical form (Figure 7.22).

7.7   VEGA HEDGING IS NOT JUST SIMPLY OFFSETTING OVERALL VEGA EXPOSURE

If we assume that volatility is constant then the concept of vega is pretty much irrelevant: in a world where volatility does not change, there is no need to hedge (nor to measure) the sensitivity of the price of the option against something that is not going to change. In practice, however, the empirical evidence suggests that implied volatility changes over time. As such, it is important to measure vega and to be able to implement a vega-hedging strategy when appropriate. But this is not the end of the story. Hedging the vega of an out-of-the-money option, for example, with an at-the-money straddle is, most likely, not going to mitigate against the risk of a change in the slope or in the convexity of the volatility skew. In other words, using a straddle will allow the hedger to immunize his or her positions with respect to parallel shifts in the volatility skew (at least at inception) but will provide little or no benefit in the case of a change in the slope or in the convexity of the skew itself (as the straddle price is not affected by these types of movements). To express the same concept slightly differently, recall that the straddle carries little or no dVega/dSpot or dVega/dVol.

To sum up, the concept of vega hedging is not just a simple procedure of offsetting the overall vega exposure of a position. Rather, it has to focus on the higher-order derivatives such as dVega/dSpot or dVega/dVol and, therefore, probably has to involve risk reversals and butterflies. Only in this case the hedger will be able to control (or try to control) the risk arising from changes in the vega exposure due to changes in spot prices or volatility and, thereby, achieve much more robust vega hedging.

In the following section, we will introduce an extension of the Black–Scholes framework based on the idea of being able to build a portfolio that is not only vega neutral but is also neutral with respect to changes in the steepness of the volatility skew and of its convexity. In other words, neutral with respect to dVega/dSpot and dVega/dVol. This approach, also called the Vanna–Volga approach, due to its strong focus on these two quantities, is typically used for hedging certain exotic derivatives, in particular, in the FX space. The following section will introduce the Vanna–Volga framework.

7.8   HEDGING VOLATILITY RISK: A BRIEF INTRODUCTION OF THE VANNA–VOLGA APPROACH

As we shall soon see, certain exotic derivatives can show a significant dVega/dSpot (vanna) and/or dVega/dVol (volga) exposure that could be costly to ignore. The Vanna–Volga approach allows option traders to quantify the magnitude of the dVega/dSpot and dVega/dVol[7] exposures of certain options, so that their price can be adjusted accordingly.

What we plan to present here is merely an introduction, since a full discussion on this topic is well beyond the scope of this book.

The starting point when pricing an exotic option is to measure the dVega/dSpot and the dVega/dVol. This can be done easily by recalculating the option vega for a different level of spot price and for a different level of volatility.

At this point, we have to introduce the following two ratios:

vanna ratio = vanna of the exotic option/vanna of the risk reversal
volga ratio = volga of the exotic option/volga of the butterfly

These two ratios will help us to understand the quantity of the risk reversal and of the butterfly that could be traded to hedge (at least locally) the vanna and the volga of the exotic option. At this stage, we also need the following:

vanna contribution = Market price of the $RR - RR$ priced with σ_{50} on both strikes
volga contribution = Market price of the $BF - BF$ priced with σ_{50} on all strikes

These two quantities are a measure of how "wrong" the prices of a risk reversal and a butterfly are if the actual volatility smile is ignored and only the 50 delta volatility is used to price all the options.

---

[7] Even if in the standard Black–Scholes framework the volatility is assumed to be constant, it is still possible and meaningful to calculate the derivatives of the option price (or of other Greeks) with respect to the volatility itself.

We can now define:

$$\text{vanna cost} = \text{vanna ratio} \times \text{vanna contribution}$$
$$\text{volga cost} = \text{volga ratio} \times \text{volga contribution}$$

The last two quantities are a measure of "how wrong" the price of the exotic option is if we price it within the Black–Scholes framework, i.e., ignoring the impact of the steepness and of the convexity of the skew. We can, therefore, adjust the price obtained in the Black–Scholes framework (which we will call the BSPrice) for the exotic option using the two quantities we have just calculated. The Vanna–Volga price (VVPrice) of our exotic will therefore be equal to:

$$\text{VVPrice} = \text{BSPrice} + \text{vanna cost} + \text{volga cost}$$

The approach thus described is quite a simplistic formulation of the Vanna–Volga approach but it should provide an intuitive and practical way to tackle the consequences of a Black–Scholes framework that does not incorporate any skew effect. The Vanna–Volga approach is sometimes also called "trader's rule of thumb".

7.9 THE VOLATILITY SMILE – ONE STEP FURTHER

7.9.1 Introduction

Some assets, such as commodities or single stocks, tend to exhibit higher price volatility than other assets and this often comes with a more pronounced volatility smile, especially for short tenors. It is, therefore, important to understand the properties of the volatility smile, which can significantly affect the quality of pricing of derivatives and the quality of the calculation of their associated Greeks. We will see in this section how a "bad" smile can render a trading book unmanageable, how it can give derivative prices that are not in line with the market, and, in extreme cases, we will see how the smile can seemingly offer arbitrage opportunities, meaning that some derivatives with positive payoffs will turn out to have negative prices when priced with a "bad" smile.

We will also see how to estimate the term structure of volatility. The concept of "factors" will be introduced and, in particular, we will look at their importance for the pricing of derivatives on assets based on forward prices. Finally, we will briefly introduce the concept of stochastic volatility and discuss the pros and cons of using it. If addressed rigorously, most of these topics would involve complicated mathematics. We aim instead to provide here some intuition behind the quantitative aspects of volatility that impact the daily life of practitioners.

7.9.2 Why and how to build a smile

As discussed in section 7.7, quoting option prices and managing the impact of the volatility smile is necessary because, as useful as the Black–Scholes model is, it is based on some very strong assumptions, i.e., that the implied volatility of an option does not depend on the particular parameters of the option (i.e., the strike and the expiry) and that it does not change over time. However, this is not true in the real world. Volatility changes with the option specifics and with market conditions and this must be reflected in how options are priced in the real world. In mathematical jargon, this is expressed by saying that volatility is stochastic. Some pricing models take this into account explicitly and are therefore called stochastic volatility models.

Stochastic volatility models are complicated, however, and difficult to manage in practice. Moreover, for most options trades, it is not necessary to take on the additional complications and aggravations of using stochastic volatility models. They are never needed for options with European payoffs, for example.

When we introduced the concept of volatility smile/skew, we discussed the possible reasons for its existence and how it is typically reflected in market quotes. We also noted that, regardless of the reason why skew exists, it has to be taken into account when pricing options. Data on volatility smiles is collected and stored by analysts and traders for future use. In many assets, this is done by storing the implied volatility quotes at a predetermined set of delta points. Alternatively it could be done as a function of strike or moneyness or some other variables.

Again, regardless of the way in which the data on the smile is collected in a system, it will generally only be a small set of data points, usually an ATM point and one to three other delta points each for put and call maturity. A trading book will contain options with many more strikes and tenors, however. Any relevant pricing system will be required to compute implied volatility for any arbitrary strike. This is done by taking the points actually quoted in the market and calibrating a continuous function that returns an implied figure for the implied volatility corresponding to a given strike. There are two possible approaches that can be used to construct a smile function, a functional form and an empirical interpolation.

Functional form. This approach uses a mathematical function, inspired either by some prior financial mathematical model or by some view of the typical behaviour of the volatility market. A simple example approach, to illustrate the idea (although we would not recommend doing it this way), could be to use a parabola to interpolate across a smile that has three points. Any functional form for the smile will have a certain number of parameters and, consequently, it needs to match the number of volatility quotes available. As a minimum, a functional form for a smile will need three parameters; one to match the ATM volatility, one for the overall skew (i.e., the volatility difference between a given out-of-the-money call and the corresponding out-of-the-money put) and one for the overall smile curvature.[8]

Some examples of functional forms that are in commercial use are:

- The Vanna–Volga smile has been used with FX and precious metals, where three-point smiles are common. It is a form in which the implied volatility of an option at any arbitrary strike is computed by simulating a hedge which uses the three available options in the market to balance the vega, vanna and volga of the new option. This approach was introduced in section 7.8.
- The SABR smile is a functional form inspired by a very simple stochastic volatility model, which has seen extensive use in fixed income markets especially. It works best for assets that exhibit low volatility and so is rarely used in commodity markets.
- The SVI smile is a functional form inspired by more sophisticated stochastic volatility models, like the Heston model, which can handle more complicated smile shapes than both the Vanna–Volga and SABR smiles. In particular, it can handle the high volatilities and smiles typical with commodity markets.

Empirical interpolation. In this case, there is no attempt to impose a mathematical shape on the smile and, instead, the quotes available in the market data are taken as exact and some algorithm is used to do a "join-the-dots exercise". However, this approach needs some level

---

[8] Alternatively, one could think of this as the absolute level of the ATM volatility, the absolute level of the out-of-the-money call volatility and the absolute level of the out-of-the-money put volatility.

Table 7.3   Comparison between functional form and empirical interpolation

	Functional form	Empirical interpolation
Pros	Naturally smooth smile with the associated "good" properties Extrapolation comes for free	Always matches all market quotes exactly
Cons	May not reproduce market quotes exactly	Requires extra effort to handle extrapolation Will likely introduce discontinuities in the smile shape in the attempt to reproduce all quotes exactly

of sophistication and that it is not advisable to join the dots with straight lines between the quoted points. Note that it must be possible to compute implied volatilities for strikes which are more out-of-the-money than the available quoted calls and puts, i.e., the algorithm must be capable of extrapolation as well as interpolation.

A common approach is to use cubic splines, or some variation of them, to interpolate the implied volatility as a function of delta. Cubic splines are available in Excel.

In Table 7.3, we summarize the pros and cons of functional form smiles versus empirically interpolated smiles.

7.9.3   Smile arbitrage

The most important property that a "good" smile form must have is that the smile does not offer arbitrage opportunities. For example, a European option with a positive-only payoff profile cannot have a negative price. This can never happen when pricing a single vanilla European option but it can happen when pricing a strategy or portfolio or portfolio of options.

To be clear, if a trader is using a "bad" skew, i.e., one that offers arbitrage opportunities, he or she may literally be giving away money. In practice, if a smile can be arbitraged (or, "is in arbitrage"), some of the option prices generated from the smile will be wide off the market and the associated Greeks and the hedges will also be widely off the mark, potentially causing losses on both vanilla and exotic portfolios. It is clearly very important to check that a smile is not in arbitrage and, in fact, that it is not even near arbitrage.

At this point, an example may be useful. Consider an out-of-the-money call spread on oil. Let us say that today is the first of March and that the December forward contract for oil is at F dollars per barrel. The call spread is composed of a long call at strike K_1 and a short call at the higher strike K_2. Assuming that the implied volatility at K_1 is σ_1, the corresponding price of the long call option with strike K_1 can be calculated easily with the Black formula. Let's assume that its price is equal to $\$V$. There is an arbitrage if the price of the short call option with strike K_2 is equal to or higher than $\$V$, which corresponds to an implied volatility at K_2 of σ_2 or larger. This is equivalent to saying that the implied volatility associated with the strike K_2 cannot be higher than a level that makes the price of the call option with strike K_2 higher than the price of the option with strike K_1 (since $K_1 < K_2$).

The above reasoning can be applied to a call spread where K_2 is larger than K_1 only by a small amount, an infinitesimal amount mathematically speaking. It can be shown in that case that the no-arbitrage condition for a call spread can be seen as a condition on the maximum slope that the smile can have. A similar reasoning can also be applied in the case of a put spread, in which case it implies that a well-defined smile cannot have a too large negative slope.

Another, and more common in practice, example of arbitrage is the butterfly arbitrage. In this case the strategy is composed by three options at three strikes separated by an interval ΔK: K_1, K_2 and K_3, where $K_1 = K_2 - \Delta K$ and $K_3 = K_2 + \Delta K$. The strategy consists in a long call at K_1, a double-notional short call in K_2 and another long call in K_3. This gives a positive payoff between K_1 and K_3, with maximum level ΔK corresponding to strike K_2; outside the $[K_1, K_3]$ interval the payoff is zero.

In the case of the butterfly arbitrage, what matters is that the values of the two long options at K_1 and K_3, priced with Black and Scholes according to the volatility smile, must add up to a larger value than the double-notional option at strike K_2.

Similarly to the call spread case, this reasoning can be applied to the case in which ΔK is infinitesimal. This translates into a condition on the curvature of the smile, which cannot be too low.

7.9.4 Volatility surface

So far in this discussion, we have concentrated on how to interpolate the smile in order to price a payoff at an arbitrary strike, which is not directly quoted in the market. We will now look at how volatility behaves when it comes to option expiries that are not readily quoted in the market. There are two distinct cases to be handled here: options based on the spot prices of assets and options based on specific forward prices of assets (for example, oil or base metals).

Spot-based assets. In the case of spot-based assets, the volatility quotes are usually available on a set of rolling tenors. For example, there might be volatilities available for options expiring in 1 business day, 1 week, 2 weeks, 1 month, 1 quarter, 1 year, 2 years and 3 years, etc.

In this case, the volatility of an option expiring on a date between two tenors is generally computed by interpolating the two smiles whose expiries are just before and just after the expiry date of the option in question. The function that returns the implied volatility at an arbitrary tenor and strike is called the volatility surface.

Forward-based assets. This case is more complicated. For each forward expiry for the underlying asset (for example, a December contract on Brent Oil), there is generally an expiry for the associated options that is typically from zero to a few days earlier.[9] In order to specify a European option, the strike and expiry are not sufficient. One also needs to specify the forward contract underlying the option. In general, there will be a difference between the price of two options with the same strike and expiry but a different underlying forward. In order to be able to price an arbitrary European option on a forward-based asset, one volatility surface must be constructed for each forward. We discuss next how this can be done.

7.9.5 Volatility time dependence in forward-based assets

For the moment, consider the case of a forward-based asset (with forwards expiring monthly) without a volatility smile but with different implied volatilities for the ATM options associated with each monthly forward contract. Under most market conditions, the general pattern is that volatilities are highest at the shorter end of the curve, with the volatilities falling at a decreasing

---

[9] In some cases, for example agricultural commodities, the option expiry can be a much longer period before the expiry of the forward.

Table 7.4 Example of volatility term structure

Forward expiry	Option expiry	Volatility
31 Jan 2012	21 Jan 2012	35.08%
29 Feb 2012	19 Feb 2012	34.22%
31 Mar 2012	21 Mar 2012	33.41%
30 Apr 2012	20 Apr 2012	32.65%
31 May 2012	21 May 2012	31.93%
30 Jun 2012	20 Jun 2012	31.26%
31 Jul 2012	21 Jul 2012	30.64%
31 Aug 2012	21 Aug 2012	30.05%
30 Sep 2012	20 Sep 2012	29.49%
31 Oct 2012	21 Oct 2012	28.97%
30 Nov 2012	20 Nov 2012	28.48%
31 Dec 2012	21 Dec 2012	28.02%
31 Jan 2013	21 Jan 2012	27.59%
28 Feb 2013	18 Feb 2013	27.19%
31 Mar 2013	21 Mar 2013	26.81%
30 Apr 2013	20 Apr 2013	26.45%
31 May 2013	21 May 2013	26.12%
30 Jun 2013	20 Jun 2013	25.81%
31 Jul 2013	21 Jul 2013	25.51%
31 Aug 2013	21 Aug 2013	25.24%
30 Sep 2013	20 Sep 2013	24.98%
31 Oct 2013	21 Oct 2013	24.73%
30 Nov 2013	20 Nov 2013	24.50%
31 Dec 2013	21 Dec 2013	24.29%

rate progressively to an approximately constant level at the long end of the curve. Consider the hypothetical example of a volatility term structure on 1 Jan 2012 shown in Table 7.4.

While, in practice, there are always variations in the shape of volatility term structures for specific assets, this is a very common pattern. So, what does this structure tell us about the early volatility of an option? Consider the following example: what is the appropriate implied volatility of an OTC option expiring on 21 Dec 2012 referenced to the 30 Jun 2013 forward, whose listed option expires on 20 Jun 2013.

This answer is not available explicitly from the market but we can take a view. We can assume, for example, that the future period ahead behaves in a similar way to that implied by the market structure of volatilities. So, we could argue that (since there is a 6-month difference between the two option expiries) the ratio of volatilities between the OTC option expiring in Dec 12 and the listed option expiring in Jun 13 should be approximately the same as the ratio between the prompt volatility (Jan 2012) and the volatility 6 months later (21 Jul 2012), i.e., 30.64%/35.08% = 0.87. This would give as an estimate for the implied volatility on the OTC option of 0.87 ∗ 25.81% = 22.54%.

In this way, the pattern of volatilities associated with each forward contract in the market tells us something about the term structure of early volatilities of each individual forward contract.

The above example is by no means the only possibility. The important take-away is that, in order to be able to compute all the volatilities on a forward-based asset, one needs to make some assumptions, to build a model out of those assumptions and then to be able to verify that the model makes sense. A rigorous analysis of all such models is outside the scope of this book but some important points to consider are below.

7.9.6   Models of forward-based asset volatilities

There are many such models but they have some characteristics in common:

1. The long ends of price curves tend to have volatilities flattening out eventually.
2. The short ends tend to have different (generally higher) volatilities and they tend to move in a semi-independent way from the long-end volatilities. In most cases, however, the short- and long-end volatilities move in a partially correlated way, this needs to be taken into account by the model.
3. A skew correction must be part of the model so that all vanilla options available in the market data are priced within the market bid–ask spread.
4. Some assets require a more complicated model function and possibly the introduction of extra factors. Assets with seasonality are the most obvious example.

7.9.7   Calibrating a model of forward-based asset volatilities

The most obvious way to test that a model makes sense is to calibrate it to observable prices in the market. Any model will have parameters (e.g., the correlation between volatilities at the short and long end of the curve, the relative importance of the short end). Calibrating a model for forward-based assets means finding the values of the model parameters which best correspond to known data. There are two main ways to do this:

1. Historical analysis. Historical series of forward levels and/or volatilities are studied statistically to estimate the model parameters. This is mathematically straightforward but it ignores the current information available in the market. As a consequence, we would argue that this approach should be used as either a sanity check or as a last resort if it is impossible to estimate model parameter from the available market data.
2. Market instruments. The model parameters are calculated using available market prices of those derivatives that are affected by the term structure of volatility. Examples of such products are early-expiry vanilla options, swaptions (the option to enter into a forward-starting swap) and, to some extent, calendar spreads (an option on the spread between two different forwards).

To assess whether a model is appropriate for a particular underlying asset, ensure that the model's parameters do not change too much from one day to the next and that the implied prices of any options that were not part of the calibration process are in line with any available in the market. If, however, the parameters jump from one day to the next, then it may be time to look for a different model.

7.10   PRICING EXOTIC OPTIONS[10]

The examples that we have discussed so far in this chapter have been limited to simple options. Any portfolio of vanilla Europeans, for instance, requires only the knowledge of the

---

[10] Exotic options will be described in more detail in Chapter 8.

market-implied volatility to be priced. Other products are somewhat more complicated, for instance Asian options or swaptions, although there still is an analytic approximation that can be computed in a relatively simple way.

Finally, there are more exotic products for which no good analytical approximation is available. Some examples of such products are:

1. Barrier trades: receiving the payoff is conditional on the asset reaching (for "in" barriers) or not reaching (for "out" barriers) a certain contractual level. The payoff itself can be anything from a fixed amount of cash to another option.
2. Callable trades: these trades have, in principle, a series of cash flows but they can be terminated before maturity either at the discretion of one of the counterparties or according to some combination of conditions. For example, in TARNs, when the total of previous cash flows has reached a certain amount.
3. Multi-asset trades: even simple basket trades are difficult to price with sufficient precision using an analytic technique. This becomes even more difficult with more complicated multi-asset payoffs like best-of/worst-of options and basket auto-callable trades.
4. Financial models of a physical facility: for example, gas storage deals, where a financial institution essentially rents gas storage tanks and dictates when to fill them with gas or, conversely, when to sell the gas inside.

These trades are, in most cases, path dependent: a future cash flow depends not only on the future state of the market but also on the price history of the market since the inception of the trade.

For such trades, an approach is needed which can be used, not only to compute the possible states of the market at the derivative's expiry, but also the path of the market during the life of the trade. The most generally applicable approach, in this case, would be the Monte Carlo technique that we described earlier.

7.11   DIFFERENT TYPES OF VOLATILITY

7.11.1   Volatilities discussed so far

Thus far, we have touched upon two types of volatility:

1. Market-implied volatility, constructed from the prices of those European options available in the market and interpolated to all possible expiries and strikes.
2. Step volatilities used in Monte Carlo, PDEs and binomial/trinomial tree techniques, which were mentioned earlier but not properly defined.

In this section, we will expand in more detail the way in which different types of volatility are defined and used in pricing.

7.11.2   Forward-starting volatility

In the case of a Black–Scholes spot process, with no smile and no time-dependent volatility, the issue is simple. The volatility used in the Monte Carlo simulation is the same as the market-implied volatility of the asset. So, if the implied volatility for the underlying asset is 24.5% then the volatility used to generate the Monte Carlo path will be 24.5% for any time step and for any value of S, the spot level.

Table 7.5 Example of
volatility term structure

Tenor	Market volatility
1d	30%
2d	29%
3d	28%

In practice, however, the market-implied volatility will depend upon the strike (i.e., there is a smile) and on the option expiry, due to the volatility term structure (both in the case of spot-based and forward-based assets). This needs to be reflected in the pricing model used in the Monte Carlo simulation and the equation, in this case, will take a form:

$$S(k) = S(k-1) * [\text{yield}(t) * dt + \text{vol}(t, S) * W * \text{sqrt}(dt)]$$

which states, explicitly, that the volatility depends on time, t, and the spot level, S. In addition, note the dependence of the yield on time.

From a previous discussion on the construction of the volatility surface (sections 7.1, 7.3 and 7.4), we can recall that we have a known market-implied volatility, vol_mkt(T, K), as a function of maturity T and strike K. On the other hand, in a Monte Carlo simulation, we have a step volatility vol(t, S) as a function of simulation time t and spot level S. Unfortunately, the two are not the same. To see why this is the case, ignore smile for a moment and consider the example of an ATM volatility term structure for a spot-based asset shown in Table 7.5.

Now, assume that a Monte Carlo simulation needs to be constructed to price a 3-day barrier. There will be three Monte Carlo steps: from evaluation date to 1d, from 1d to 2d, from 2d to 3d.

To compute each step's volatility, consider the following. Since the first step goes from the evaluation date to the first volatility quote available in the market, we can consider the implied volatility constant for the duration of the step. This is exactly like a Black–Scholes process with maturity 1 day. Consequently, the Monte Carlo step volatility is 30%.

For time step two, it is tempting to think that the Monte Carlo step volatility is 29% but this would be a mistake. We need the "average" volatility for the 2 days to be 29%. As we saw above, the first step volatility is 30%. If the step volatility for the second this step is 29%, then the average overall volatility for the first 2 days would be somewhere between 30 and 29%. If this were the case, however, then the overall Monte Carlo volatility from evaluation date to 2d would not match the market-implied volatility of 29%.

The correct way to compute the step two volatility is to match the total variance in the market for 2d with the total variance along a Monte Carlo path from the evaluation date to 2d. For any option tenor, the market total variance is the square of the volatility times the tenor. For a Monte Carlo path, the total variance is the sum of each step's variance; a step's variance, in turn, is the product of the square of the step volatility times the step's time interval. This gives us the following equation:

$$\text{vol\_mkt}^2(2d) * 2d = \text{vol}^2(1) * dt + \text{vol}^2(2) * dt$$

where vol(1) and vol(2) are the Monte Carlo step volatilities of the first and second steps. Replacing with the numbers above, the remaining unknown quantity is the second step's volatility:

$$(29\%)^2 * 2 = (30\%)^2 * 1 + \text{vol}^2(2) * 1$$

Solving the above gives the value vol(2) = 27.96%. In order to obtain an overall volatility of 29% across the first two steps, the second step's volatility vol(2) has to decrease more than the spot-implied volatility does.

The volatility for step three can be computed in two mathematically equivalent ways. One is to match the market total variance for $3d$ with the sum of the corresponding three Monte Carlo step variances:

$$\text{vol\_mkt}^2(3d) * 3d = \text{vol}^2(1) * dt + \text{vol}^2(2) * dt + \text{vol}^2(3) * dt$$

But the sum of the first two steps' variances, as noted in the previous step, is the same as the total market variance for $2d$. Reworking the above equation, we get:

$$\text{vol}^2(3) * dt = \text{vol\_mkt}^2(3d) * 3d - \text{vol\_mkt}^2(2d) * 2d$$

and vol(3) = 25.88%.

In general, given two times s and t, s is less than t, where the market-implied volatility is known and without smile, the volatility "vol" that solves the equation:

$$\text{vol}^2 * (t - s) = \text{vol\_mkt}^2(t) * t - \text{vol\_mkt}^2(s) * s$$

is called the forward-starting volatility between s and t.

7.11.3 Local volatility

When smile is introduced to the volatility surface, the mathematics needed to compute the implied volatility that would be used in a Monte Carlo step becomes considerably more complicated, and a detailed treatment is outside of the scope of this book. The principle remains the same, however. The volatility surface for implied volatilities in the market, vol_mkt(T, K), allows one to price any vanilla option given its expiry T and strike K. There is one and only one function vol(t, S), called the local volatility, which is consistent with vol_mkt(T, K) in the sense that a process whose instantaneous volatility is vol(t, S) will result in the same vanilla European option prices as the Black–Scholes formula price from the market volatility.[11]

In practical terms, this means that the price of any portfolio of vanilla European options, in a Monte Carlo simulation using the local volatility as the step volatility, will converge (for a large number of paths) to the Black–Scholes price of the portfolio. The same will be true of the price of vanilla options computed by PDEs, where applicable.

7.11.4 The limits of local volatility

At the start of this chapter, we mentioned that the basic Black–Scholes model is based on very strong assumptions, i.e., that an option's implied volatility does not depend on the parameters of the particular trade (i.e., strike and expiry) and that it does not change over time. Within the

---

[11] This can be demonstrated but it is not important for our discussion.

previous paragraphs, we have gone beyond some of these simplifications, with the introduction of smile, of the volatility term structure and, as a consequence, of local volatility.

One of the assumptions remains, however. In all models discussed above, volatility does not change over time. Unfortunately, we have a problem. The concept of local volatility implies that, given market prices available today, we know all the future volatilities of an asset, for any future time and any asset price. How does this apparent paradox affect pricing? Does it mean that the prices obtained with the techniques mentioned so far are wrong?

Well, option pricing is not about forecasting. For instance, when we compute the current price of an option according to its implied volatility and the Black–Scholes formula, we are not saying anything about the value that the option will eventually have at expiry. We would need a working crystal ball to do that. What we are saying is that it is possible to set up an arbitrage-free hedging strategy that will reproduce the value of the option, no matter the future behaviour of the market. Similarly, when using the local volatility in Monte Carlo pricing, we are just using current market data to build Monte Carlo paths that are equally probable *based on the information available today*. The model does forecast a volatility for tomorrow but it is not automatically invalidated if the volatility tomorrow is different.

Second, it can be demonstrated that, given the surface of implied volatility (or equivalently the local volatility), the price of all European payoffs, or any combination of European payoffs, is unique. In other words, any stochastic model that produces the same volatility surface will work exactly the same for all European payoffs.

So what is left? Payoffs in which the combinations of fixings at different times are important in determining the price. Examples of such payoffs are:

1. Performance options, also known as forward-starting options. Such option prices are based on the performance of assets between two future times t_1 and t_2, with $t_1 < t_2$.
2. Cliquets. These are portfolios of forward-starting options, with a global cap (or floor) on the total value of the strip.
3. Barriers. Consider, for instance, a knock-in barrier. It can only knock in once. The probability of touching the barrier at a given time heavily depends on the fixings at all previous times.

Consider the case of performance options in particular. As time elapses and reaches the date t_1 of the first fixing, performance options become simple European options and their value depends only on the market volatility. However, the market volatility in $t1$ will be different to the market volatility that we expect based on the market data at inception. Moreover, the time value of the option depends asymmetrically on the future volatility: if the volatility decreases from now until t_1, the price can only go down to zero while, if the volatility increases, the option price can increase indefinitely. In the models seen so far, however, the time value of an option comes from the future changes of the asset's price, not from changes in volatility. So, what sort of model is needed to incorporate the extra optionality of a performance option?

7.11.5 Stochastic volatility models

In this family of models, volatility can change through time, like the asset price itself, i.e., volatility is a stochastic process. For instance, in a Monte Carlo simulation of an asset under a stochastic volatility model, two paths are computed: a volatility path and an asset path. The steps in volatility are computed using a coefficient representing the variability of volatility, often (and sometimes improperly) called the vol-of-vol, short for the volatility of volatility. The steps in asset price are then computed using this dynamic volatility.

Having a stochastic volatility automatically creates a volatility smile. To understand this, compare two Monte Carlo paths of a stochastic volatility model:

1. In path one, volatility drops sharply and stays low for most of the path. Consequently, the asset price is not likely to change much and will reach the end of the path relatively near to the ATM level.
2. In path two, the volatility rallies, and is very high for most of the path. Here the asset price is likely to move a lot and to reach the end of the path either at a very high or a very low level.

When averaging across all paths in the Monte Carlo, paths ending far from the ATM level will have experienced, on average, a higher volatility than paths ending near ATM. In other words, a volatility smile is generated.

Similarly, but in a slightly more complicated manner, correlation between the changes in asset price and the changes in volatility tend to create skew. A positive correlation creates a high call skew, while a negative correlation creates a high put skew.

Thanks to the relationship between the stochastic volatility process and the smile implied by the model, it is possible to calibrate a stochastic volatility model that reproduces approximately the smile in the market.

Stochastic volatility models used in practice tend to have other parameters so that they also match the term structure of volatility, although these tend to be very model specific and outside the scope of this introduction.

Despite all this, there are significant drawbacks in stochastic volatility models:

1. European option prices cannot be reproduced perfectly, only approximately. Stochastic volatility models might be appropriate for exotic trades but they may not be appropriate for vanilla instruments.
2. The calibration of such models can be unstable, resulting in jumps in mark-to-market profit and loss.
3. If one calibrates such models using vanilla option prices, they could still give prices for exotics (cliquets, barriers...) that are not in line with prices observed in the market. Conversely, if one calibrates models using prices for exotics, the models might not be able to get near to the price of the vanillas.

To overcome some of these limitations, a further family of models is needed.

7.11.6 Local-stochastic volatility models

These models put together the characteristics of local volatility and stochastic volatility:

1. Volatility is stochastic, with its own vol-of-vol, as above...
2. ... but the actual volatility is adjusted with a local volatility correction, which is such that the prices of all European options are reconstructed exactly.

Local-stochastic volatility (LSV for short) models allow one to reproduce concurrently market prices of both exotics and vanilla options. The vanilla volatilities are matched by construction and the stochastic volatility parameters can be calibrated to the exotic prices.

This characteristic resolves issue 1 and 3 in section 7.11.5. However, a caveat remains. First, in many markets there is not enough liquid data on exotic trades to calibrate reliably an LSV model. The main exceptions are probably FX and gold market. Second, the calibration of an LSV model might also be unstable, making the use of the model difficult for anything more than initial pricing. Third, it is often difficult to calibrate a model so that the prices of options with wildly different maturities are all reconstructed correctly. In this case, the wisest path might be to avoid trading some products altogether!

SUMMARY

In this chapter, we looked at implied volatility across different strikes and across different option maturities. In the Black–Scholes world, volatility is constant. In the real world, however, we have a volatility surface. In general, for non-commodities, the volatility term structure tends to be upward sloping and reflects the additional risk and liquidity premia present at the back end of the volatility term structure. For certain commodities, however, such as oil and natural gas, the implied volatility term structure can be structurally downward sloping.

Even across similar maturities, however, there can be significant differences in the volatility curve. Volatility smiles and skew can be traded and we also looked at ways in which investors can take a view on the shape of the volatility curve by trading various option strategies.

Finally, we looked at the different "types" of volatility and we discussed some of the ways in which traders attempt to model volatility.

Exotic Derivatives

8.1 EXOTIC DERIVATIVES WITH FIXED PAYOFFS

In this section, we are going to introduce and describe exotic derivatives with fixed payoffs. Due to this feature, the price of the underlying asset measured on or at certain date(s) (or, more generally, its path within a certain timeframe) will determine only the *occurrence* of the payoff and not the amount of the payoff itself.

8.1.1 European digital options

A European-style *digital option*, sometimes referred to as a *binary option, all-or-nothing or cash-or-nothing option*, will pay out a fixed amount if the underlying asset is above (in the case of digital call options) or below (in the case of digital put options) a certain strike at a certain date (option expiry).

The European digital option is perhaps the simplest derivative one can imagine, since it requires just one observation that determines the binary event.

In the example below, we will assume a generic payoff of $1. Any other digital payoff can obviously be obtained by scaling up this payoff as appropriate (e.g., a $100 payoff can be thought of as a portfolio of 100 identical digital options each with $1 payoff).

Figure 8.1 shows the payoff of a European digital call ($1 payoff) on a generic underlying with strike equal to $100.

As the payoff is fixed, the price of the derivative is generally expressed as a percentage amount of the fixed payoff.

Therefore, if we say that the price of this digital is 45%, we mean that we have to pay $0.45 to enter this contract that can potentially pay out $1; or that we have to pay $45 premium if the payoff is $100.

8.1.2 One touch and no touch options

As we just described, the occurrence of the fixed payoff in case of a European digital option is determined only with respect to the price of the underlying asset observed at expiry. However, it is clearly possible to define derivatives with fixed payoff that will take place if the price of the underlying asset touches (or does not touch) a certain level (which we will call "barrier") during the life of the option. Generally, whether the barrier has been touched or not is determined based on continuous observation of the underlying price (typically in FX or certain commodities) or based on daily fixing (for instance, by observing only the closing values of an equity index or an exchange-traded commodity). It is worth mentioning that if the barrier observation is not continuous but is based, say, on daily fixings, the intraday dynamic of the underlying price will not be relevant for the purpose of assessing whether the barrier has been reached or not. Sometimes a payoff can be also defined based on the path of the underlying price with respect to two barriers, as we will shortly define.

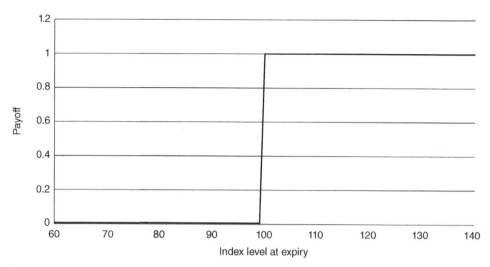

Figure 8.1   Payoff profile of a digital call option with 100 strike

In the case of just one barrier, we can define the following options:

- *One touch option*: the fixed amount will be paid out if the barrier is ever touched by the underlying price during the life of the option (i.e., at any time prior to expiry or at expiry). If the barrier is ever touched, the direction of the underlying price after the event is going to be irrelevant: as long as the price of the underlying asset touches the barrier once, the option will pay out the fixed amount (in which case, depending on the agreement, the payoff can take place as soon as the barrier is touched or at the option expiry). Sometimes the one touch option is also called "American digital option" (i.e., a digital option with the possibility of exercise at any time), but we prefer the more common definition of one touch option.
- *No touch option*: the fixed amount will be paid out if the barrier is never touched by the underlying during the life of the option (i.e., at any time prior to expiry or at expiry). As in the one touch case, different ways of observing the barrier can be agreed (i.e., based on continuous observations or at predetermined fixings).

As in the case of European digital, the prices of the one touch and no touch options are also generally expressed as a percentage of the fixed payoff.

Compared to the price of the corresponding European digital, we can observe that the price of one touch is going to be higher under the same conditions as it has more chances to expire in-the-money; it is also worth noting that, in general, increasing the frequency of the observation (say from daily to continuous) will increase the chance of reaching the barrier, increasing the price of the one touch option and reducing the price of the corresponding no touch option.

Also, we can define a sort of one touch–no touch parity: as the probability to touch the barrier is one minus the probability not to touch it, we will obviously have that the sum of the price of a one touch and the price of a no touch with same barrier and expiry will be equal to 100% (we are expressing these prices in percentage terms and ignoring the presence of the discount factor for simplicity[1]).

---

[1] Taking into account the discount factor, the sum of the two prices will have to be equal to the discount factor itself.

In case of two barriers, we can define the following options:

- *Double touch option*: the fixed amount will be paid out if either barrier is ever touched by the underlying price during the life of the option (i.e., at any time prior to expiry or at expiry).
- *Double no touch option*: the fixed amount will be paid out if no barrier is ever touched by the underlying price during the life of the option (i.e., at any time prior to expiry or at expiry). As in the one touch case, different ways of observing the barrier can be agreed (i.e., based on continuous observations or at predetermined fixings).

It goes without saying that in this case, one barrier will have to be above and one below the current price of the underlying asset (otherwise the barrier that is furthest out will have no impact).

8.1.3   Combinations of fixed payoff options

It is common to combine more than one fixed payoff option to obtain a highly customized derivative.

We will now present an example and discuss the relevant decomposition into individual options. Let us assume that an investor buys the following structure:[2]

Underlying: Gold
Initial Date: 2 January 2013
Expiry Date: 3 June 2013
Observation Dates: daily closing price from Initial Date to Expiry Date
Notional: $2,000,000
Spot price: $1,600/oz
Barrier1: $1,700/oz
Barrier2: $1,800/oz
Barrier3: $1,900/oz
Payoff1: 5% of the Notional
Payoff2: 10% of the Notional
Payoff3: 20% of the Notional

Payoff payments are dependent on the following:

- If on any Observation Date, the price of gold reaches $1,700 (inclusive) but does not reach $1,800, then the option pays out 5% of the notional at maturity, i.e., $100,000.
- If on any Observation Date, the price of gold reaches $1,800 (inclusive) but does not reach $1,900, then the option pays out 10% of the notional at maturity, i.e., $200,000.
- If on any Observation Date, the price of gold reaches $1,900 (inclusive), then the option pays out 20% of the notional at maturity, i.e., $400,000.
- In any other case the option pays out $0 at maturity.

Analysing the payoff profile, it can be easily decomposed into three one touch options with the same expiry (3 June 2013), different barrier levels (1,700, 1,800 and 1,900) and daily observation. The payoff of the first one touch option (with barrier equal to $1,700) will be

---

[2] This structure can be embedded in a structured product. In Chapter 10, structured products will be analysed in more detail.

equal to \$100,000. Also the payoff of the second one touch option (with barrier equal to \$1,800) will have to be equal to \$100,000. This is because if \$1,800 is ever reached (with \$100,000 payoff), also \$1,700 would have been reached (for obvious reasons, with \$100,000 payoff too) and the sum of the two payoffs will be equal to \$200,000, matching the definition of the product. If \$1,900 is ever reached, the investor will receive an additional \$200,000 (therefore the total will be \$400,000, again matching the payoff profile of the structure).

This is an example of more complex derivative that can be decomposed in simpler individual options. At this point it should be clear that the price of the overall structure on gold will have to be equal to the sum of the prices of the individual components. Going back to our example, if we assume that the prices of the three individual one touch options are respectively 30%, 25% and 15%, the price of the overall structure can be calculated multiplying these percentage prices for the respective payoffs and adding the results. In other words:

$$\text{Total price} = 30\% \times \$100,000 + 25\% \times \$100,000 + 15\% \times \$200,000 = \$85,000$$

The total price can be also expressed as a percentage of the notional, i.e., 4.25%.

8.2   OTHER COMMON EXOTIC DERIVATIVES

8.2.1   Barrier options

A *barrier option* is an arrangement such that, if the price of the underlying asset crosses a preset *barrier (or trigger) level*, at some time before expiration, then an option is either activated ("knocked-in") or an existing option is deactivated ("knocked-out"). Barrier options are an extension of vanilla options. Standard calls and puts have payoffs that depend on the strike, while barrier options have payoffs that depend on the strike and the barrier.

- Where the option is activated, with the price of the underlying asset hitting a barrier, it may be known as an "up-and-in", "knock-in" or "down-and-in" option.
- Where the option is deactivated (or extinguished), with the price of the underlying asset hitting a barrier, it may be known as an "up-and-out", "knock-out" or "down-and-out" option.

For example, assume a European-style call option on a US equity with an underlying spot price of \$10 and a knock-out barrier set at \$12. This option will behave like a vanilla European call, except if the spot price of the equity moves above \$12. At this point, the option "knocks-out". Note that the option does not reactivate if the spot price falls back below \$12. Once the option is knocked-out, it is knocked-out permanently.

Barrier options come in eight different permutations. The four main types of standard barrier options are:

- *Up-and-out*. The spot price is below the barrier level and has to move up for the option to be knocked-out.
- *Down-and-out*. The spot price is above the barrier level and has to move down for the option to be knocked-out.
- *Up-and-in*. The spot price is below the barrier level and has to move up for the option to be activated.
- *Down-and-in*. The spot price is above the barrier level and has to move down for the option to be activated.

In addition, each barrier type can take the form of either a call or a put – hence, the total of eight permutations.

Note that, of these eight, four will knock-in or knock-out when the options are in-the-money (for instance, an *up-and-in* call option with strike 10 and barrier 12 or an *up-and-out* call option with same strike and barrier). These are called *reverse barrier options*. They can pose significant hedging challenges for the seller. On the other hand, if the option is knocked-in or knocked-out when it is out-of-the-money (for instance, a *down-and-in* call option with strike 10 and barrier 8 or a *down-and-out* call option with same strike and barrier) it is normally called *regular barrier option*.

As in the case of one touch or no touch options, in the case of barrier options the barrier can be monitored continuously or with a certain frequency. It is also worth noting that if the barrier is only monitored at expiry, the barrier option can be expressed as a combination of a European vanilla and a digital option; we will leave the decomposition to the reader.

Sometimes in the case of knock-out options a rebate can be agreed and it is going to be paid out if the barrier is hit, triggering the knock-out even for the option. Rebates can be simply thought of as one touch options that pay out when a barrier is triggered.

Barrier options tend to be cheaper (sometimes even considerably cheaper) than vanilla options with the same strike and maturity. As such, barrier options tend to be thought of as lower-cost options. Of course, the cost saving is not a free lunch and the buyer of a barrier option is giving up some of the protection (or some upside) that would be afforded by a vanilla option. In a sense, a barrier option allows a buyer to purchase insurance or protection (or simply take a view) that more accurately represents his/her view on the possible future price moves of the underlying asset. For example, if you want to hedge against a drop in the price of an equity (currently priced at $5) but you are also willing to bet that the price will not go below $3, then you can buy the reverse knock-out put barrier option and pay less premium than the vanilla put option.

As should be clear from the preceding paragraph, buyers of barrier options are able to use them to gain exposure to future market scenarios that are more complex than the simple bullish or bearish view implied by standard call and put options. By choosing a barrier option rather than a vanilla option, the buyer avoids paying for those scenarios he/she thinks are highly unlikely. Alternatively, he/she can enhance his/her return by selling a barrier option that pays off only under scenarios that he/she thinks are highly improbable.

As another example, suppose that a stock is trading just above a key support level. An investor believes that the price of the stock is going to rise from the current level but that, if it happens to drop below the support level, it will continue to fall further. The investor can buy a down-and-out call that gets knocked-out if the stock falls below the support level at any point before the option expiration date. In this way, the investor has avoided paying for the scenario in which the stock declines substantially and then rises again since he/she believes this to be unlikely.

It is very common to embed barrier options in structured products; for instance, as we will discuss in Chapter 10, a down-and-in put can be used to build non-principal-protected products, or an up-and-out call can be used to provide cheaper upside exposure, as we will analyse in more detail.

In–out parity

In the world of barrier options, the put–call parity relationship is replaced by the *in–out parity*. *Note that this is only true for European-style options without rebate.* Combining one "knock-in" option and one "knock-out" option with the same strike, barrier and termination date is equivalent to the vanilla option. This follows from simple arbitrage. Simultaneously holding the "knock-in" and the "knock-out" option guarantees that exactly one of the two will pay out identically to a standard European option while the other will be worthless.

So:

- The price of a down-and-in call (put) plus the value of a down-and-out call (put) is equal to the price of a vanilla call (put).
- The price of an up-and-in call (put) plus the price of an up-and-out call (put) is equal to the price of a vanilla call (put).

8.2.2   Asian options

Asian options are options on the average value (geometric or arithmetic) of the underlying asset price from inception to expiry. They are sometimes called "average price" options. Their payoffs depend on a weighted combination of events over a certain period. In order to calculate the average, prices can be sampled daily or, more commonly, sampled discretely.

There are two common types of Asian options:

- The option's payoff is based on the difference between the average price of the underlying asset over a specific period of time and the strike price. This is sometimes called a fixed strike. The payoff of an Asian call option with fixed strike is Max(Average Underlying – Strike,0) and the payoff of an Asian put option with fixed strike is Max(Strike – Average Underlying, 0). The traded average price options (TAPO) traded on the London Metals Exchange are an example of this type of option.
- The option's exercise price is the average of the underlying asset price over a specific period of time versus the final price. This is sometimes called a floating strike. The payoff of an Asian call option with floating strike is Max(Final Price – Average Strike,0) and the payoff of an Asian put option with floating strike is Max(Average Strike – Final Price, 0). Such options are common in electricity markets and are used by hedgers whose primary risks are related to the average price of the underlying electricity market/product.

When thinking about the valuation of Asian options, one must not only consider the current price of the asset but also the "running average". This is the average price of the asset from inception until the valuation date. The option value is then a function of the underlying price, the running average price and the other usual suspects, such as time to maturity, implied volatility, etc. Wilmott (2006) calls this strong path dependency to differentiate from the weak path dependency of, for example, barrier options.

Benninga (2008) argues that Asian options are particularly useful when the user is selling the underlying asset through the option period and is therefore exposed to the average price and where there is danger of price manipulation in the underlying. The Asian option mitigates the effect of manipulation since it is based not on a single price but on a sequence of prices.

It is important to note that the payoff from an Asian call option cannot be higher than the average payoff of n plain vanilla call options expiring on each observation date. This condition holds because the Asian option is written on the average underlying price, i.e., it is possible for observations higher and lower than the strike price to offset each other before the option payoff formula is applied. On the other hand, when taking the average option payoff this offset will not take place, i.e., the individual options will be in-the-money or out-of-the-money and only afterwards would the average payoff be calculated.

To recap, the payoff of an Asian call option with fixed strike:

$$\text{Max}(\text{Average Price} - \text{Strike}, 0)$$

where:

$$\text{Average Price} = \frac{\sum_{i=1}^{n} S_i}{n}$$

Payoff of average of call options:

$$\frac{\sum_{i=1}^{n} \text{Option}_i}{n}$$

where:

$$\text{Option}_i = \text{Max}(S_i - \text{Strike}, 0)$$

Asian call option payoff $\leq$ Payoff of average of call options (where as usual we indicated with S_i the price of the underlying asset at time i). The same logic applies to an Asian call option with a floating strike and to an Asian put option with a fixed or floating strike.

Since Asian options are written on an average price, the underlying price for the Asian option (i.e., the average price) will generally be less volatile than the underlying price measured only at the expiry date. We should expect Asian options to be cheaper than the corresponding European options. Since there is no closed formula for pricing arithmetic Asian options, analytical approximations can be used although these are outside the scope of this book. Alternatively, it is possible to price Asian options using Monte Carlo.

8.3 EUROPEAN DIGITAL OPTIONS: PRICING AND GREEKS

8.3.1 Pricing European digital options

The price of the generic $1 payoff European digital option can be calculated as the discounted risk-neutral probability of the price of the underlying ending up above (for digital calls) or below (for digital puts) the strike price at expiry. In the Black–Scholes framework, there is a very simple formula to calculate the probability of the underlying being above the strike price at expiry. The probability is equal to $N(d_2)$ where, once again, the function $N(x)$ is the cumulative probability distribution function for a standardized normal variable (i.e., the probability that a standardized normal variable will be less than x) and:

$$d_2 = \frac{\ln(S/K) + (r - \sigma^2/2)(T - t)}{\sigma\sqrt{T - t}}$$

where as usual S is the spot price of the underlying asset, K is the strike price of the digital, r the risk-free interest rate expressed with continuous compounding, σ is the volatility and $T - t$ is the time to expiry.

The probability calculated using $N(d_2)$ is with reference to the event occurring at the expiry date (T). To obtain the price of the digital at any given time t, where $t \leq T$, one needs to discount this probability, i.e., one has to multiply it by the relevant discount factor $DF(t, T)$. In other words, the price of the digital call is:

$$DF(t, T) N(d_2)$$

It is useful to recall that this is a risk-neutral probability, i.e., it has nothing to do with the expectations that individual market participants have of the probabilities of the price movements. Rather, it is related to the replication cost of the payoff assuming that some basic assumptions hold.[3]

It is also worth mentioning that the formula $DF(t, T)N(d_2)$ is for a digital call with a \$1 payoff (more accurately we should say a payoff equal to 1 unit of currency). When pricing a generic digital call with a payoff of, say, W dollars (or W units of currency), one simply has to multiply formula above by W. Another way to think of it might be that $DF(t, T)N(d_2)$ is the percentage of the digital payoff W.

As with vanilla options, there is a sort of put–call parity for digital options that is quite intuitive. Buying a digital call is financially equivalent to selling a digital put.

Assume that a trader buys a digital call. He or she is going to pay a premium, say 40% of the payoff. In return, he or she will receive the payoff at expiry if the price of the underlying is above a certain strike price at the option expiry. Ignoring, for now, the effect of discount factors (we could also assume that interest rates are zero), we will show that the position is equivalent to a sale of a digital put at the same strike price where the premium is 60% of the payoff. The 60% digital put premium is equal to 100% − price of digital call, i.e., 40%. The equivalence of the two strategies will hopefully be clear from the following scenario analysis:

Scenario 1: The price of the underlying asset is above the strike price when the option expires. The call is in-the-money and the put is out-of-the-money.

- If the trader had bought the digital call option for 40% of the payoff, he or she is going to receive 100% of the payoff at expiry since the digital call option expires in-the-money and the total profit will be (100% − 40%) × payoff, i.e., 60% of the payoff.
- If the trader had sold the digital put option for 60% of the payoff, he or she is going to pay zero at expiry since the digital put option has expired out-of-the-money and the total profit will be 60% × payoff, the same as above.

Scenario 2: The price of the underlying asset is below the strike price when the option expires. The call is out-of-the-money and the put is in-the-money.

- If the trader had bought the digital call option for 40% of the payoff, he or she will receive a zero payoff at expiry (because the digital call option expires out-of-the-money) and the total net loss will be equal to the premium paid, i.e., a loss of 40% × payoff.
- If the trader had sold the digital put option for 60% of the payoff, he or she will have to pay the full payoff at expiry since the digital put option expired in-the-money and the total loss will be (60% − 100%) × payoff = − 40% × payoff, the same as above.

Therefore, buying a digital call option (i.e., betting on a certain event happening) is equivalent to selling a digital put option with same strike and expiry (i.e., selling the bet that that event will not happen). Put another way, we can say that the price that one has to pay to place a bet on a certain event happening (a digital call) has to be equivalent to the price one has to receive to sell the opposite bet, i.e., that that event is not going to happen (a digital put).

Need more convincing? What if the trader simultaneously buys a digital call and a digital put (with the same strike, expiry and payoff)? The trader has bet both that the underlying

---

[3] For a summary of the key assumptions underlying the Black–Scholes framework, refer to section 5.4.

price will move such that the call is exercised and that the put is exercised. Ignoring bid–offer spreads for the moment, the trader is going to receive the full 100% payoff under any market environment. Arbitrage considerations suggest that for this trade not to offer a guaranteed risk-free profit to the buyer (and the seller) then the total price paid for making the two bets (one for the event to happen and the other one for the event not to happen) must be equal to the total payoff itself appropriately discounted. If this is not the case, a straightforward arbitrage opportunity can be exploited:

- If the total price (of buying both bets) is lower than the present value of the digital payoff, it is obviously profitable to buy both bets, thereby getting the digital payoff at expiry with 100% probability.
- If the total price (of buying both bets) is higher than the present value of the digital payoff, the opposite strategy of selling both bets and having to pay the digital payoff with 100% probability will clearly be chosen to generate a risk-free profit (arbitrage).

To sum up, ignoring bid–offer spreads, if the price of a digital call is $DF(t, T)N(d_2)$, then the price of the corresponding digital put (i.e., with same strike, expiry and payoff) will be equal to $DF(t, T)(1 - N(d_2))$.

In Figure 8.2, we present the evolution over time of the price of a digital call with strike equal to \$100. In the right-hand portion of the chart, one can see the evolution of the digital option price over time for an in-the-money option (convergence to 100% payoff), whereas the left-hand portion shows the price convergence to zero. Close to the strike, where the uncertainty is greatest, the price of the digital option is, rather unsurprisingly, close to 0.5.

At this point, we would note the similarity of the chart of the price of a digital call option with the one of the delta of a vanilla call option. We will explain the significance of this observation in more detail later in this chapter.

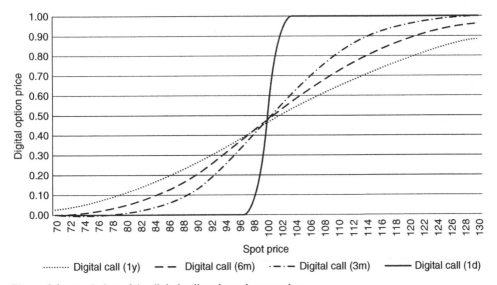

Figure 8.2 Evolution of the digital call option price over time

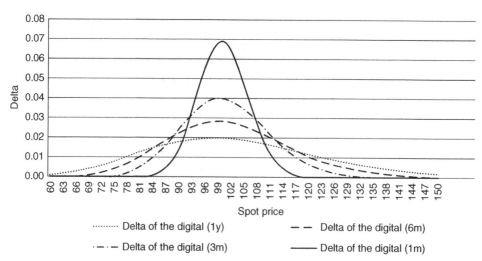

Figure 8.3   Evolution over time of the Delta of a digital call

8.3.2   The Greeks of a digital option

The delta of a digital option is relatively simple to understand (at least from a qualitative point of view). In the case of a long position in a digital call (or a short position in a digital put), the delta is going to be positive since there will be a gain arising from an increase in the price of the underlying asset. The price rise increases the probability of the digital call option expiring in-the-money or reduces the probability of the digital put option expiring in-the-money. Conversely, a short position in a digital call (or a long position in a digital put) will have negative delta.

We can deduce from the argument above that the sign of the delta of an individual digital option cannot flip from positive to negative or vice versa. Instead, it will always stay either positive or negative.

That said, it is important to understand that the magnitude of the delta of a digital option can change substantially through time, exhibiting highly unstable dynamic behaviour. As Figure 8.3 shows,[4] the delta will be high whenever there is a possibility that even a small change in the price of the underlying asset can cause an in-the-money option to become out-of-the-money or vice versa. It is natural to expect an option to be in this position when the underlying asset price is trading in close proximity to the strike price and when the option expiry is reasonably close. This is a function of the "all or nothing" nature of the digital option. In other cases, when the price of the underlying asset is trading relatively far from the strike and/or is far enough away from the option expiry, the delta will exhibit a much "flatter" shape. This is because a small change in the price of the underlying asset is not going to have a significant impact on the probability of the digital event taking place and so it will not have a significant impact on the price of the digital option itself. Even in this case, however, one should expect the value of the delta to be maximized when the price of the underlying asset is relatively close to the strike price since this is the level where the option payoff will be ultimately determined.

---

[4] The chart shows the evolution over time of the delta of a digital call option on a generic asset with a strike set at 100.

Analytically the delta of a digital call option can be calculated as:

$$DF(t, T) \frac{N'(d_2)}{S\sigma\sqrt{T-t}}$$

where d_2, S, σ and $T - t$ are as before and:

$$N'(x) = \frac{1}{\sqrt{2\pi}} e^{-x^2/2}$$

At this point, we would highlight the similarity of Figure 8.3 with that of the gamma of a vanilla call option. This is probably not too surprising given that we highlighted in section 8.3.1, the similarity of the price function for a digital call option with that of the delta of a vanilla call option. Qualitatively, the Greeks of the digital option can be thought of as higher orders of the Greeks of a vanilla call option (i.e., the price of a digital has the same shape of the delta of a vanilla, the delta of a digital has the same shape of the gamma of a vanilla and so on . . .).

Graphing the first derivative of the delta function in Figure 8.3 will give the gamma function for the digital call option. We invite interested readers to do this and then to compare this result with Figure 7.9, which shows the call spread gamma as a function of the underlying price. They will be similar. We will explain the significance of this comparison in more detail later in this chapter.

Analytically, the gamma of a digital call option can be calculated using the following formula:

$$-DF(t, T) \frac{d_1 N'(d_2)}{S^2\sigma^2(T-t)}$$

where d_2, S, σ and $T - t$ are as before and d_1 is defined in section 5.4.

Turning to the vega of a digital option. The first point to note is that the buyer of a digital option (either a call or a put) will tend to have a long vega exposure when the option is out-of-the-money and a short vega exposure when the option is in-the-money. This is unlike the vega exposure of a vanilla call or put option where the buyer is always long vega.

Using the same techniques that we have used before to assess the Greeks qualitatively, it should be relatively easy to see why it should be the case that the buyer of a digital option can see his or her vega exposure switch signs. When a digital call is in-the-money, for example, the buyer will end up getting the payoff if the underlying does not subsequently cross the strike (which would then cause the option to be out-of-the-money). In this situation, the buyer of the digital option benefits if the spot price of the underlying asset exhibits as little volatility as possible. Hence the short vega exposure. On the other hand, the buyer of an out-of-the-money digital option will want the price of the underlying to cross the strike in order for the option to expire in-the-money. The buyer therefore wants volatility in order to avoid the price of the underlying staying below the strike price (in the case of the digital call) or above the strike (in the case of the digital put). Hence the long vega exposure.

Obviously, the exact opposite is true for the seller of a digital option (either a call or a put). The seller will be long vega when the option is in-the-money (the seller needs the underlying asset price to cross the strike in order to avoid having to pay the digital amount at expiry) and short vega when the option is out-of-the-money (the seller does not want the underlying asset price to cross the strike, otherwise he or she will have to make payment of the digital amount at expiry).

Qualitatively, the vega of a digital call option looks similar to the vega of a call spread. We will now explain shortly the reason for the comparison of the risk profile of the digital call option and the risk profile of the call spread. Analytically, the vega function for a digital call option is as follows:

$$-df(t,T)\frac{d_1 N'(d_2)}{\sigma}$$

where d_2, t, T and σ are as before and d_1 is defined in section 5.4.

Given the discussion on vega it should be relatively easy to assess theta. Rather unsurprisingly, theta is going to have the opposite sign to vega (and also of gamma). Again a simple example will show why this is the case. When the digital call is in-the-money, a buyer will get the full payoff if the underlying asset price does not cross the strike. It should be easy to see that the buyer benefits from the simple passage of time. Every day that the underlying asset price stays where it is, the probability of the option expiring in-the-money will increase. Hence, the long theta exposure. On the other hand, the buyer of an out-of-the-money digital option will need the price of the underlying to cross the strike in order for the option to expire in-the-money. From a vega point of view, the buyer needs volatility in order that the price of the underlying does not stay below the strike (for the buyer of a digital call) or above the strike (for the buyer of a digital put). From a theta point of view, this translates into an equivalent (albeit opposite) problem, i.e., that the passage of time works against the holder. Every day that the underlying price does not move significantly, it is a "wasted" day since the underlying asset loses an opportunity to get closer to the strike price. Hence, the short theta exposure.

Again, the exact opposite is true for the seller of a digital option (either a call or a put). The seller will be short theta when the option is in-the-money (time works against the seller) but will be long theta when the option is out-of-the-money (time works in favour of the seller).

8.3.3 Incorporating volatility skew into the price of a digital option

It should be clear from the discussion of vega in section 8.3.2, that a digital option is affected by a strong dVega/dSpot since the sign of its vega can sometimes switch from positive to negative and vice versa if the price of the underlying asset changes sufficiently. To a certain extent, therefore, the price of a digital option and its Greeks tend to have something in common with the risk reversal that we discussed in section 7.5.3. Recall that risk reversals are strongly affected by the dVega/dSpot and that their price strongly depends on the steepness of the volatility smile. Hence, also the price of a digital option is strongly affected by the volatility smile. In this section, we present a very simple method that allows one to use the information embedded in the steepness of the smile around the strike of the digital option. In order to do so, however, we will focus first on how a European digital can be replicated by a call spread (in the case of a digital call) or by a put spread (in the case of a digital put).

Let us begin with an example. Imagine that we want to price a European digital call on a generic index (denominated in US dollars) with strike price equal to 100 index points and payoff equal to $10. If we build the 90–100 call spread (long one unit of a 90 call and short one unit of a 100 call), it is easy to observe that such a call spread offers a payoff that is equal to or greater than the payoff of the digital call option. In Figure 8.4, the area underneath the solid line (the payoff at expiry for the call spread) is clearly larger than the area underneath the dotted line (the payoff at expiry for the digital option).

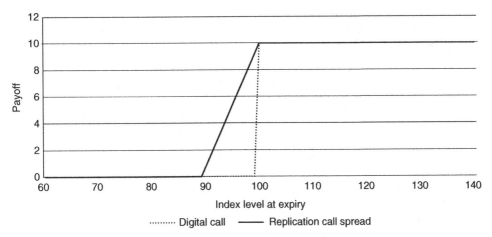

Figure 8.4   90 - 100 call spread vs. digital option with 100 strike and 10 payout

Since the payoff from the call spread is always equal to or greater than the payoff from the digital option, we can conclude that the price of the digital option has to be lower than the price of the replicating call spread (otherwise an obvious arbitrage opportunity will arise). The price of the call spread can easily be calculated from the Black–Scholes formula by using the appropriate level of implied volatility for the two different strikes consistent with the volatility skew.

Alternatively, we could have built the call spread in a slightly different way, i.e., with the lower strike equal to the strike of the digital 100 and the higher strike at 110. The resulting 100–110 call spread, unlike the call spread described in Figure 8.4, can never pay out more than the digital option, as highlighted by Figure 8.5. This time around, the area underneath the solid line (the payoff for the call spread) is clearly smaller than the area underneath the dotted line (the payoff for the digital option).

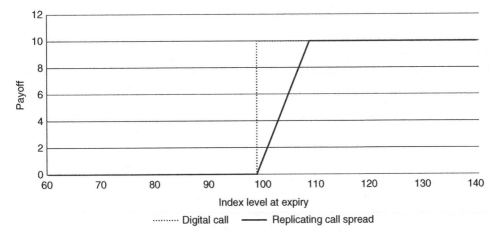

Figure 8.5   100 - 110 call spread vs. digital option with 100 strike and 10 payout

We can deduce that the price of the digital option has to be higher than the price of the replicating call spread. Of course, the 100–110 call spread price can be easily calculated with the Black–Scholes formula, taking into account the appropriate level of volatility for each strike consistent with the skew of the underlying asset.

This exercise, although very simple, offers a good starting point to understand how to embed the volatility skew into the price of a European digital option. As such, it is a significant step forward when compared with the earlier discussion around the pricing of the European digital. In that discussion, when we assumed risk-neutral probability, we were not able to embed any skew.

Looking back at the formulae that we presented for pricing a digital call or a digital put, one can see that volatility only appears once. Even if this volatility is assumed to be the one consistent with the underlying volatility digital option strike, there is no way to embed in the formula $DF(t, T)N(d_2)$ the slope of the volatility skew itself. Moreover, as can be seen from spreadsheet "Chapter 8 – Digital Options", in most cases, the slope of the volatility skew around the strike of the digital may affect the price of the digital option even more than the absolute level of volatility itself. Please refer to the spreadsheet "Chapter 8 – Digital Options" to better understand this issue.

To be clear, expressing the price of the digital as the price of a call spread does not mean that we cannot conceive of digital option prices as, essentially, probabilities of events occurring at expiry. To "convert" these prices back to probabilities, we would simply need to divide the prices by the maximum payoff of the call spread, which, by construction, is also equal to the payoff of the digital option. Moreover, depending upon how one builds the call spread, one would find either an upper limit or a lower limit for the price of the digital expressed as a probability. For instance, if the price of our 90–100 call spread turns out to be $5 and the price of the 100–110 call spread turns out to be $4, then we could conclude that the "true" price of the digital option is within the $4 to $5 range or that the risk-neutral probability of the event occurring at expiry (i.e., the underlying price to be above 100 index points) is within a 40 to 50% range. These numbers have been obtained simply by dividing the price of the two call spreads by the digital payoff of $10.

At this point, we should note that, what may seem to be a worthwhile method of embedding the skew in the price of our digital call option may also give us a relatively wide range, e.g., 40–50%. From time to time, we may need to "tighten" this range to increase the accuracy of our price. The way to do it is to reduce the difference of the strikes of the call spreads and increase the leverage or notionals traded. Again, an example will be helpful to clarify this. Instead of replicating the payoff of our 100 digital call option via a 90–100 call spread and a 100–110 call spread, we could perhaps halve the difference between the two strikes (say from 10 to 5 index points). In this case, however, we have to double the size of the call spread so that we keep the total payoff equal to 10, to be consistent with the payoff of the digital option.

In other words, we are reducing the difference between the two strikes by a factor of 2 and increasing the leverage (i.e., the number of options that are required) by the same factor in order to preserve the maximum payoff.

Compared with the previous example, we are reducing the areas where the call spreads do not accurately replicate the payoff of the digitals; in this way we are able to reduce the difference between the "overestimating" and the "underestimating" call spreads, with a meaningful increase in accuracy of our pricing.

Clearly, we can keep on reducing the difference between the two strikes of the call spreads and increasing the leverage of the options accordingly (as we did in the previous example).

The replication of the digital payoff will be more and more accurate; the price of the "overestimating" and the "underestimating" call spread will both converge to the "true" price of our digital option.

So, how do the prices calculated in this way compare with the price of the digital option that one could have obtained using the $DF(t,T)N(d_2)$ formula? As interested readers can discover, playing around with spreadsheet "Chapter 8 – Digital Options", for relatively flat volatility skews around the strike of the digital, the price calculated by the $DF(t,T)N(d_2)$ formula (i.e., ignoring the effect of the skew) will look comfortably within the range obtained using the call spreads. As one increases the slope of the volatility skew around the strike of the digital option, however, one can see that the range derived from the "overestimating" and "underestimating" call spreads can significantly deviate from the price of the digital calculated using the $DF(t,T)N(d_2)$ formula. Again it is very important to stress that, in some cases, the slope of the volatility skew around the strike of the digital option can matter even more than the absolute level of volatility itself.

As a rule of thumb it should be noted (and we invite interested readers to replicate these cases) that, whenever the skew is downward sloping (or, more precisely, downward sloping beyond a certain level), the price of the digital call obtained via call spread replication tends to be higher than the one calculated ignoring the contribution of the skew. Conversely, whenever the skew is upward sloping (or, more precisely, upward sloping beyond a certain level), the price of the digital call obtained via call spread replication tends to be lower than the one calculated ignoring the contribution of the skew.

Obviously the opposite is true for digital put options (since these can simply be priced as 1 minus the digital call price).

Being able to build a replicating strategy for a digital call option via a call spread still leaves a very important question unanswered, i.e., what is the nature of the link between the slope of the volatility skew around the strike price of the digital (or, more generally, the shape of the volatility skew) and the probability that the price of the underlying will be above or below that strike price at expiry?

We can rephrase this question as a sort of paradox. First, consider an upward-sloping volatility skew. Using calls, the upward-sloping curves means essentially that, *in volatility terms*, the further out-of-the-money the upper strike call is, the more expensive it gets; again, we stress that this is in volatility terms, not in price terms. For very upwardly-sloped skews, however, the price of digital calls seems to be reduced by the shape of the skew itself (the more upward sloping is the skew around the strike, the cheaper the digital call becomes). This would appear to be inconsistent with what our intuition tells us. How can an increased price (in volatility terms) of the out-of-the-money call options be consistent with a reduced price for the corresponding digital call? After all, it would seem obvious to expect that an increased price for the vanilla call (reflected in the higher volatility) could be driven by an increased probability of that vanilla call ending up in-the-money.[5] As the previous examples have shown, however, the opposite is true. How can this apparent paradox be reconciled?

Think about this. When a vanilla option gets more expensive due to increased volatility of its spot price, it does not mean that the probability of the option finishing in-the-money is necessarily increased. The most appropriate way to understand this concept of *increased volatility* is really that the potential payoff associated with the option finishing in-the-money

---

[5] This is the same as saying that the digital call with the same strike should get more expensive since its price should be an immediate reflection of this increased probability.

is bigger. We must not forget that the driver of the price of a vanilla option is not only the probability of the option being in-the-money at expiry but also *by how much* that option can be in-the-money. On the other hand, the driver of the price of a digital option is simply the (discounted) probability of the option being in-the-money at expiry. Consequently, it is not inconceivable that one could have different prices for a European digital call option (i.e., different probabilities of the underlying being above the strike at expiry) associated with the same price for a vanilla option. It would simply mean that a lower price of the digital (i.e., a lower probability) would be balanced by a higher potential payoff for the vanilla option for it to have the same price. And, vice versa, a higher price for the digital (i.e., a higher probability) would have to be balanced by a lower potential payoff on the vanilla option.

8.4 OTHER EXOTIC OPTIONS: PRICING AND GREEKS

8.4.1 Pricing common barrier options

It can be shown that, in a Black–Scholes framework, the price of a barrier option on non-dividend paying assets can be calculated as follows.

Price of a down-and-in call when $B \leq K$:

$$\text{CallD\&}I = S\,(B/S)^{2\varphi}\,N\,(y) - Ke^{-rT}\,(B/S)^{2\varphi-2}\,N\left(y - \sigma\sqrt{T}\right)$$

where:

$$\varphi = \frac{r + \sigma^2/2}{\sigma^2}$$

$$y = \frac{\ln\left[\dfrac{B^2}{SK}\right]}{\sigma\sqrt{T}} + \varphi\sigma\sqrt{T}$$

and, as usual, S is the spot price of the underlying asset, K is the strike price of the option, B is the barrier level, r is the interest rate (continuous compounding), σ is the volatility and T is the time to expiry.

From the parity relationship already discussed, we can deduce that the price of a down-and-out call, in this case ($B \leq K$), is equal to the price of the corresponding vanilla call minus the price of the down-and-in call that we just calculated.

Price of a down-and-out call when $B \geq K$:

$$\text{CallD\&}O = SN\left(x_1\right) - Ke^{-rT}N\left(x_1 - \sigma\sqrt{T}\right) - S\left(\frac{B}{S}\right)^{2\varphi}N\left(y_1\right)$$

$$+ Ke^{-rT}\,(B/S)^{2\varphi-2}\,N\left(y_1 - \sigma\sqrt{T}\right)$$

where:

$$x_1 = \frac{\ln\left[\frac{S}{B}\right]}{\sigma\sqrt{T}} + \varphi\sigma\sqrt{T}$$

$$y_1 = \frac{\ln\left[\frac{B}{S}\right]}{\sigma\sqrt{T}} + \varphi\sigma\sqrt{T}$$

From the parity relationship, we find that the price of a down-and-in call, in this case ($B \geq K$), is equal to the price of the corresponding vanilla call minus the price of the down-and-out call that we just calculated.

Price of an up-and-in call when $B > K$:

$$\text{CallU\&I} = SN\left(x_1\right) - Ke^{-rT}N\left(x_1 - \sigma\sqrt{T}\right) - S\left(\frac{B}{S}\right)^{2\varphi}\left[N\left(-y\right) - N\left(-y_1\right)\right] +$$
$$+ Ke^{-rT}\left(B/S\right)^{2\varphi-2}\left[N\left(-y + \sigma\sqrt{T}\right) - N\left(-y_1 + \sigma\sqrt{T}\right)\right]$$

From the parity relationship, we find that the price of an up-and-out call, in this case ($B > K$), is equal to the price of the corresponding vanilla call minus the price of the up-and-in call just calculated.

It is worth noting that if $B \leq K$, the value of an up-and-out call has to be equal to zero since, if the option is in-the-money, the barrier should have been triggered. Moreover, in the same case, the value of an up-and-in call has to be equal to the value of the corresponding vanilla because, in order for the option to be in-the-money, the barrier should have triggered.

For the barrier put options we have the following formulae.

Price of an up-and-in put when $K \leq B$:

$$\text{PutU\&I} = -S\left(B/S\right)^{2\varphi}N\left(-y\right) + Ke^{-rT}\left(B/S\right)^{2\varphi-2}N\left(-y + \sigma\sqrt{T}\right)$$

where:

$$\varphi = \frac{r + \sigma^2/2}{\sigma^2}$$

$$y = \frac{\ln\left[\frac{B^2}{SK}\right]}{\sigma\sqrt{T}} + \varphi\sigma\sqrt{T}$$

and, as usual, S is the spot price of the underlying asset, K is the strike price of the option, B is the barrier level, r is the interest rate (continuous compounding), σ is the volatility and T is the time to expiry.

From the parity relationship already discussed, we can deduce that the price of an up-and-out put, in this case ($K \leq B$), is equal to the price of the corresponding vanilla put minus the price of the up-and-in put just calculated.

Price of an up-and-out put when $K \geq B$:

$$\text{PutU\&O} = -SN\left(-x_1\right) + Ke^{-rT}N\left(-x_1 + \sigma\sqrt{T}\right) + S\left(\frac{B}{S}\right)^{2\varphi}N\left(-y_1\right) +$$
$$- Ke^{-rT}\left(B/S\right)^{2\varphi-2}N\left(-y_1 + \sigma\sqrt{T}\right)$$

where:

$$x_1 = \frac{\ln\left[\frac{S}{B}\right]}{\sigma\sqrt{T}} + \varphi\sigma\sqrt{T}$$

$$y_1 = \frac{\ln\left[\frac{B}{S}\right]}{\sigma\sqrt{T}} + \varphi\sigma\sqrt{T}$$

From the parity relationship, we find that the price of an up-and-in put, in this case ($K \geq B$), is equal to the price of the corresponding vanilla put minus the price of the up-and-out put just calculated.

Price of a down-and-in put when $K > B$:

$$\text{PutD\&}I = -SN\left(-x_1\right) + Ke^{-rT}N\left(-x_1 + \sigma\sqrt{T}\right) + S\left(\frac{B}{S}\right)^{2\varphi}\left[N\left(y\right) - N\left(y_1\right)\right] +$$

$$-Ke^{-rT}\left(B/S\right)^{2\varphi-2}\left[N\left(y - \sigma\sqrt{T}\right) - N\left(y_1 - \sigma\sqrt{T}\right)\right]$$

From the parity relationship, we find that the price of a down-and-out put, in this case ($K > B$), is equal to the price of the corresponding vanilla put minus the price of the down-and-in put just calculated.

It is worth noting that if $K \leq B$, the value of a down-and-out put has to be equal to zero since, if the option is in-the-money, the barrier should have been triggered. Moreover, in the same case, the value of a down-and-in put has to be equal to the value of the corresponding vanilla because, in order for the option to be in-the-money, the barrier should have been triggered.

8.4.2   Greeks of common barrier options

What we will try to develop here is an intuition about the Greeks of barrier options and their behaviour. In this section, we will focus on up-and-out calls allowing interested readers the chance to use their newly found intuition to consider the behaviour of the Greeks for the other kinds of barrier options.

It will be useful to start from a simple example. Assume that a trader is long a 3-month option on a certain underlying (say an equity index or an FX rate), with spot price equal to 110, strike K equal to 100 and up-and-out barrier level B equal to 120. We will assume an implied volatility at 12.5% and, for simplicity, interest rates set equal to zero. Using the formula that we have just presented, we calculate a price for this up-and-out call (we note incidentally that this is a *reverse knock-out* option as it would be in-the-money when it can be knocked-out) equal to 7.04, significantly (and unsurprisingly) cheaper than the 10.18 price of the corresponding vanilla option, which can easily be verified using the Black–Scholes formula.

As we have done previously, we will start with the profile of the delta of this option.

Since this is a call option, it would be reasonable to expect a trader who is long this option to be long delta since an increase in the spot price is clearly required for his or her option to be in-the-money. This delta cannot be greater than the delta of the corresponding vanilla option, however, since, if the underlying price gets close to the 120 barrier level, the probability of the option being knocked-out increases significantly. In other words, the trader would like the underlying price to go higher but not too much, to avoid the risk of incurring a knock-out

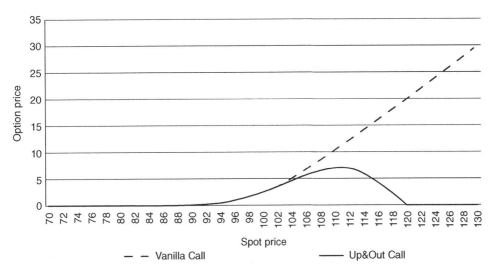

Figure 8.6 Comparison between Vanilla and U&O Call

event. Hence, the option will have a positive delta but it will be lower than the delta of the corresponding vanilla. Should the underlying price get close to the barrier level, however, the sign of the delta will flip to negative. For instance, if the underlying price reaches 119 (i.e., just below the 120 barrier), the delta will likely be negative since a further increase in the underlying price will probably lead to a knock-out event. In other words, there is a level of the price beyond which the trader is going to prefer a lower payoff with higher probability than a marginally higher payoff with very high probability of losing everything.

Figure 8.6 depicts the behaviour of the U&O call option price as a function of the spot price of the underlying asset showing also a comparison with respect to the behaviour of the corresponding vanilla call option.[6]

As the chart clearly shows, when the spot price is sufficiently far from the 120 barrier, the up-and-out call option (solid line) has the same (or similar) behaviour as the corresponding vanilla option (dotted line). As the price of the underlying approaches the barrier, however, the prices of the two options diverge sharply. The first derivative of the price of the up-and-out with respect to the price of the underlying is the delta of the up-and-out option. So, as long as the underlying is not too close to the barrier, the delta of the up-and-out call is positive (i.e., the solid line is upward sloping, as is the dotted line representing the corresponding vanilla call). When the barrier is sufficiently close, however, the sign of the delta flips to negative. This can be deduced from the slope of the solid line in Figure 8.6, which becomes negative for spot prices higher than about 111; any further price increase beyond a certain point increases the probability of triggering a knock-out event, which would cause the option to expire worthless.

In any case, as the barrier is touched, the option disappears and so does its delta. Figure 8.7 depicts the behaviour of the delta with respect to the price of the underlying. Note that, since

---

[6] In Figures 8.7–8.11, the Greeks have not been calculated analytically. Instead, we have calculated the difference between the price of the option and the price of the same option where one input parameter has been shifted. For example, to calculate the vega, we shift the volatility by 1% and calculate the impact on the price of the option. Likewise, to calculate the delta we shift the price of the underlying by $0.01 and evaluate the option price impact, and so on.

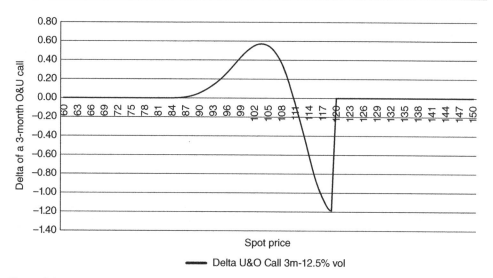

Figure 8.7   U&O call delta as a function of spot price

the value of the delta cannot be higher than the value of the delta of the corresponding vanilla, the delta of the up-and-out is capped at 1. On the other hand, there is virtually no limit to the negative values that the delta may assume when the underlying price is close to the barrier. Note also the sharp discontinuity of the delta when the barrier is hit.

Figure 8.7 also helps to understand the shape of the gamma function of the up-and-out option. It will be positive for very low spot prices (when the exotic option behaves in line with the corresponding vanilla option) and negative for higher levels of the spot, where the proximity of the barrier is such that the behaviour of all of the various Greeks gets distorted significantly. Obviously if the barrier is touched the gamma will immediately collapse to zero.

How should one expect the delta of the barrier option to change as a consequence of the passage of time? To answer this question, we need to note that, to the extent that the spot price is away from the barrier, the price and the Greeks of the exotic option will converge towards those of the regular vanilla option as time passes. This generally implies a progressive increase in the level of the delta for in-the-money options and a decrease in the level of the delta for out-of-the-money options.

Figure 8.8 shows a comparison of the delta for our up-and-out at inception and after 2 months, i.e., when the residual tenor is 1 month. Ignoring the area in the immediate proximity to the barrier, the delta of the barrier option with residual tenor of 1 month tends to be significantly higher than the delta of the barrier option with the longer tenor (provided that the option has not been knocked-out). Moreover, as time passes, the level of the spot price that sees the delta flip from positive to negative gets progressively higher (all else being equal) and that, for barrier options with shorter tenor, the discontinuity around the barrier can be significantly larger than the same option with a longer tenor.

What about the behaviour of the delta with respect to implied volatility? To a certain extent and from a pure qualitative point of view, the effect on the delta of an increased level of the implied volatility is similar to that for a longer option tenor. Higher volatility implies a higher probability of hitting the barrier at some time; however, when volatility is sufficiently low,

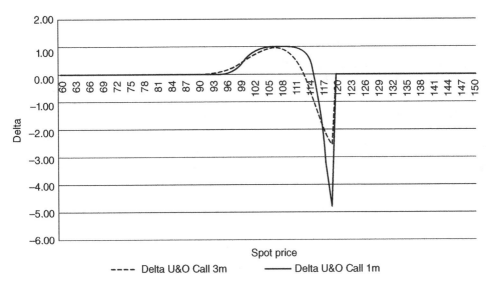

Figure 8.8   Evolution of the delta of an U&O call over time

the probability of hitting the barrier at some point will be significantly lower as the barrier level gets more and more out of reach. The resultant behaviour of the delta of our up-and-out call of a higher implied volatility regime can therefore be summarized as: compared with the delta observed in a low volatility regime, the delta in a high volatility regime will generally be lower, its convergence to the delta of the corresponding vanilla will be slower and the point where the delta flips into negative territory will be lower.

Figure 8.9 highlights these results. It is also worth noting the extent of the discontinuity, which is much higher in the case of low volatility. This depends on the fact that, for higher

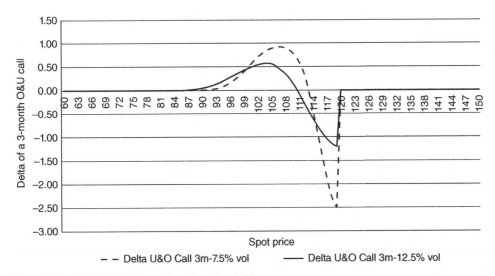

Figure 8.9   U&O call delta as a function of volatility

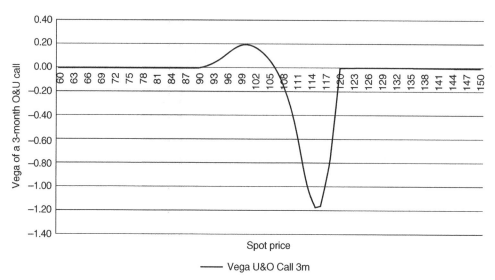

Figure 8.10 U&O call vega as a function of the underlying price

levels of volatility, the probability of hitting the barrier is also higher and therefore the impact on the Greeks of hitting the barrier (hence the discontinuity in the Greeks) is lower compared with a lower volatility regime.

From the analysis, it should be clear what to expect regarding vega and its behaviour. When the barrier is sufficiently far away, the vega of the exotic will be similar to the vega of the corresponding vanilla. In other words, we should expect a positive vega for the option buyer. As the spot price of the underlying asset approaches the barrier, however, we should expect the sign on the vega to move to negative territory; again, the buyer would like the price of the underlying asset to stay as close as possible (but obviously not beyond) the barrier level. A high level of implied volatility around the barrier is not desirable, since it would increase the probability of the underlying either dropping (reducing significantly, if not negating, the potential payoff of the barrier) or increasing beyond the barrier level (which is even worse since it would knock out the entire option, thereby causing the payoff to be zero by definition). Figure 8.10 summarizes the vega exposure as a function of the spot price.

From this chart is should be possible to visualize dVega/dSpot by simply taking the first derivative. For low levels of the underlying price, the slope of the chart is initially positive (i.e., positive dVega/dSpot). This has nothing to do with the barrier option since it would also be observed in the corresponding vanilla. For higher underlying prices, we expect the vega of the vanilla to converge slowly to zero (without ever turning negative) but, as the chart shows, in the case of the barrier option, the vega does initially turn negative as the underlying price approaches the barrier and then rapidly converges to zero as it gets closer and closer to the barrier.

This chart is similar (at least from a quantitative point of view) to the chart of the vega of a risk reversal presented earlier in Figure 7.15. The major difference is that, in case of a barrier option, the convergence to zero on the right-hand side is much sharper due to the effect of the barrier. That aside, this analysis should reinforce the idea of the risk reversal as a potential hedging instrument for those derivatives that show a significant dVega/dSpot (as highlighted in section 7.8 on the Vanna–Volga method).

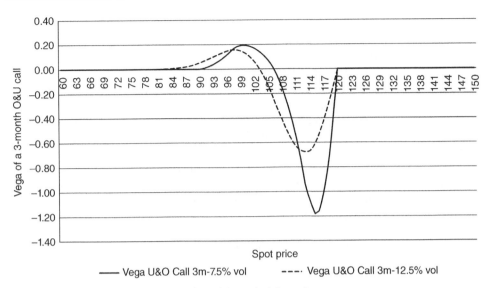

Figure 8.11   U&O call vega as a function of the underlying price

Finally, with the passage of time and, assuming that the option has not been knocked-out, there will be a convergence of the vega of the barrier option to the vega of the regular vanilla.

What about vega as a function of the volatility itself? Consider Figure 8.11. It is possible to deduce the sign of dVega/dVol from the difference between the dotted line and the solid line. The chart shows the evolution of the vega for a higher volatility regime (dotted line) and a lower volatility regime (solid line). When the difference is positive (i.e., the dotted line is above the solid line), dVega/dVol is positive (i.e., vega is higher for higher level of volatility). Conversely, when the difference is negative (i.e., the dotted line is below the solid line), dVega/dVol is negative (i.e., vega is lower, or more negative, for higher level of volatility).

As we have pointed out previously, in the case of delta, when volatility is low and/or the underlying price is sufficiently far from the barrier, the behaviour of the barrier option will not be too dissimilar from the corresponding vanilla option, i.e., positive dVega/dVol for out-of-the-money options and virtually no dVega/dVol for at-the-money or close-to-at-the-money options (the dotted line is initially above the solid line). For higher levels of the underlying price, higher volatility will increase the probability of the option expiring worthless (either out-of-the-money or because of the occurrence of a knock-out event). This will imply a lower option price (and also a negative vega) should implied volatility exceed a certain level; dVega/dVol is negative (dotted line below the solid line). For levels of the underlying price very close to the barrier, however, the negative vega in the case of low volatility tends to be "stronger" than in the case of high volatility. In case this is not obvious, think about it. When the underlying price is very close to the barrier, in a low volatility regime, a marginal increase in volatility can have a much bigger impact than in the case of a high volatility regime. Consequently, we should expect the dotted line to go back above the solid line, signalling a positive dVega/dVol.

To sum up, for increasing levels of the underlying price, the sign of dVega/dVol will be initially positive, turn negative and then positive again unless the barrier is hit (in which case it will sharply move to zero).

8.4.3 Greeks of Asian options

These tend to be similar (at least from a qualitative standpoint) to the Greeks for a vanilla option of the same basic call or put type.

Consider first the delta. It is natural to assume that the buyer of an Asian call option has a long delta exposure. The buyer profits from an increase in the price of the underlying asset since it tends to increase the chance of a higher average price, leading to a higher potential payoff. Conversely, the buyer of an Asian put option will have a short delta exposure.

Vega, gamma and theta also tend to be of the same sign as those on same-kind (i.e., call or put) European options although they are generally lower in magnitude due to the effect of the averaging. On any observation date, since the contribution to the average price on that date is then known, a certain degree of uncertainty about the final payoff is removed. For example, when the underlying price is known for all observation dates except the final one, the underlying price observed on the last observation date will affect the option payoff only marginally due to the averaging feature of Asian options. Consequently, on any observation date, the Greeks of an Asian option will decline in magnitude, since the uncertainty regarding the final averaging is reduced.

SUMMARY

In this chapter, we introduced the more regularly traded exotic derivatives. We began with digital options, which have a fixed payoff, and then moved onto barrier options and Asian options. In all cases, we spent time on the basic structure of the option as well as describing, in some detail, their associated Greeks. In particular, we noted that the Greeks of the digital option can be thought of as higher orders of the Greeks of a vanilla option. On the other hand, the Greeks of Asian options tend to be qualitatively similar to the Greeks of a vanilla option of the same basic call or put type. The Greeks of barrier options also show similarities to those of vanilla options, although, of course, they show clear discontinuities at the barriers.

9

Multi-Asset Derivatives

In the following chapter, we will analyse some typical risks that arise from multi-asset derivatives. In particular, we will focus on correlation risk for basket options and the correlation/cross-gamma risk for best-of and worst-of options.

From a pure pricing point of view, Monte Carlo simulation tends to be the most common approach (in some cases, the only possible approach). Monte Carlo simulation was described in detail in Chapter 5.

9.1 BASKET OPTIONS

9.1.1 Basket option definition and Greeks

A basket option is an option written on a basket of underlying assets. As a first approximation, we can think of a basket option (either a call or a put) like a vanilla option written on a "single underlying" where the single underlying is the basket itself. This approximation allows us to analyse the Greeks of the basket option in a similar way to the Greeks of a vanilla option. The buyer of, say, a basket call option on two equity indices (which we will call Index A and Index B for simplicity) will have the following exposures:

- Long delta exposure on the basket. The buyer will profit if the value of the basket increases and this can ultimately be seen also as a long exposure on the individual basket constituents (Index A and Index B).
- Long gamma exposure on the basket. As the level of the basket increases, so does the basket delta and when the level of the basket decreases, so the corresponding delta will fall. When analysing the gamma of the individual underlying indices, it is interesting to observe that any increase in the price of an individual index (say Index A) will increase the level of the whole basket (all else being equal). Therefore, due to the long gamma at basket level, the delta of the other basket constituents will increase. In our example, an increase in the value of Index A will not only increase the delta of Index A itself but also the delta of Index B. This is because any individual underlying will trigger a change in the *whole* basket delta and, therefore, on the delta of all other basket constituents. Generalizing, let us define the quantity $dDelta_i/dPrice_j$ with $i \neq j$, i.e., the first derivative of the delta of the basket constituent i with respect to the price of another basket constituent j. Based on the above, we expect $dDelta_i/dPrice_j$ to be a positive quantity. $dDelta_i/dPrice_j$ is often called *cross-gamma* as it refers to the change in delta of one underlying with respect to the change in price of another underlying.
- Long vega exposure on the basket. Not surprisingly, the basket call option that we have just described will have a long exposure with respect to the volatility of the basket. The reason is exactly the same as with the case of options on individual underlying assets. The higher the volatility, the higher is the replicating cost of the payoff of the derivative and also the higher the potential payoff of the option. But what are the drivers of the volatility of the

Figure 9.1   Sensitivity of a basket option to the correlation

basket? Certainly the volatility of the individual basket constituents (σ_A and σ_B) but also the correlation among them ($\rho_{A,B}$).

At this point, it may be useful to recall the formula for the variance of a basket (σ^2_{Basket}) expressed as a function of the variance of the individual basket components when the basket is composed of only two components (A and B) with weights w_A and w_B respectively and with $w_A + w_B = 1$:

$$\sigma^2_{Basket} = w^2_A \sigma^2_A + w^2_B \sigma^2_B + 2\rho_{A,B} w_A \sigma_A w_B \sigma_B$$

The basket volatility σ_{Basket} is simply obtained by taking the square root of σ^2_{Basket} (the basket variance). As the formula shows, the basket volatility is also a positive function of the correlation between the basket constituents. So, for higher level of correlation, we should observe a higher price for the basket option, since the higher correlation will increase the basket volatility and that will increase the option price as the flow chart in Figure 9.1 summarizes.

9.1.2   Cross-gamma and correlation revisited

In section 9.1.1, we introduced the concepts of cross-gamma and the sensitivity of the option price to correlation in the case of basket options. The two concepts have been introduced separately but it is now worth demonstrating that they are actually closely linked. Let us revisit the example of a call option written on the basket of Index A and Index B. We said when introducing the concept of cross-gamma that, as the price of Index A increases, so will the delta of Index B (of course the delta of the Index A will also increase). If the correlation between Index A and Index B is positive then, when the price of Index A increases, triggering a higher level of delta for Index B, the price of Index B is also likely to increase due to the positive correlation. Consequently, the increase in the value of Index B is now even more valuable to the option buyer since the individual delta of Index B is higher due to the increase in the price of the other underlying (Figure 9.2).

Figure 9.2   Cross gamma for basket options

Needless to say, the same dynamic applies when an increase in the price of Index B triggers a higher level of delta for Index A, again with the additional benefit arising from the fact that the value of Index A is also likely to increase due to the positive correlation.

In other words, in a context of positive cross-gamma, it is desirable that the individual underlying assets have positive correlations between themselves to take advantage of the increased individual delta that occurs when the price of the other basket constituents increase.

This discussion also applies in the case of a decrease in the price of a constituent of the basket. When the value of Index A decreases, it will trigger a lower level of delta for Index B. This time around the price of Index B is also likely to decrease due to the positive correlation but this will cause a lower loss to the option buyer since the individual delta of Index B is now lower due to the decrease in the price of the other underlying.

9.2 BEST-OF AND WORST-OF OPTIONS

9.2.1 Best-of and worst-of definitions

Best-of and worst-of options are call (or put) options written on the best performing or on the worst performing underlying asset, respectively, on a given set of underlying assets. The best performing asset is the one that exhibits the highest percentage appreciation or the smallest percentage decline from trade date to expiry date while, by extension, the worst performing asset is the one with the highest percentage depreciation or the smallest positive return over the same period.

Unlike basket options, it is worth noting that the best-of (or worst-of) options are written on an *individual* underlying asset chosen from a set of available underlying assets according to the relative performance. We will see how this plays a crucial role in the pricing and hedging of these derivatives.

Assuming that the option is in-the-money, the payoff of a best-of call option is calculated at expiry by comparing the return of the best performing asset to the predefined strike using the following formula:

$$\text{Best-of call payoff} = \text{Max}(0, \text{BestPerformingAsset}) \times \text{Notional}$$

where Notional refers to the amount of money invested on the product; and BestPerformingAsset is the performance of the best performing asset in the set of underlying assets and is measured as follows:

$$\frac{(\text{BestAssetPrice}_{\text{Final}} - \text{Strike})}{\text{Divisor}}$$

where $\text{BestAssetPrice}_{\text{Final}}$ is the price of the best performing asset at the expiration date of the option and Strike and Divisor can be any level but in general the initial price of the best performing asset is used as both, i.e., the price at the initial date of the option. It is common that the initial date coincides with the trade date. The reason why the Strike and the Divisor tend to be the initial price is just because it makes it easier for investors to follow the performance of the products, i.e., how the product has evolved since the date the trade was put on.

By putting the Strike and the Divisor equal to the initial price the payoff becomes:

$$\text{Best-of call payoff} = \text{Max}\left(0, \left(\frac{\text{BestAssetPrice}_{\text{Final}}}{\text{BestAssetPrice}_{\text{Initial}}} - 1\right)\right) \times \text{Notional}$$

where BestAssetPrice$_{\text{Initial}}$ is the price of the best performing asset at the initial date of the option. Similarly, the payoff of a Worst-of call option is calculated according to the following formula:

$$\text{Worst-of call payoff} = \text{Max}(0, \text{WorstPerformingAsset}) \times \text{Notional}$$

where WorstPerformingAsset is the performance of the worst performing asset in the set and is measured as follows:

$$\left(\frac{\text{WorstAssetPrice}_{\text{Final}} - \text{Strike}}{\text{Divisor}} \right)$$

where WorstAssetPrice$_{\text{Final}}$ is the price of the worst performing asset at the expiration date of the option.

As in the case of the Best-of call payoff, the Strike and Divisor can be any level but in general the initial price of the worst performing asset is used as both, as it makes it easier for investors to follow the performance of the products, i.e., how the product has evolved since the date the trade was initiated.

By putting the Strike and the Divisor equal to the initial price the payoff becomes:

$$\text{Worst-of call payoff} = \text{Max} \left(0, \left(\frac{\text{WorstAssetPrice}_{\text{Final}}}{\text{WorstAssetPrice}_{\text{Initial}}} - 1 \right) \right) \times \text{Notional}$$

where WorstAssetPrice$_{\text{Initial}}$ is the price of the worst performing asset at the initial date of the option. The Best-of put option is defined as follows:

$$\text{Best-of put payoff} = \text{Max} (0, \text{BestPerformingAsset}) \times \text{Notional}$$

where BestPerformingAsset is the performance of the best performing asset in the set and it is measured as follows:

$$\left(\frac{\text{Strike} - \text{BestAssetPrice}_{\text{Final}}}{\text{Divisor}} \right)$$

where BestAssetPrice$_{\text{Final}}$ is the price of the best performing asset at the expiration date of the option.

As with the call payoff, the initial price of the best performing asset tends to be used as Divisor and Strike.

By putting the Strike and the Divisor equal to the initial price the payoff becomes:

$$\text{Best-of put payoff} = \text{Max} \left(0, \left(1 - \frac{\text{BestAssetPrice}_{\text{Final}}}{\text{BestAssetPrice}_{\text{Initial}}} \right) \right)$$

where BestAssetPrice$_{\text{Initial}}$ is the price of the best performing asset at the initial date of the option. Lastly the Worst-of put is defined as follows:

$$\text{Worst-of put payoff} = \text{Max}(0, \text{WorstPerformingAsset}) \times \text{Notional}$$

where WorstPerformingAsset is the performance of the worst performing asset in the set and it is measured as follows:

$$\left(\frac{\text{Strike} - \text{WorstAssetPrice}_{\text{Final}}}{\text{Divisor}} \right)$$

where WorstAssetPrice$_{Final}$ is the price of the worst performing asset at the expiration date of the option.

Again, the initial price of the worst performing asset tends to be used as Divisor and Strike. By putting the Strike and the Divisor equal to the initial price the payoff becomes:

$$\text{Worst-of put payoff} = \text{Max}\left(0, \left(1 - \frac{\text{WorstAssetPrice}_{Final}}{\text{WorstAssetPrice}_{Initial}}\right)\right) \times \text{Notional}$$

where WorstAssetPrice$_{Initial}$ is the price of the worst performing asset at the initial date of the option.

Let us go through an example:

Basket = (Gold, Brent, Copper)
Initial date: 2 Jan 2013
Expiry date: 3 June 2013
GoldPrice$_{Initial}$ = $1,500/oz = GoldStrike = GoldDivisor
BrentPrice$_{Initial}$ = $100/bbl = BrentStrike = BrentDivisor
CopperPrice$_{Initial}$ = $7,600/MT = CopperStrike = CopperDivisor
Notional = $1,000,000

Let us assume the possible final values for the three different assets at expiry date as shown in Table 9.1.

So, how are best-of and worst-of options used? In the case of worst-of call option, they provide a lower-cost alternative to vanilla call options. Note that, in this case, lower cost may not necessarily imply "cheaper". Whether an option is rich or cheap depends upon the expected payoff relative to the cost and a low-cost option with a low payoff may be "rich" relative to a higher-cost option with a much higher payoff.

Buying a best-of call option provides the investor with the opportunity to benefit from the best payoff of a set of underlying assets, at a lower cost than buying individual vanilla options on all the underlying assets. Buying a best-of call option covering two underlying assets is generally a higher cost than buying a single vanilla option but less costly than buying two vanilla options.

On the other-hand, the payoff of a worst-of call option is the lower of the payoffs of a vanilla option on each asset. Buying a worst-of call option with two underlying assets is generally

Table 9.1 Scenario analysis for Best-of/Worst-of call and put

	Gold	Brent	Copper
AssetPrice$_{Final}$	$1,800/oz	$90/bbl	$7,650/MT
AssetPerformance	$\frac{1,800}{1,500} = 120\%$	$\frac{90}{100} = 90\%$	$\frac{7,650}{7,600} = 100.66\%$
BestPerformingAsset	Gold: 120%		
WorstPerformingAsset	Brent: 90%		
Best-of call payoff	Max(0, 120%–1) × $1,000,000 = $200,000		
Worst-of call payoff	Max(0, 90%–1) × $1,000,000 = $0		
Best-of put payoff	Max(0, 1–120%) × $1,000,000 = $0		
Worst-of put payoff	Max(0, 1–90%) × $1,000,000 = $100,000		

lower cost than buying just one vanilla option but, of course, the holder of the worst-of call would only receive a payoff if both of the underlying assets are above the strike at expiry.

The symmetric rationale applies to best-of and worst-of put options.

As we will see in Chapter 10, when embedded in structured products, the worst-of call (for example, embedded in a guaranteed product) exposure to correlation will cut the cost of the option. When embedded in a "reverse convertible", the high premium received from the implicit sale of a worst-of put can significantly increase the coupon paid to the investor but its risk can sometimes be extremely high, as we will discuss in Chapter 10.

9.2.2   The price and the Greeks of best-of and worst-of options

Pricing best-of and worst-of options generally requires Monte Carlo techniques that in this case will have to be applied to multiple assets. In the spreadsheet "Chapter 9 – Best-of and Worst-of Options" we will show some examples based on two underlying assets. Simulating more than one underlying obviously requires an assumption that has to be made on the correlation between the various assets. As we will shortly see in more detail, assumed and then realized correlations will have a huge impact on prices and risks of best-of and worst-of options.

To understand better the risks of best-of and worst-of options, it is worth taking a moment to consider the effect of dispersion. High dispersion means that the returns from the underlying assets are very different from each other. Narrow or low dispersion means that the returns from the underlying assets are very similar to each other. For high levels of dispersion, one can expect a high return from the best performer and a low return from the worst performer, although the average or combined performance of the underlying basket of assets could remain unchanged. Similarly, lower dispersion leads to lower returns from the best performer and higher returns for the worst performer, with the basket return unchanged. To appreciate the effect of correlation and volatility on best-of and worst-of options, it is necessary to understand how they affect dispersion. If the pairwise correlations between the underlying assets are low, then the returns of the underlying assets will be much more varied. If the pairwise correlations between the underlying assets are high, however, the returns of the underlying assets will be broadly similar.

Higher volatility will also likely lead to asset returns with large deviations from the average return. In other words, higher volatility will also tend to lead to higher dispersion. In a sense, volatility and correlation are related and, hence, high volatility will have a direct and an indirect impact on option pricing.

9.2.3   Best-of call

Best-of call options have higher cost than any vanilla option written on each individual constituent of the set of underlying assets. This is because, by definition, the payoff of a best-of call option is always equal to or higher than the payoff of each individual call option on the same underlying assets.

Let us analyse the Greeks in more detail assuming the case of a buyer of a best-of call option on two equity indices (Index A and Index B). The buyer is going to have the following exposures:

- Long delta exposure on each individual underlying. The buyer will profit if the value of at least one underlying increases and this can ultimately be seen also as a long exposure to each underlying within the set (Index A and Index B in this example). The higher the number of underlying assets having a positive performance, the better it is for the best-of call option buyer since it will raise the probability that the price of at least one underlying is going to be above the strike when the option expires (remember that for best-of calls even if only one underlying is above the strike, the option will expire in-the-money). In any case, as the option expiry approaches, the delta will become more and more concentrated towards the best performing underlying since it is the one that has the greatest chance of ending up above the strike when the option expires.

- Long gamma exposure on each individual underlying and, in particular, on the one that, during the life of the option, is registering the best performance. As the price of at least one underlying asset increases, so does its individual delta, in particular if the price increase is related to the underlying that is registering the best performance given that it has the highest chance of ending up above the strike when the option expires. Conversely, when the price of any underlying decreases, its corresponding individual delta will fall. Crucially, when analysing the gamma of an individual underlying, it is interesting to observe that any increase in the price of one individual index (say Index A) will increase the level of its delta (all else being equal) but, due to its better relative performance, the delta of the other index (Index B) will *decrease*. This is because any individual underlying will trigger a change in the *overall relative performance of each constituent*. Generalizing, if we again consider the cross-gamma, i.e., the quantity $dDelta_i/dPrice_j$ with $i \neq j$, or the first derivative of the delta of the underlying i with respect to the price of another underlying j, based on the discussion above, we expect $dDelta_i/dPrice_j$ to be a *negative* quantity.

- Long vega exposure on each underlying and, in particular, on the one that, during the life of the option, is registering the best performance. The reason is exactly the same as the case of options on individual underlying assets. The higher the volatility, the higher is the cost of replicating the payoff from the option and also the higher the potential payoff. During the life of the option, the vega of the best performing underlying (in the case of a best-of call option) will converge to the vega of the corresponding vanilla option and the vega of the other underlying assets will progressively disappear. Therefore, unlike the previous example seen in 9.1.1, in the case of best-of options there is no concept of "basket vega" or "basket volatility".

- Short correlation exposure. Higher dispersion leads to a higher payoff for a best-of call option as it increases the chances of at least one underlying ending up above its strike. Since a decrease in correlation leads to higher dispersion, a best-of call option buyer is short correlation.

As the impact of the correlation is crucial to understanding the price dynamics of these options, we summarize these concepts with the flow charts in Figure 9.3.

In general we can also add that the higher the forward prices for the individual underlying assets, the higher the price of the call option on the best performing asset. The lower the forward prices for the individual underlying assets, the lower the price of the call option on the best performing asset. Since higher interest rates and lower dividends increase forward prices, a buyer of a best-of call is long rho and short dividends.

9.2.4 Best-of put

Symmetrically to best-of call, best-of put options will have lower costs than any vanilla put option written on each individual constituent of the basket of underlying assets. This is because, by definition, the payoff of a best-of put option is always equal to or lower than the payoff

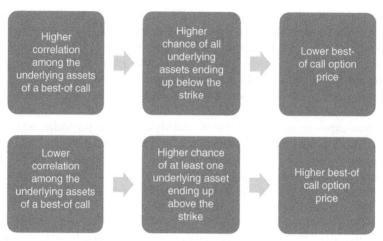

Figure 9.3   Sensitivity to correlation for best-of call options

of each individual put option on the same underlying assets. Lower cost implies that they can offer increased potential leverage making them attractive for certain investors.

The buyer of a best-of put written on two indices A and B is going to have the following exposures:

- Short delta exposure on each individual underlying. The buyer will profit if the value of all underlyings decrease below their respective strikes and this can ultimately be seen also as a short exposure to each underlying within the set (Index A and Index B in this example). It is important to remember that for a best-of put, if only one underlying is above the strike, the option will expire worthless; it is therefore crucial that all underlying assets are below the strike. As the option expiry approaches, the delta will become more and more concentrated towards the best performing underlying provided that it has a chance of ending up below the strike when the option expires.

- Mixed gamma exposure on each individual underlying. Gamma can be long for the particular underlying asset that, during the life of the option, happens to have high probability of being the best performer at expiry. Once it is clear which underlying index will end up being the best performer, its gamma will start behaving like the gamma of a vanilla put option, i.e., as the price of each underlying asset increases, so does its individual delta (converging to zero) and, vice versa, when its price decreases, its corresponding individual delta will get lower (converging to –1). Whenever there is not enough clarity on which underlying asset is most likely to be the best performer, each individual gamma will tend to be negative. It is not difficult to see why. Any decrease in the price of an individual index (say Index A) will *increase* the level of its delta (all else being equal its delta will get closer to zero) since it increases the chance of not being the best performing asset; hence, the negative gamma. However, due to the better relative performance of the Index B compared with Index A in this case, the delta of Index B will now *decrease* (all else being equal its delta will get closer to –1 provided that Index B is below its respective strike). This is because any individual underlying will trigger a change in the *overall relative performance of each constituent* and therefore on their delta. To summarize, we can identify two potential factors of the gamma of a best-put option that drive it in opposite directions: the first factor is very similar to the typical gamma of an individual vanilla, and it will prevail when during the life of the trade one underlying is likely to be the best performer asset (making the option buyer long gamma on that particular asset); the second factor is due to the "dispersion effect" and tends to drive the gamma in the opposite direction (making the option buyer short gamma on that particular asset). Generalizing, if we again consider the cross-gamma, i.e., the quantity $dDelta_i/dPrice_j$ with $i \neq j$, or the first derivative of the delta of the underlying i with respect to the price of another underlying j, based on the discussion above, we expect $dDelta_i/dPrice_j$ to be a *positive* quantity (positive cross-gamma) whereas $dDelta_i/dPrice_i$ can be either a *positive or a negative* quantity (mixed individual gamma). It goes without saying that, if the best performing underlying is such that the best-of put option is quite likely to be out-of-the-money, all individual gammas and all possible cross-gammas will converge to zero.

- Vega exposure can be also mixed (for the same reason as the gamma that we just analysed). On the one hand, higher volatility leads to a higher put option price, whereas, on the other, it may increase the dispersion reducing the price of the option. Therefore, there is no concept of the "basket vega" or "basket volatility". Again, if the best performing underlying is such that the best of put option is quite likely to be out-of-the-money, all individual vegas will converge to zero.

- Long correlation exposure. As it should be clear from the discussion about gamma of best-of put options, higher dispersion leads to a lower payoff for a best-of put option as it increases the chances of at least one underlying ending up above its strike making the option worthless. Since a decrease in correlation leads to higher dispersion, a best-of put option buyer is long correlation.

Let us summarize again these concepts with the flow chart in Figure 9.4.

We should also note that the higher the forward prices of the individual underlying assets, the lower the price of the put option on the best performing asset. Of course, the lower the forward prices of the individual underlying assets, then the higher the price of the put option on the best performing asset. Since higher interest rates and lower dividends increase forward prices, a buyer of a best-of put is short rho and long dividends.

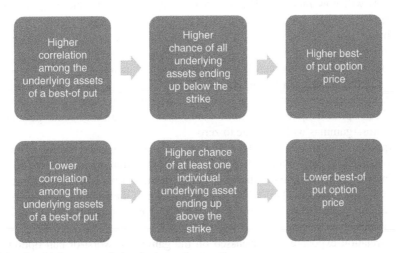

Figure 9.4   Sensitivity to correlation for best-of put options

9.2.5   Worst-of call

Similarly to best-of puts, worst-of call options will have lower cost than any vanilla call option written on each individual constituent of the basket of underlying assets. This is because, by definition, the payoff of a worst-of call option is always equal to or lower than the payoff of each individual call option on the same underlying assets.

Again lower cost implies that they can offer increased potential leverage; in general it is also easier to embed a worst-of call option in a structured product due to its lower cost compared to a regular vanilla call option, as we will see in Chapter 10.

Let us now analyse the exposures that the buyer of a worst-of call written on the two indices A and B is going to have:

- Long delta exposure on each individual underlying. The buyer will profit if the value of all underlying assets increases and this can ultimately be seen as a long exposure on each underlying within the set (Index A and Index B in this case) since the higher the number of the underlying assets having a positive performance, the better it is for the worst-of call option buyer, since there is a higher probability that all underlying assets are going to be above the strike when the option expires. In any case, as the option expiry approaches, the delta will get more and more concentrated on the worst performing underlying as it is the one that is most likely to end up driving the payoff of the worst-of option.

- Mixed gamma exposure on each individual underlying. Gamma can be long for the particular underlying asset that, during the life of the option, happens to have high probability of being the worst performer at expiry. Once it is clear which underlying index will end up being the worst performer, its gamma will start behaving like the gamma of a vanilla option (i.e., as the price of each underlying asset increases, so does its individual delta and, vice versa, when its price decreases, its corresponding individual delta will get lower). Whenever there is not enough clarity on which underlying asset is most likely to be the worst performer, each individual gamma will tend to be negative. Any increase in the price of an individual index (say Index A) will *decrease* the level of its delta (all else being equal) since it increases the chance of not being the worst performing asset; hence, the negative gamma. However, due to the better relative performance of the Index A compared with Index B, the delta of Index B will now *increase*. This is because any individual underlying will trigger a change in the *overall relative performance of each constituent* and therefore on their deltas. Generalizing, if we again consider the cross-gamma, i.e., the quantity $dDelta_i/dPrice_j$ with $i \neq j$, or the first derivative of the delta of the underlying i with respect to the price of another underlying j, we expect $dDelta_i/dPrice_j$ to be a *positive* quantity (positive cross-gamma), whereas $dDelta_i/dPrice_i$ can be either a *positive or a negative* quantity (mixed individual gamma). It goes without saying that, if the worst performing underlying is such that the worst-of call option is quite likely to be out-of-the-money, all individual gammas and all possible cross-gammas will converge to zero.

- Vega exposure can also be mixed (for the same reason as the gamma that we just analysed). On the one hand, higher volatility leads to a higher put option price, whereas, on the other, it may increase the dispersion reducing the price of the option. There is no concept of the "basket vega" or "basket volatility" in this case. Again, if the worst performing underlying is such that the worst-of call option is quite likely to be out-of-the-money, all individual vegas will converge to zero.

- Long correlation exposure. As discussed on the gamma of worst-of call options, higher dispersion leads to a lower payoff for a worst-of call option as it increases the chances

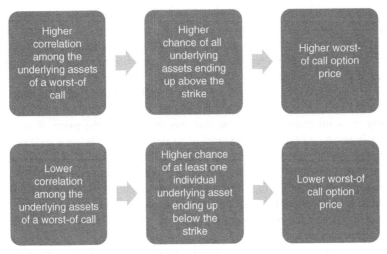

Figure 9.5   Sensitivity to correlation for worst-of call options

of at least one underlying ending up below its strike making the option worthless. Since a decrease in correlation leads to higher dispersion, a worst-of call option buyer is long correlation. See Figure 9.5.

We conclude this section noting that the higher the forward prices of the individual underlying assets, the higher the cost of the call option on the worst performing asset. Since higher interest rates and lower dividends increase forward prices, a buyer of a worst-of call is long rho and short dividends. This is the same as for the best-of call.

9.2.6   Worst-of put

Also worst-of put options can be analysed within the same framework used so far. Similar to best-of call, worst-of put options have higher costs than vanilla options written on individual constituents of the set of underlying assets. This is because, by definition, the payoff of a worst-of put option is always equal to or higher than the payoff of each individual put option on the same underlying assets.

Let us analyse the Greeks in more detail assuming again the case of a buyer of a worst-of put option on two equity indices (Index A and Index B). The buyer is going to have the following exposures:

- Short delta exposure on each individual underlying. The buyer will profit if the value of at least one underlying decreases below the strike and this can be seen also as a short exposure to each underlying. The higher the number of underlying assets underperforming, the better it is for the worst-of put option buyer since it will raise the probability that the price of at least one underlying is going to be below the strike when the option expires (remember that for a worst-of put even if only one underlying is below the strike, the option will expire in-the-money). In any case, as the option expiry approaches, the delta will become more and more concentrated towards the worst performing underlying since it is the one that has the greatest chance of ending up below the strike when the option expires.

- Long gamma exposure on each individual underlying and, in particular, on the one that, during the life of the option, is registering the worst performance. As the price of at least one underlying asset decreases, so does its individual delta if, in particular, the price decrease is related to the underlying that is registering the worst performance and that, consequently, has the highest chance of ending up below the strike when the option expires. Conversely, when the price of any underlying increases, its corresponding individual delta will be higher. Similar to the case of best-of call option, when analysing the gamma of an individual underlying, it is interesting to observe that any increase in the price of one individual index (say Index A) will increase the level of its delta (all else being equal) but, due to its better relative performance, the delta of the other index (Index B) will *decrease*. This is because any individual underlying will trigger a change in the *overall relative performance of each constituent*. Generalizing, if we again consider the cross-gamma, i.e., the quantity dDelta$_i$/dPrice$_j$ with $i \neq j$, or the first derivative of the delta of the underlying i with respect to the price of another underlying j, based on the discussion above, we expect dDelta$_i$/dPrice$_j$ to be a *negative* quantity.
- Long vega exposure on each underlying and, in particular, on the one that, during the life of the option, is registering the worst performance (as in the case of options on individual underlying assets). During the life of the option, the vega of the worst performing underlying will converge to the vega of the corresponding vanilla put option and the vega of the other underlying assets will progressively disappear. Again, there is no concept of "basket vega" or "basket volatility".
- Short correlation exposure. Higher dispersion leads to a higher payoff for a worst-of put option as it increases the chances of at least one underlying ending up below its strike. Since a decrease in correlation leads to higher dispersion, a worst-of put option buyer is short correlation.

Again, we summarize these concepts with the flow charts in Figure 9.6.

Finally, the higher the forward prices of the individual underlying assets, the lower the price of the put option on the worst performing asset and vice versa. Since higher interest rates

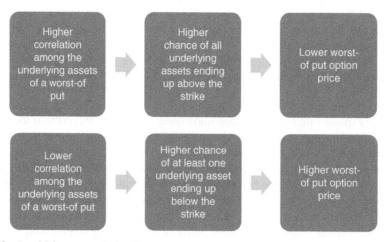

Figure 9.6   Sensitivity to correlation for worst-of put options

Table 9.2 Delta exposure

	Call	Put
Best-of	long	short
Worst-of	long	short

Table 9.3 Gamma and vega exposure (including its impact on dispersion)

	Call	Put
Best-of	long	unclear
Worst-of	unclear	long

Table 9.4 Cross-gamma exposure

	Call	Put
Best-of	short	long
Worst-of	long	short

Table 9.5 Correlation exposure

	Call	Put
Best-of	short	long
Worst-of	long	short

and lower dividends increase forward prices, the buyer of a worst-of put is short rho and long dividends.

We can now summarize the previous analysis in Tables 9.2 to 9.5.

9.2.7 Cross-gamma and correlation revisited (again ...)

It is worth demonstrating that the concepts of cross-gamma and sensitivity of the option price to correlation are the two sides of the same coin. Let us revisit the example of a worst-of call option written on Index A and Index B (this analysis can be extended to all best-of and worst-of options). When we analysed the gamma profile of a worst-of call option, we observed that as the price of Index A increases, the delta of Index B increases, since it is the most likely to be the worst performing underlying. If the correlation between indices A and B is positive then, when the price of Index A increases (triggering a higher level of delta for Index B), the price of Index B is also likely to increase due to their positive correlation. Therefore, the increase in the price of Index B is now even more valuable to the option buyer since the individual delta of Index B is higher due to the increase in the price of the other underlying (assuming that the price increase of Index A is greater than that of Index B). See Figure 9.7.

Figure 9.7   Cross gamma effect when Index A is higher

Figure 9.8   Cross gamma effect when Index A is lower

The same dynamic applies when an increase in the price of Index B triggers a higher level of delta for Index A, with the additional benefit arising from the fact that the price of Index A is also likely to increase due to the positive correlation.

In other words, in a context of positive cross-gamma, from the point of view of the buyer of a worst-of call option, it is desirable that the individual underlying assets are positively correlated to take advantage of the increased individual delta arising from increases of the prices of other basket constituents.

This discussion is also applicable to the case of a fall in the prices of the individual assets. If the price of Index A falls, it will trigger a lower level for the delta of Index B. This time around, the price of Index B is also likely to decrease due to the positive correlation but this will cause a lower loss to the option buyer since the individual delta of Index B is now lower due to the decrease in the price of the other underlying. See Figure 9.8.

9.3   QUANTO DERIVATIVES

Thus far, we have worked under the assumption that the currency of denomination of the derivative payoff is the same as the currency of the underlying asset. This is the case, for instance, of USD-denominated derivatives written on gold or crude oil (which are denominated in USD) or on the S&P 500 equity index (which is a basket of USD-denominated stocks and therefore USD denominated) or any other USD-denominated assets. It is, of course, possible to trade derivatives denominated in a currency different to that of the currency of denomination of the underlying asset. Examples of this are very common in the structured products world; for instance, when Europeans (who may want EUR-denominated products) are offered commodity derivatives or structured products denominated in EUR (commodities are typically USD denominated). In this case, we have a EUR-denominated investment with an embedded EUR-denominated derivative payoff on a USD asset. This kind of derivative is commonly called a "quanto", with the indication of the currency of denomination of the derivative payoff itself ("quanto EUR" in the last example).

The expression "call option on gold, quanto EUR" refers to a gold option where the currency of denomination of the payoff is EUR, irrespective of the foreign exchange rate between EUR and USD.

For instance, if we assume that the spot price of gold is \$1,600/oz, an ATM spot call on gold quanto EUR will have the following payoff assuming a notional of 1 ounce:

$$\text{Max}(\text{Gold}_{\text{Final}} - 1,600, 0) \text{ taken as EUR quantity}$$

If the price of gold at expiry ($\text{Gold}_{\text{Final}}$) is equal to \$1,700/oz, then the option payoff will be equal to EUR 100 for each ounce of gold that was defined as the notional.

Returning to the example and assuming that the option was traded with a notional of 1 ounce, the seller of the option will have to pay out EUR 100 to the buyer since the price of the underlying was \$100 higher than the strike. Again, we stress that the EUR/USD rate has no implication whatsoever in the determination of the EUR payoff.

When trying to price this kind of quanto derivative, it would be tempting to start from the USD price of the corresponding plain vanilla option (USD denominated and equal to, say, \$25) and then assume for the price of the quanto derivative an amount in EUR equal to the USD option price adjusted by the spot rate. By extension, it would be tempting to apply the Greeks for the plain vanilla options to hedge the payoff at expiry. Unfortunately, this would not work.

It would work, in principle, if the EUR/USD rate were unchanged for the entire life of the option. Foreign exchange rates are volatile, however, and often, especially in the case of commodities, movements in EUR/USD and movements in the price of the underlying asset show significant correlation.

An example will show how this can affect the replication cost of our gold call option quanto EUR and, therefore, its price. Our starting point should be that if, on the one hand, the level of the EUR/USD rate is not directly affecting the payoff of the option, it is definitely affecting the number of ounces that have to be traded to delta hedge the quanto option. Let us assume, for simplicity, that the quanto option has a notional of 100 ounces and is about to expire with a very high probability of being in-the-money (assume it is now nearly a delta 1 option). In this case, for every dollar move in the price of gold, the value of the option will move by EUR 100 (EUR 1 for each ounce of notional), irrespective of the EUR/USD rate. How many ounces of gold will the option seller have to own to hedge this exposure? The option seller will have to own a number of ounces such that, if the price of gold goes up by \$1, then the profit will be EUR 100. If we assume that the EUR/USD rate is equal to 1.25 and does not change (we will shortly remove this rather unrealistic assumption), then the number of ounces will be equal to $100 \times \text{EUR/USD}$, i.e., 125 ounces. As should be clear, the delta-hedging strategy is affected by the EUR/USD rate. Obviously, as the FX rate goes up or down, the seller of a quanto option will have to buy or sell gold to hedge the option.

So, in the situation just described (gold call option quanto EUR, with option delta equal to 1) and a EUR/USD rate of 1.25, the option seller will have to own 125 ounces of gold. If the FX rate goes to 1.28, however, the option seller will have to buy 3 additional ounces of gold to keep the overall net delta exposure at zero. On the other hand, if the FX rate drops to 1.23, the option seller will have to sell 2 ounces to maintain delta neutrality.

What would seem just a mechanical exercise of tracking the FX rate and adjusting the delta hedge accordingly, however, is in fact complicated by the fact that a change in EUR/USD rate tends to be quite correlated with a change in the price of gold. Far from being just a relation that can be proven empirically, a positive correlation between gold and EUR/USD has potentially a large impact on the cost of replicating a quanto option and, by extension, on its price. This is because, as EUR/USD rate goes higher and the option seller has to buy more gold, the price of gold will also likely be higher due to the positive correlation. Conversely, as EUR/USD goes lower, the price of gold that the option seller will receive will also be lower due to the positive correlation between the two assets. This creates a "buy high, sell low" situation that is not too different from that which we observed in the case of a short gamma position. Consequently, we should expect the gold call option quanto EUR to be more expensive than the corresponding plain vanilla option. The price of the option is based on the cost of replicating/hedging the exposure and, as we have just seen, the actual cost of hedging will be higher due to the positive correlation between gold and EUR/USD.

The impact of the correlation between the price of the underlying asset and the currency of denomination of the quanto option can also be seen from a different angle. Thus far, we have analysed it from the perspective of a change in the FX rate that triggers a delta rebalancing at different prices. We would get the same result, however, if we adopted the point of view of a change in the price of the underlying that triggers a need for a rebalancing of the FX exposure. Let us see how this would work. Assume that we own 125 ounces of gold to hedge the exposure arising from the quanto derivative described above. If gold moves up by $10, our profit on the delta-hedging side would be equal to $1,250. This amount will have to be converted into EUR (since the option we are hedging is EUR denominated). If EUR/USD is unchanged at 1.25, we would get EUR 1,000 from our delta hedging activity. Given the positive correlation with the price of gold, however, EUR/USD is likely to be higher than the initial price of 1.25, implying a EUR profit of less than EUR 1,000. Conversely, in the case of a fall in the price of gold of $10, the resulting loss of $1,250 is amplified in EUR terms since, this time around, the EUR/USD rate would likely be lower (again because of the positive correlation with gold) causing a potential loss greater than EUR 1,000.

Irrespective of which moves first, the FX rate or the price of the underlying, the option seller, during the hedging process, faces lower profits or higher losses arising from the positive correlation between underlying asset and the currency of denomination of the derivative being hedged.

What also emerges from this example is that this additional cost does not just apply to options. In the example above, we were working, for simplicity, on a delta 1 call option and we assessed that there is indeed an additional cost for the quanto feature. This implies that the "optionality" *per se* might not be the main driver of the additional cost that is actually linked to the need to own the underlying asset as a hedge. Let us consider another example, the sale of a quanto straddle (i.e., quanto call and quanto put with the same strike). To the extent that the delta is negligible (which may be the case if we are sufficiently far from the expiry), we should not expect to suffer a meaningful loss from the process that we described above; we would not need to hold much of the underlying asset and, as a consequence, we would not have significant profit or loss arising from delta-hedging activity (i.e., no dollars that have to be exchanged into EUR).

In every derivative with a quanto feature, an adjustment to the price has to be made with respect to the correlation between the underlying asset and the currency of denomination of the derivative itself. This adjustment arises from the additional cost (or reduced cost, in the case of negative correlation) to rebalance the delta exposure of the derivative when the FX rate changes.

As a first approximation, it is possible to say that the impact of the quanto adjustment is proportional to the delta of the derivative. In other words, *what seems to be affected by the presence of the quanto feature is not its volatility but the forward of the underlying asset used to price the derivative* (otherwise we could not explain why a delta 1 option – which is by definition vega neutral – is significantly affected by the quanto adjustment, whereas the delta-neutral straddle – which has a very high vega – is not).

So, is the correlation between the underlying asset and the currency of denomination of the derivative payoff the only factor affecting the price of the quanto derivative? Again, let us try to use intuition to assess if a quanto derivative has any additional sources of cost (other than the correlation that we have just discussed). Recall the example above. The adjustment in the price arises from the additional hedging cost.[1] Intuitively, if the underlying asset price has very little volatility, even in the presence of strong correlation with the FX rate, then the impact of the quanto adjustment would be minimal; the trader will have to rebalance the delta exposure at prices of the underlying that are relatively similar (due to the low volatility). In the extreme (and unrealistic) scenario of an underlying asset with volatility very close to zero, the impact of the quanto adjustment would be meaningless. Conversely, if the volatility of the underlying asset is very high, the cost of having to rebalance as the FX rate moves up and down (or the cost of having to trade the FX exposure as the price of the underlying moves up and down) could be considerable.

When looking at the volatility of the FX rate, similar logic would apply. So, the correlation between the underlying asset and the FX rate, the volatility of the underlying asset and the volatility of the relevant FX rate amplify the effect that each factor would have on its own. If just one of these three were zero (or very close to zero), however, the quanto adjustment would be close be zero.

Analytically, it can be shown that the quanto feature causes a shift in the level of the forward such that:

$$\text{Quanto forward} = \text{Underlying forward} \times \exp(\rho_{\text{FX,Underlying}} \times \sigma_{\text{FX}} \times \sigma_{\text{Underlying}})$$

where the underlying forward is expressed in its currency of denomination, $\rho_{\text{FX,Underlying}}$ is the correlation between the FX rate and the underlying asset, σ_{FX} is the volatility of the FX rate and $\sigma_{\text{Underlying}}$ is the volatility of the underlying asset.

It can easily be seen that, due to the multiplication of the three factors in the formula (the correlation between the underlying asset and the FX rate, the volatility of the underlying asset and the volatility of the FX rate), if any factor is zero or very close to zero, the overall price adjustment due to the quanto property will tend to be extremely low. Conversely, for very high levels of the two volatilities and of the correlation, the price adjustment (in absolute terms) can be meaningful (causing a potentially big discrepancy between the quanto forward and the forward of the underlying asset). This is consistent with the intuition of the three factors amplifying each other and the possibility of a single factor reducing drastically the impact of the quanto adjustment if it is sufficiently close to zero.

9.4 "COMPO" DERIVATIVES

Another set of derivatives denominated in a currency other than the currency of denomination of the underlying is *"compo" derivatives*.

---

[1] Which, as we have shown, is due to the difference in the cost of the underlying asset that the hedger has to trade as the FX rate moves or due to the difference in the FX rate that the hedger has to trade as the price of the underlying asset changes.

We say that a derivative is "compo" if its underlying asset is converted into a currency different from the original currency of denomination. A typical example is represented by a call option written on gold converted into EUR but how does this conversion take place? Let us assume that the spot price of 1 ounce of gold in USD terms is equal to $1,600 and that spot EUR/USD is 1.25. The price of gold in EUR terms will be equal to 1,600/1.25 = 1,280 EUR/oz. It is now possible to define a derivative payoff on this new asset (gold traded in EUR). For instance, we could define a European call option with a 1,350 strike written on gold in EUR. To assess if the option is in- or out-of-the-money at expiry, the price of an ounce of gold traded in EUR will have to be calculated (as a ratio of the USD price of 1 ounce of gold and the EUR/USD rate prevailing at expiry). For instance, if at expiry the price of gold in USD terms is 1,800 and the FX rate at expiry is 1.28, the price of gold in EUR is going to be 1,800/1.28 = 1,406.25 and the option will expire in-the-money with a payoff of EUR 56.25 per ounce. Conversely, if at expiry, the price of gold in EUR is below the strike price, the call option will expire out-of-the-money.

What we have just described is effectively a EUR-denominated derivative on a EUR-denominated asset (since, even if gold is USD denominated, its price is converted into EUR at the prevailing FX rate for the purpose of calculating the derivative payoff).

We probably need to spend a little time now to convince ourselves that the forward of the gold price converted into EUR is only affected by the EUR interest rate curve and not by the USD curve (nor by the correlation between the EUR/USD rate and price of gold). This may seem counterintuitive at first glance. If one buys 100 ounces of EUR-denominated gold, 3 months forward, the ideal scenario is for the price of gold to go up and the FX rate to go down, suggesting that one may be short correlation. It is not the case, however.

Or, more correctly, it is not the case in the risk-neutral world. Recall, in the risk-neutral world, the only factors that matter are those affecting the replication cost of the derivative and, in this case, it is relatively easy to show that here correlation does not affect the replication cost. To understand this, we use a simple example. Imagine that we are asked to enter a 1-year forward contract on EUR-denominated gold on 1 million EUR notional. The replication strategy will consist simply of borrowing 1 million EUR at the prevailing interest rate (say 5%), converting it to USD at the prevailing FX rate (to obtain $1.25 million) and buying 1,250,000/1,600 ≈ 781 ounces of gold. When the forward matures, we will have to sell the gold at the prevailing market price (obtaining an amount in USD), convert the proceeds into EUR at the prevailing FX rate and repay the EUR amount borrowed (EUR 1,050,000 including the interest rate). Therefore, if we price the forward at EUR 1,050,000, we are perfectly able to meet the obligation under the forward contract and any arbitrage opportunity is excluded. This simple example shows that USD interest rates and the volatilities of the FX rate and the underlying asset as well as the correlation between them are not affecting the forward price of EUR-denominated gold, which is affected only by the EUR interest rate (in this example, we have been ignoring any storage cost or convenience yield arising from the gold holding).

When we analyse the volatility of the EUR-denominated gold, however, it is easy to see that this is clearly affected by not only the individual volatilities of the FX rate and the underlying asset but also by their correlation. After all, the price of the EUR-denominated gold can be expressed as a ratio (USD-denominated gold price divided by the EUR/USD rate). If the numerator and the denominator of a ratio are positively correlated, the volatility of the ratio will tend to be lower, while, in the case of negative correlation, the volatility of the ratio will be much higher. In case of compo derivatives, therefore, there is indeed an impact of the correlation between the price of the underlying asset and the FX rate. This impact does not feed through to the price of the derivative via a change in the forward of the underlying asset, however, (as in the case of quanto derivative) but via its volatility. The immediate consequence of this is that, unlike in the case of a quanto, the compo forward is not affected by the correlation between the FX rate and the underlying asset price (the reason being that the compo forward has no vega).

What are impacted (unlike in the case of a quanto) are those derivatives that are heavily dependent on volatility (such as vanilla options and straddles/strangles). Consequently, if we buy a straddle or a strangle (or an individual vanilla) written on gold converted into EUR (or, more generally, on one underlying asset converted into a different currency), the long vega exposure that we are going to have can be seen also as long vega exposure on both the underlying asset and the FX rate and as a negative exposure on the correlation between them. Since this correlation exposure is derived from the option vega, it will tend to disappear if, during the life of the trade, the vega converges to zero (due to the option being deeply in-the-money or deeply out- of-the-money or simply through the impact of time decay).

SUMMARY

In this chapter, we analysed the typical risks that arose from multi-asset derivatives and, in particular, we focused on correlation risk for basket options and the correlation/cross-gamma risk for best-of and worst-of options. We discussed quantos and compos and went through examples for each. We also noted in passing that Monte Carlo simulation tends to be the most common approach (often the only possible approach) to pricing.

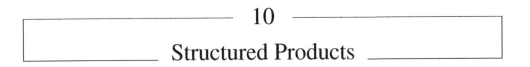

10

Structured Products

Suggesting an investment in a *structured product*, given the aftermath of what has become known as the Global Financial Crisis, may well not be the best way to start a conversation with a prospective client, such is the tarnished reputation of the asset class.

It is certainly likely that many structured products had been created in the past for the benefit of the issuer rather than for the user but to dismiss all of them as irrelevant, overpriced and lacking in transparency would be a pity. Structured products come in many shapes and sizes and can offer extremely efficient solutions to the particular needs of many investors, especially those investors who cannot access directly the over-the-counter derivatives markets. In a sense, structured products are designed to meet specific needs that cannot be met from the standardized financial instruments available to the majority of investors.

10.1 DEFINITION

Before we discuss some of the main characteristics of structured products, we will describe what we mean by the catch-all term *structured product*.

The United States' Securities and Exchange Commission defined structured products as "securities whose cash flow characteristics depend upon one or more indices or that have embedded forwards or options or securities where an investor's investment return and the issuer's payment obligations are contingent on,[1] or highly sensitive to, changes in the value of underlying assets, indices, interest rates or cash flows". Hardly pithy, is it? If definitions are meant to explain, then the SEC's attempt lacks intuitive appeal.

A simpler definition is that they are pre-packaged investment products based on a single security or a basket of securities whose returns are linked to, but unlike, direct exposures to the underlying. Note that the scope of assets that can form part of a structured product is so wide that trying to describe a "typical" structured product is meaningless. So, perhaps a better way to proceed would be to highlight certain features that many, if not most, structured products include and then describe some of the more common ones. We do this next.

10.2 COMMON FEATURES

In this chapter, we will focus mainly on structured products in bond format (structured bonds or structured notes). Typically, these kinds of structured products:

1. offer income or capital appreciation but usually not both;
2. have easily defined but highly customized risk and return profiles (in particular, they may offer capital protection if held until maturity);
3. are linked to liquid, publicly traded assets;

---

[1] The returns are contingent in the sense that the structured product provides a return dependent on the movements in the price of the underlying asset.

4. have, in general, maturities of between 6 months and 5 years but can be as short as 3 months and longer than 10 years;
5. are designed to be held until the maturity date, although they can often be unwound at any point before the expiry date at a cost.

Since structured products tend to be highly customized, one criticism is that the implicit costs associated with these products are less than transparent to the end-users/investors. For the more sophisticated investors, this may not be a valid criticism. For less sophisticated clients, however, frequently the target market for structured products, particularly in Europe, the criticism may have some merit.

10.3 PRINCIPAL PROTECTION

A feature of many structured products is a "guarantee" of protection on the principal invested if the product is *held to maturity*. The principal protection can be set at 100% of the notional invested or at a lower percentage, say 80%. The amount of protection, however, will clearly have a bearing on the prospective return from the structured product.

For example, assume that an investor invests $100 in a principal-protected structured product maturing after 5 years. Against this, the issuer of the structured product could simply invest in a zero-coupon bond that has the same final maturity. This bond might cost $90 dollars to buy but after 5 years it will repay the final $100. With the remaining $10 from the original $100 invested, the issuer could purchase other assets to generate an income or capital return such as a call option on an equity instrument, currency or commodity. If, however, the principal protection is set at $80, then the issuer would only need to invest $72[2] in the zero-coupon bond and there would be $28 available to invest in other assets as opposed to $10. In theory, of course, the investor could do all of this himself or herself although this may not be possible in practice.

So, in the example above, the investor gets some element of principal protection (whether 100% or 80% of the initial investment) and, for the return component, whatever is earned from the risky asset. If the money is invested in a call option, there will be a positive return as long as the option does not expire worthless. If it does, the investor receives nothing in excess of the initial investment or the capital protection level agreed.

At this point, however, we need to be very clear about the extent of the principal protection being offered. For the majority of structured products, the principal protection is offered by the issuer. The zero-coupon bond in which the investor's money is placed will generally be a bond from the issuer. Consequently, if the issuer defaults then the principal will not necessarily be protected. Instead, the structured product investor becomes another creditor of the bankrupt issuing entity. Since the price of the zero-coupon bond for a given issuer is a function of both the general level of interest rates prevailing in the market place and the credit spread applicable to the issuer, in environments of high interest rates and high credit spreads for the issuing firm (i.e., the lower is the price of the zero-coupon bond), the higher is the amount that can be used to finance the embedded option. Note, however, that the issuance of structured products constitutes a form of borrowing for the issuing firm, i.e., a new structured product raises capital for the issuing firm for use across their other trading operations.

---

[2] The zero-coupon bond generates a return of $10 on an investment of $90 over the life of the investment, i.e., a total return of 11.1%. If, however, the final amount required at the end of the period is just $80, then the issuer only needs to invest $72 in the zero-coupon bond since an 11.1% return on $72 is $8, giving a total of $80 at the end of the period.

In practice, the amount that can be spent on the embedded option is the residual amount left once the capital protection features of the structure have been put in place and any related costs have also been taken into account.

10.4 THE BENEFIT TO THE ISSUER

The advantages of structured products as far as the investor is concerned are simple. Structured products offer access to assets and payoffs that the investor might otherwise not be able to achieve.

On the other hand, why would a financial institution want to issue structured products? The answer is that the issuer achieves cheaper funding. Structured products are essentially liabilities of the financial institutions that issue them.[3] The money that the institutions raise from selling structured products funds their other activities and this partly helps to explain why the risk–reward profile of the structured products should be better for investors than the direct risk–reward profile of investing in the underlying asset. The investor is not simply investing in the underlying asset. He or she is investing in the underlying asset and simultaneously making a loan to the issuing financial institution. This loan involves a bet on the creditworthiness of the financial institution that is the issuer.

In our example thus far, we have an investor putting money into a structured product. The investor receives any future gain from the underlying asset and some degree of capital protection on the initial investment (assuming that the issuer is still in existence 5 years hence). This sounds like a win–win situation. All upside and no downside. How can this be? Clearly the investor has swapped the risk of lower asset prices for the risk that the issuer is unable to repay the structured product at maturity.

Is it a good deal for the issuer? It will be if it is able to borrow money cheaper than it otherwise would, i.e., if it has borrowed the $100 at less than it would have to pay elsewhere. Why might it be able to borrow money more cheaply through a structured product than through a normal bond? Because it is offering a payoff profile to the investor that he or she would otherwise not be able to achieve.

Is it a good deal for the investor? This will depend upon whether he or she has been able to access a payoff that might not otherwise have been available (and if the spreads and commissions paid implicitly by the investor to achieve these exposures are not egregious!). Presumably, if the investor has taken the decision to invest in a structured product rather than a vanilla instrument, it is because the structured product offers some payoff benefit. If so, he or she may be willing to accept a lower potential return on the money invested relative to returns demanded by other lenders to the issuer.

What has effectively happened here is that the investor has lent money to the issuer (the investor has made a risky loan), taken the interest payment up-front and bought an at-the-money spot call option with this payment. Whether all this, with the benefit of hindsight, still turns out to have been a good decision depends upon the future price performance of the

---

[3] One of the most important but perhaps least understood risks involved in investment in structured products is the risk associated with the credit quality of the issuer. Although the cash flows from structured products are derived from the assets underlying the notes, the products themselves are liabilities of the financial institution that issues them. The majority of structured products are issued by large, global financial institutions but, as we have seen in recent years, these same large global financial institutions are not always too-big-to-fail. While asset-backed securities tend to be issued through so-called bankruptcy-remote, third party vehicles, structured products tend not to be.

underlying asset on which the call option is written and whether the issuer is still in existence 5 years hence.

10.5 REDEMPTION AMOUNTS AND PARTICIPATION

Let us look at a slightly more detailed example where we focus on the redemption profile of the structured note. In other words, how much money we get back at maturity. For instance, we could start with a redemption amount linked to the price of crude oil such that, for every 1% appreciation in the oil price, the redemption amount increases by 1%. Assuming 100% principal protection, our structured product will thus be linked to the performance of the crude oil price but only to the extent that this performance is positive. In the case of negative price performance, the redemption amount will be floored at 100% of the capital initially invested in the product.

Summarizing the key elements of our structured note:

- Underlying asset: crude oil
- Maturity: 5 years
- Redemption amount if the product is held until maturity: 100% participation in the appreciation of the price of crude oil with 100% principal protection
- Currency of denomination: USD
- Notional: $1,000,000
- Cost of the issuer's zero-coupon bond: 90% of Notional, or $900,000
- Amount left to finance the embedded option: 10% of Notional, $100,000

Assuming a call option with a strike price equal to the current price of a barrel of crude oil, say $100/bbl, a forward price of $95/bbl, a volatility of 25% and a discount factor of 0.9, we can use the Black formula to get the price, $17.15. As a percentage of the spot price of oil, this clearly exceeds our constraint of 10%, however.

What can we do at this point? On the face of it, the call option that we were planning to embed in our product is too expensive given current market conditions. Fortunately, we can apply some changes to our redemption condition such that we force the call option price to be 10% of the spot price.

Let us look at a couple of possibilities.

1. We can reduce the participation in the appreciation of the crude oil price. Thus far, we were working on the assumption that for each 1% appreciation of the price of crude oil, the redemption amount would grow by 1%. We can reduce this number. If we reduce this participation level to approximately 58%, then the cost of our call option would be roughly 58% of 17.15%, i.e., approximately 10%. In this case, for each 1% appreciation in the price of crude oil, the redemption amount will increase by 0.58%.
2. We can embed a cap to the overall redemption amount of the note. In this case, the embedded option would no longer be a plain vanilla call but, rather, a call spread. For instance, a call spread with the lower strike at $100 and the higher strike at $147.5 would cost approximately $10, or 10% of the current spot price of crude oil. In this case, we keep the initial level of 100% participation up to the cap, although the obvious drawback is that if the underlying asset subsequently moves up by more than 47.5%, the buyer of the structured note will no longer participate in this upside.

The previous example shows how it is possible to modify the redemption function to force the price of the embedded option to meet a certain constraint. Given what we have described so far, we can express in terms of a formula the redemption amount at maturity of our structured product (redemption for simplicity).

Initial case:

$$\text{Redemption} = \text{Notional} \times \left[100\% + \max\left(\frac{\text{CrudeOil}_{\text{Final}} - \text{Strike}}{\text{Divisor}}, 0 \right) \right]$$

where:

$\text{CrudeOil}_{\text{Final}}$ = Price of a barrel of crude oil at the expiry date of the product;
$\text{Strike} = \text{CrudeOil}_{\text{Initial}}$ = Price of a barrel of crude oil at the inception of the product;
$\text{Divisor} = \text{CrudeOil}_{\text{Initial}}$

We also discussed two possible variations:
Variation 1 (lower participation in the appreciation of the underlying):

$$\text{Redemption} = \text{Notional} \times \left[100\% + \text{Participation} \times \max\left(\frac{\text{CrudeOil}_{\text{Final}} - \text{Strike}}{\text{Divisor}}, 0 \right) \right]$$

where Participation is the leverage factor that defines how much the Redemption will participate in the appreciation of the underlying positive performance; it was equal to 58% in our example.
Variation 2 (participation unchanged but total redemption amount capped):

$$\text{Redemption} = \text{Notional} \times \left[100\% + \min\left(\text{Cap}, \max\left(\frac{\text{CrudeOil}_{\text{Final}} - \text{Strike}}{\text{Divisor}}, 0 \right) \right) \right]$$

where Cap is the maximum percentage level of appreciation of the underlying asset in which the buyer of the structured note will participate; it was equal to 47.5% in our example.

Note that both variations offer principal protection at maturity; in the case of a depreciation in the oil price, the redemption would be floored at 100% of the Notional.

It should be clear from the previous examples that structured products with principal protection (or partial protection) are often thought of as a combination of a zero-coupon bond (redeeming at the desired level of principal protection) and a long position in an embedded option with the desired payout.

As discussed in Chapter 9, structured product payoffs tend to be defined in percentage terms. This is exactly what we are doing here. The choice of the divisor is particularly important since it is the variable that allows us to translate the payoff into percentage terms. As the Notional is described in units of currency (USD in this case) and the underlying asset is described in unit of currency per unit of underlying asset (USD/barrel), the divisor is crucial in transforming the change in the price of the underlying asset (in USD/barrel) into a percentage appreciation that can be applied to the Notional (units of currency).

For instance, if we assume that the initial price of crude oil is equal to \$100/bbl and its final price is equal to \$120/bbl, we need to transform the \$20/bbl appreciation into percentage terms if we want to apply it to the Notional. In this case, assuming that the divisor equals the initial price of \$100/bbl, we can easily calculate the percentage appreciation as 20/100 = 20%. The 20% can easily be applied to the Notional (say \$1,000,000) to obtain a redemption amount equal to \$1,200,000 (assuming 100% participation).

This is economically equivalent to saying that the investors who bought this structured product are taking a position on a number of barrels equal to the ratio Notional/divisor, or

10,000 barrels. To convince yourself that this is the case, multiply this number of barrels by the final price that we assumed in our example, to obtain $10,000 \times 120 = \$1,200,000$. This is exactly the same amount as calculated above. Of course, when the participation is not equal to 100%, these figures will have to be adjusted accordingly.

This simple example shows that, from a pure financial point of view, it is always possible to express the notional as a number of units of underlying asset (number of barrels in this case). In practice, however, the notional will tend to be expressed in units of currency. Hence, the importance of the divisor.

10.6   PRINCIPAL AT RISK: EMBEDDING A SHORT OPTION

So far, we have discussed the case of 100% principal protection and the case of 80% principal protection obtained by reducing the amount invested in the zero-coupon bond. In practice, however, there is a more common way to structure products with principal at risk: a short position in an option (typically a put option or a variation of a put option) can be embedded such that, if it is in-the-money when the structured product matures, the principal amount invested may get eroded. The product can be structured such that the minimum redemption amount is equal to zero (the investor loses the entire amount invested).

The premium received from the implicit sale of an option can be used either to finance the cost of providing upside participation or to provide a fixed coupon or a stream of fixed coupons that are higher than the ones that would be payable by a fixed coupon bond issued by the same entity with the same maturity.

Recall the previous example in section 10.5 where we had to finance a call option with a price of 17.15% but we only had 10% available. We could cover the remaining 7.15% by embedding a short position in a put option with a strike roughly equal to \$69.3/bbl (or 69.3% of the price of crude oil at inception). With 25% implied volatility, this would generate a premium of around 7.15% that we can use to finance our call option. In this case, we can keep a participation of 100% and we do not need to impose a cap on the potential upside. On the other hand, of course, in the case of a sharp fall in the price of crude oil, the redemption amount may be considerably less than the amount invested at inception. In particular, in the extreme case of crude oil prices going to zero, the payoff of the embedded short put option will be equal to 69.3%, implying a redemption amount equal to 30.7% of the Notional. In terms of a formula, this case can be represented as follows:

If $\text{CrudeOil}_{\text{Final}} < 69.3\% \times \text{CrudeOil}_{\text{Initial}} = 69.3\% \times \text{Divisor}$:

$$\text{Redemption} = \text{Notional} \times \frac{\text{CrudeOil}_{\text{Final}}}{\text{Divisor}}$$

Otherwise:

$$\text{Redemption} = \text{Notional} \times \left[100\% + \max\left(\frac{\text{CrudeOil}_{\text{Final}} - \text{Strike}}{\text{Divisor}}, 0 \right) \right]$$

where $\text{CrudeOil}_{\text{Final}}$, $\text{CrudeOil}_{\text{Initial}}$ and Divisor were as before.

Figure 10.1 is the redemption profile in this case defined as a function of the price of crude oil that could be observed at maturity. The chart clearly highlights the upside participation given by the embedded long call option (with strike at \$100) and the downside exposure given by the embedded short put option struck at \$69.3. The redemption amount in the chart is expressed as percentage of Notional.

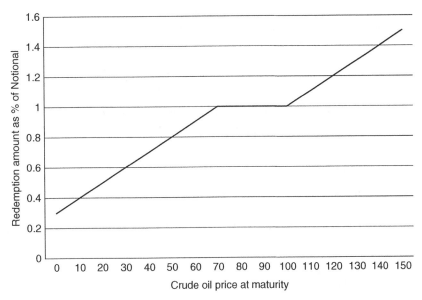

Figure 10.1 Redemption profile of the structured note linked to Crude Oil

10.7 MORE COMPLICATED PAYOFFS

The payoff profiles for structured products may be much more complicated than that of a simple vanilla call or call spread combined with a vanilla put or put spread. In this section, we will describe briefly some notable common examples.

10.7.1 "Shark fin" notes

This product is obtained by embedding an up-and-out call (with rebate). Given the shape of the payoff function, the product is sometimes called a "shark fin". We will look at a 1-year USD-denominated "shark fin" note on gold.

Underlying: Gold
Observation dates: continuously, i.e., observations intra-day
Notional: $3,000,000
$Gold_{Initial}$: $1,500/oz
$Gold_{Final}$: Price of an ounce of gold at the expiry date of the product
Call Strike: $1,500/oz
Barrier level: $1,800/oz
Rebate: 5% of Notional

This option starts in "activated' mode as follows:

- If, at any point in time, the price of gold rises to $1,800/oz, the call is deactivated but the rebate is activated and the redemption amount will be equal to (100% + Rebate) × Notional.

- If the price of gold never reaches $1,800/oz during the life of the product, then the embedded call option does not get knocked out and the investor will keep the exposure to the price of gold, struck at $1,500/oz, i.e., the redemption amount will be equal to:

$$\text{Notional} \times \left[100\% + \max \left(\frac{\text{Gold}_{\text{Final}} - \text{Strike}}{\text{Gold}_{\text{Initial}}}, 0 \right) \right]$$

- Clearly this implies that if the price of gold ends up below $1,500/oz, the embedded call will expire worthless and the redemption amount will be equal to the Notional.

10.7.2   Reverse convertible notes

Barrier options can easily be embedded in structured products. One example is the so-called "reverse convertible note" that can be structured using a down-and-in put option. We will consider a 1-year USD-denominated reverse convertible note on Brent Crude.

Underlying: Brent Crude
Observation dates: every business day during the life of the product
Notional: $1,000,000
Coupon: 8% of Notional
Brent Crude$_{\text{Initial}}$: $100/bbl
Brent Crude$_{\text{Final}}$: Price of a barrel of Brent Crude at the expiry date of the product
Put Strike: $100/bbl
Barrier level: $70/bbl

This product works as follows:

- If, on any observation date, the price of Brent drops to or below the barrier level, then the put is activated and the investor will have the following redemption amount at maturity:
  - If the price of Brent is below the strike price ($100/bbl), then the redemption amount will be equal to Notional × (Coupon + Brent$_{\text{Final}}$/Brent$_{\text{Initial}}$). This is basically equivalent to a combination of (100% + Coupon) × Notional and a short position in the put option struck at $100/bbl.
  - If the price of Brent is at or above the strike price ($100/bbl), the redemption amount will be simply equal to (100% + Coupon) × Notional (economically this is equivalent to saying that the embedded put option expires out-of-the money and the capital invested is not eroded).
- If the price of Brent never reaches $70/bbl on any observation date, then the put option is not going to be activated and the redemption amount will simply be equal to (100% + Coupon) × Notional.

10.7.3   Range accrual notes

The investor receives a coupon which depends on how many days the price of the underlying asset has been within a certain range. Consider the following example where we describe a 1-year USD-denominated range accrual on the S&P 500 Index.

Notional = $1,000,000
Conditional coupon: 6% of Notional

S&P500$_{\text{Initial}}$ = 1,416
Lower barrier: 1,204
Higher barrier: 1,628
Daily observations:
Redemption = Notional × (100% + n/total × 6%)

where n is the number of business days in which the closing level of the S&P 500 Index has been within the range defined by the lower and upper barriers and *total* is the total number of observations during the life of the product. This can be seen as the investor being long a strip of daily digital call options with strike 1,204 and being short a strip of daily digital call options with strike 1,628; the payoff of each digital option is equal to 6% × Notional/n. Again, several variations can apply. For instance, the coupon can be paid at different frequencies during the tenor of the structure, not only at maturity as illustrated in this example.

10.7.4 Auto-callable notes

The investor can receive his or her money before the expiry of the structure if a certain event takes place. Let us illustrate this with an example, noting that we will assume no principal protection (i.e., the note-holder will implicitly be selling an at-the-money put option in this case). We will look at a 2-year USD-denominated bullish auto-callable note on gold with the possibility of early redemption at the end of the first year.

Notional: $1,000,000
Gold$_{\text{Initial}}$: $1,730/oz
Notional (oz): 578 oz
Conditional coupon: 8% of Notional
Gold$_{1Y}$ = Price of gold observed on the last business day of the first year of the life of the product
Gold$_{\text{Final}}$: Price of an ounce of gold at the expiry date of the product
Put Strike: $1,730/oz
Auto-callable barrier level: $1,730/oz

We observe the price of gold on the last business day of the first year to determine the occurrence of the *early redemption event*, defined as follows:

- If Gold$_{1Y}$ ≥ Auto-callable barrier level, the *early redemption event* occurs and the holder of the structured note receives a redemption amount equal to (100% + Conditional Coupon) × Notional;
- If Gold$_{1Y}$ < Auto-callable barrier level, nothing happens and the structures "survives" until the scheduled maturity.

At the scheduled maturity date, assuming that no *early redemption event* took place:

- If Gold$_{\text{Final}}$ ≥ Gold$_{\text{Initial}}$, redemption is equal to (100% + Conditional Coupon) × Notional;
- If Gold$_{\text{Final}}$ < Put Strike the note-holder is exposed to the downside risk arising from the short put position and the redemption will be equal to Notional × Gold$_{\text{Final}}$/Gold$_{\text{Initial}}$.

The product is not principal protected and the buyer can potentially lose his or her entire investment.

What we described here is a very simple example of an auto-callable note. There are many possible variations of auto-callable notes. Some of the additional features that can be embedded are:

- The auto-callable note can have several auto-callable barrier levels that can be observed at different frequencies, i.e., bi-annually, quarterly, monthly, etc., and these barrier levels can assume different values at different times. For example, the auto-callable barrier levels can be at 100% of the initial price after 6 months, at 110% after 1 year, at 120% after 18 months, etc.
- Conditional coupons can have a "snowballing feature". This simply means that the coupon accumulates. In our example, if the conditional coupon had a "snowballing feature", then the structure would pay 16% at maturity if $\text{Gold}_{\text{Final}}$ were above $\text{Gold}_{\text{Initial}}$ (assuming, of course, no *early redemption event* on the last business day of the first year).
- Embedded put options may not be vanilla. Down-and-in put options tend to be relatively common in the case of non-principal protected products. In any case, the embedded put will get knocked out in the case of an *early redemption event.*

10.8   AUTO-CALLABLE NOTE: PRICING AND RISK PROFILE

10.8.1   Pricing

Consider the risk profile of the auto-callable note that we just described. The risk profile is obviously a function of the way in which the auto-callable note is structured. Let us start from the simplest possible auto-callable note, i.e., a note that is subject to early redemption at par at time t_1 if, at that time, the price of the underlying asset is above a certain barrier level. If early redemption does not take place, the normal redemption (again at par) will take place at a later stage (say at time t_2). For now, we ignore the presence of any conditional coupon such that we can focus on the auto-callable feature.

In this simple case, we have the following redemption profile (assuming a notional of $100):

- $100 at t_1 if the price of the underlying at t_1 is equal to or greater than the barrier level;
- $100 at t_2 if there was no early redemption at t_1 (i.e., if, at t_1, the price of the underlying asset was below the barrier level).

Either way, the notional amount of $100 is going to be fully redeemed. The question is when the redemption will actually take place. This example, given that there are just two time steps, is relatively simple. If we define P as the probability of the underlying asset being above the barrier level at t_1, triggering early redemption, and $\text{DF}(t_0, t_1)$ and $\text{DF}(t_0, t_2)$ as the discount factors applicable at the valuation date t_0 for cash flows payable at t_1 and t_2 respectively, we can show the present value of the note as:

$$100 \times P \times \text{DF}(t_0, t_1) + 100 \times (1 - P) \times \text{DF}(t_0, t_2)$$

This formula is derived from the fact that, in case the redemption at t_1 is triggered (the event that happens with probability P), the redemption amount is paid at t_1 and therefore has to be discounted using $\text{DF}(t_0, t_1)$. On the other hand, in case the redemption is not triggered at t_1 (the event has $1 - P$ probability) the redemption amount is paid at t_2 and therefore will be discounted using $\text{DF}(t_0, t_2)$. P can be calculated using the formula for a European digital option.

Clearly, not all auto-callable notes have just two steps. In fact, most of them have several steps and this makes pricing a little more complicated. Let us assume that we have the same auto-callable notes as before but with three steps instead of two (therefore t_1, t_2 and t_3). The first step is similar to the previous example. It is about measuring the probability of being above the barrier level at t_1. The second step is to measure the probability of being above the barrier level at t_2 *conditional* on the fact that we were below the barrier level at t_1 (i.e., the auto-callable note was not previously redeemed). The third step is the residual probability (i.e., 1 – the sum of the probabilities calculated in the previous two steps). The conditional probability at the second step makes the pricing more complicated, as it makes it impossible to treat the auto-callable as a combination of simple European digital options as we did before. In this case, numerical methods are typically used to find the value of the overall structure. Auto-callable with more than three periods are simply a generalization. Please see the examples in the Excel spreadsheet "Chapter 10 – Auto-callable".

10.8.2 Risk profile

Consider the risk profile of the auto-callable note from the perspective of the seller (typically a bank). Taking the simplest case (two steps, no put option embedded) and assuming that interest rates are equal to r for all maturities, the risk can be broken down as follows. First, the possibility of early redemption at t_1 is basically equivalent to a cash flow of $100 payable at t_1. If we imagine the risk profile that the seller will be facing at t_1, there are just two possible scenarios. If the early redemption takes place at t_1, the present value of the cash flow is going to be simply $100 (we are analysing this from the perspective of the risk faced at t_1, so there is no discounting involved). If the early redemption does not take place at t_1, we assume the scheduled redemption of $100 will occur at maturity, i.e., at t_2 in our simple example. From the perspective of the seller at time t_1, the cash flow payable in t_2 will have to be discounted (the discount factor in this case is $\text{DF}(t_1, t_2)$, i.e., the present value calculated at t_1 of a cash flow payable at t_2). To sum up, the present value of the trade calculated at t_1 is going to be:

- $100 if early redemption occurs
- $100 $\times$ $\text{DF}(t_1, t_2)$ if early redemption does not occur

Assuming interest rates observable at t_1 for all maturities are r then:

$$\text{DF}\left(t_1, t_2\right) = \frac{1}{1 + r}$$

Therefore, the actual risk that the hedger is facing at t_1 is not a digital payment of $100 but a digital payment of $100 $\times$ $(1 - \text{DF}(t_1, t_2))$. This is because, if the early redemption does not take place, the scheduled redemption will still take place at the end of the following period. Basically, the redemption will take place anyway, it is only a matter of when and therefore the risk is related to the uncertainty over the time of the payment.

Generalizing, from a pure risk point of view, our two-step auto-callable can be seen as a digital call option expiring at the end of the first period with a digital payout equal to:

$$\text{Notional} \times [1 - \text{DF}(t_1, t_2)]$$

This quantity will tend to be much lower than the notional itself and therefore the associated digital risk will also be lower. In practice, there is also an additional complication due to the fact that interest rates are not constant. Embedding a dynamic interest rate (which may or may not be correlated with the underlying asset price) is a much more complicated problem, however, and is outside the scope of this book.

If a put option is embedded in the auto-callable (at the final scheduled maturity) then the risk profile of this put option will be substantially different from a vanilla put, since the embedded put is going to be significantly affected by the possibility of early redemption, which would knock out the put option. This is equivalent to saying that, whenever an early redemption occurs, the final scheduled redemption will not take place and therefore all its components will have to "disappear". Therefore, we will have some sort of up-and-out put option where the up-and-out barrier is not observed on a continuous basis but only whenever there is a possibility of early redemption. From a qualitative point of view, the risk profile of the embedded put option will be somewhere between the risk profile of a vanilla put option and the risk profile of an up-and-out put option.

10.9   ONE STEP FORWARD: THE WORST-OF DIGITAL NOTE

In Chapter 9, we introduced the concept of worst-of option. At the time, we mentioned that a worst-of call option could be a good candidate to embed in a structured product, as it tends to be significantly cheaper than the corresponding call option on the same basket of underlying assets. What we want to present here is the another typical example of a structured product, called worst-of digital call note, which provides the buyer with a digital coupon payable only if the worst performing asset is above its respective strike. This is equivalent to saying that the digital coupon will be paid only if *all* underlying assets are above their respective strikes since, if the worst performing is above its strike, than every other underlying will be.

The option embedded in this structured product could easily be priced via Monte Carlo (using the same approach that we presented for worst-of call options and simply replacing the payout formula) but there is a simpler way to think about it.

Suppose we have a price engine that can handle worst-of call options but we have to price/hedge a worst-of digital. Instead of developing a new ad-hoc engine, we could recall that a digital option can be replicated via a call spread (see Chapter 8 for a refresher). It turns out that what is true for vanilla call options and standard digital options is also true for worst-of call and worst-of digital options.

Consider an example based on two underlying assets. Assume that we have two underlying equity indexes: Index A (with a current price of 10,000) and Index B (with a current price of 1,500). Let us also assume that we want to price a worst-of digital call expiring after 1 year and struck at the current index levels. The payoff of this option (assume equal to $1) will take place only if both Index A and Index B are above their current prices (10,000 and 1,500 respectively). As we noted when we described digital options, we will define the price as a percentage of the digital payoff. Assume that we have a pricing engine (similar to the one discussed in the spreadsheet "Chapter 9 – Best-of and Worst-of Options") based on a Monte Carlo approach allowing us to price worst-of call options defined as:

$$\text{Worst-of call payout} = \text{Max}(0, \text{WorstPerformingAsset}) \times \text{Notional}$$

where WorstPerformingAsset is the lowest of:

$$\left(\frac{\text{IndexA}_{\text{Final}} - \text{StrikeA}}{10{,}000} \right)$$

and

$$\left(\frac{\text{IndexB}_{\text{Final}} - \text{StrikeB}}{1,500} \right)$$

Assuming that the notional is equal to $100, we can price two separate worst-of call options; one struck at 100% of the current value (therefore 10,000 and 1,500 for Index A and Index B respectively) and one struck at 99% of the current value of the indices (9,900 and 1,485 respectively).

We can build a portfolio P consisting of a long position in the worst-of call struck at 99% and a short position in the one struck at 100%. If the worst performing asset ends up above its initial price by a percentage amount equal to $X\%$, the worst-of call with strike 99% will pay out $(1\% + X\%)$ of notional (for instance, $16 dollars if it is 15% higher than the initial price) and the worst-of call with strike 100% will pay out $X\%$ of notional (for instance, $15 if it is 15% higher than the initial price). The value of the portfolio P at expiry will therefore be equal to $(1\% + X\% - X\%)$ of notional, i.e., $1 in this case.

If the worst performing asset ends up dropping by more than 1% from its initial value, portfolio P will be worthless since both options will expire out-of-the-money. If the worst performing asset ends up dropping less than 1% from its initial value, the portfolio P will be worth something between $0 and $1 at expiry.

What we showed in this simple example is that the portfolio P allows us to replicate the exposure of the worst-of digital (with $1 payout) with a certain degree of overestimation. This is similar to the case of the replication of a digital call option via a call spread that we discussed in Chapter 8.

It also probably goes without saying that the Greeks of the worst-of digital call option can be thought of as the combination of the Greeks of the two individual worst-of call options embedded in the portfolio P.

10.10 A REAL-LIFE EXAMPLE OF STRUCTURED PRODUCT

The following link is for an interest rate note issued by Bank of America in 2008, which matured on July 25, 2013:

http://www.sec.gov/Archives/edgar/data/70858/000119312508156166/d424b51.pdf

There is nothing particularly special about this document that we think warrants academic study. Rather, it is fairly typical and helps to highlight certain themes. The document makes very clear that the notes are senior debt securities of Bank of America, i.e., the credit risk of the note is linked to the credit quality of the issuer. The interest rate that the investor receives is variable and uncertain and may be more or less than the rate that an investor would expect to receive on a conventional fixed-rate or floating-rate debt security with the same maturity issued by the same entity. The notes have essentially been designed so that those investors who are willing to forgo guaranteed market rates of interest on their investment can earn higher interest in the case that the US Consumer Price Index (CPI) rises faster than expected.

The document also highlights that, if the investor holds the notes until maturity, he or she will receive the principal amount and any applicable final interest payment on the notes. If, however, the notes are sold prior to maturity, the investor may find that the market value of the notes is less than the principal amount of the notes.

On page 8 of the document, it says:

We cannot assure you that a trading market for the notes will ever develop or be maintained. We will not list the notes on any securities exchange. We cannot predict how the notes will trade in the secondary market, or whether that market will be liquid or illiquid. The number of potential buyers of the notes in any secondary market may be limited. (Bank of America) currently intends to act as a market-maker for the notes, but it is not required to do so. (Bank of America) may discontinue its market-making activities at any time.

To the extent that (Bank of America) engages in any market-making activities, it may bid for or offer the notes. Any price at which (Bank of America) may bid for, offer, purchase, or sell any notes may differ from the values determined by pricing models that may be used by (Bank of America), whether as a result of dealer discounts, mark-ups, or other transaction costs. These bids, offers, or completed transactions may affect the prices, if any, at which the notes might otherwise trade in the market.

In addition, if at any time (Bank of America) were to cease acting as a market-maker, it is likely that there would be significantly less liquidity in the secondary market, in which case the price at which the notes could be sold likely would be lower than if an active market existed.

If you attempt to sell the notes prior to maturity, the market value of the notes, if any, may be less than the principal amount of the notes. Unlike savings accounts, certificates of deposit, and other similar investment products, you have no right to redeem the notes prior to maturity. If you wish to liquidate your investment in the notes prior to maturity, your only option would be to sell the notes. At that time, there may be a very illiquid market for the notes or no market at all. Even if you were able to sell your notes, there are many factors outside of our control that may affect the market value of the notes, some of which, but not all, are stated below. Some of these factors are interrelated in complex ways. As a result, the effect of any one factor may be offset or magnified by the effect of another factor.

10.11 LIQUIDITY AND EXCHANGE-TRADED NOTES (ETNs)

Although structured products can clearly offer a number of benefits, one downside is the relative lack of liquidity due to the highly customized nature of the investment. Selling them before the final maturity date may be very difficult and entail having to accept a price well below that of the "fair value" price. By extension, any returns from the structured product may often not be realized until the final maturity. This is why structured products tend to be buy-and-hold investments rather than a short-term investment to take advantage of speculative investment opportunities.

Exchange-traded notes are a structured product introduced by Barclays Bank in 2006[4] and, as the name suggests, they are traded on an exchange. Other banks quickly followed suit. ETNs were an attempt to improve the liquidity of certain types of structured products by listing them on a recognized secondary market for trading. ETNs are structured to resemble ETFs (exchange traded funds) but they are different to ETFs in that they are debt instruments. Like index funds, ETNs are linked to the return of a benchmark index but, as debt securities, ETNs do not actually own the assets that they are tracking.[5] Typically, they do not offer principal protection.

---

[4] Under the banner of iPath, http://www.ipathetn.com/us/.
[5] Neither do the institutions doing the underlying hedging of the ETNs.

SUMMARY

In this chapter, we discussed the basic characteristics of structured products and described some of the considerations behind their pricing as well as the risks involved. We highlighted the principal protection afforded by many structured products but noted also that this protection is often only as good as the creditworthiness of the issuer. We also described a number of the more notable structures and discussed some of the issues around their hedging, in particular, the auto-callables. The variety of structured products available is limited only by the imagination of the human mind, however.[6] In the introduction to this chapter, we stated that "trying to describe a 'typical' structured product is meaningless", which is why we chose to highlight the features that many, if not most, structured products include. The following website is just one of many available to the interested reader, http://www.structuredproductreview.com. Clearly, we are not endorsing this particular website, rather we are using it to highlight the immense breadth of structured products available and, by extension, emphasizing the heterogeneous nature of the structured products market.

---

[6] As well as the number and variety of derivatives and underlying assets available.

Index

Index compiled by Terry Halliday

Printed and bound by CPI Group (UK) Ltd, Croydon, CR0 4YY

23/04/2025

14660950-0001